Revised by Caroly
Yakima Valley (

D1235297

Strategies and Resources for Teaching Writing

with the

Simon & Schuster Handbook for Writers

NINTH EDITION

Linda Julian, Patricia Kelvin,
Scott A. Leonard, Laurel Black,
Cynthia Myers, Edgar V. Roberts,
and Susan Loudermilk Garza

Upper Saddle River, New Jersey 07458

10 9 8 7 6 5 4 3 2 1

ISBN 13: 978-0-205-62068-5
ISBN 10: 0-205-62068-X

Printed in the United States of America

Contents

■ **PART FIVE: READING AND WRITING**
ABOUT LITERATURE: A PRIMER FOR STUDENTS
BY *Edgar V. Roberts*   **215**

■ **PART SIX: WORKPLACE AND PUBLIC WRITING**
BY *Linda Julian*   **273**

■ **PART SEVEN: INTEGRATING COMPUTERS INTO THE WRITING CLASSROOM**
BY *Linda Julian*   **295**

■ **PART EIGHT: THE ROLE OF VISUAL RHETORIC IN WRITING**
BY *Susan Loudermilk Garza*   **313**

PART ONE:
Strategies for Teaching Writing
by Linda Julian, *Furman University*

CHAPTER 1
Great Expectations

The scene is a familiar one.

"Why'd ya give me a D on this paper? I did everything you told me to. I fixed all the things you marked wrong on my rough draft. I proofread it," the student argues, slouched in a chair across from the teacher's desk, waving the heavily red-marked essay to punctuate these assertions. Suddenly, straightening the torso and looking the teacher squarely in the eye, the student delivers the coup de grâce: "I thought you liked my writing. You're just like all the rest!"

The look of betrayal, the raised voice, and the defeated posture add force to the indictment. The teacher, overcome with a split-second vision of sins of omission and commission, attempts to salvage whatever goodwill is possible, but on a subconscious level the teacher likely admits that the student's statement contains some truth. The bitterest pill to swallow, however, is the hard truth that yet another student has been alienated from the process of learning to write, perhaps irretrievably so.

Many of our students, of course, fortunately have had teachers who made the process of writing exciting, and their interest continues into our courses. Our responsibility to these students is to sustain this excitement and help them refine their skills. Unfortunately, though, we still lose some students who have been scarred by earlier classroom experiences and who are being further alienated by some of our practices, often without our full realization. But we teachers have much more power to combat these negative experiences with writing—and negative attitudes toward writing—than many of us may realize. Engendering a positive attitude about writing can make learning it an intellectual adventure rather than a dead-end road, and this positive attitude can make teaching writing more pleasurable for us teachers as well. The most important lesson we can teach is not the grammar, structure, or tone of writing but a positive attitude towards writing that makes possible a dynamic piece of prose.

This positive attitude informs the *Simon & Schuster Handbook for Writers* by Lynn Quitman Troyka and Doug Hesse. This supplement, *Strategies and Resources for Teaching Writing*, is meant to aid teachers of writing—both new teachers and experienced teachers—in using Troyka & Hesse's handbook effectively to suit the needs of their students. I offer practical suggestions for using the text in a variety of ways to accommodate different kinds of academic calendars. Like the Troyka & Hesse text, this supplement is grounded in the theory that writing is a process that can be enjoyed and taught successfully.

Teaching writing is neither an arcane science nor a hit-or-miss operation but a manageable and stimulating venture that requires careful planning, a somewhat flexible spirit, and intellectual energy. As teachers, we know that learning to write well is the most important need that most students have. At the same time we realize that students today often see writing as an amorphous, vague skill impossible to master, and they often view teachers of writing as arbitrary beings who are impossible to please. Motivated by a need to succeed in college, apathetic students of writing enter into a tug of war with us over the grades we assign their writing, paying little attention to the process itself or the important potential embodied in their work. For them, Composition 101 is more of what they've had—and they don't want it. But Composition 101 doesn't have to be this way for them. We can make it a stimulating, creative, enjoyable course that will teach them skills useful for their entire lives.

One of the critical skills we must help all students master is learning to use computers in many different ways. Teaching critical thinking skills and writing with computers and the many resources they bring through the Internet is imperative if our students are to function as learners, employees, and citizens. In addition to using the Internet for research, students can have online class discussions. They can access syllabi and class materials for courses; they can e-mail questions to classmates or the instructor; they can e-mail essay drafts to classmates or the campus's writing center for feedback. Students can design Web pages to publish their own writing and use publishing or presentational software to create documents or visual aids. They can do collaborative projects with peers in their own class or in classes across the country or around the world.

Technology enables instruction and learning to extend past the parameters of the classroom. Teachers who have been reluctant to embrace technology are finding they have to become students themselves so that they not only maintain credibility with their students and peers but also enrich their own capabilities as thinkers and writers. Part seven of this manual addresses the pedagogical needs of both experienced and inexperienced teachers of writing by attempting to show some ways technology can work well for their composition students.

Paying attention to our students' needs with regard to technology is one major positive step we can take to help them write better. Other less revolutionary changes in our preparation and attitudes about teaching writing can help our students focus on the positive rewards of learning to write.

In communicating with our students, we can begin this transformation of attitude by accentuating the positive. In both written and oral comments to the students, we need to emphasize what the students have done well in a given assignment. Certainly, we have a duty to tell them what is ineffective in a paper and what they must do to improve a piece of writing; but if we write only negative comments, we will engender or strengthen negative attitudes towards writing. (See Chapter 7 in this supplement for a discussion of evaluation.) If we communicate to the students our recognition of each student's unique abilities as a writer and our understanding that all writers, no matter how weak or ineffective, can improve, our words will fall on the ears of more willing listeners. If we communicate positive expectations, we will have more positive results.

One important key to success in teaching writing is realizing that we cannot march an entire class in lock step through a syllabus each term. In some other disciplines the nature of the material being taught warrants a more rigid syllabus, but an inflexible syllabus in a composition course is a death knell to growth and excitement. This realization does not mean we should have no syllabus or that we should have a hit-or-miss plan for the term. On the contrary, it means that we must be adept at constantly amending and revising our syllabus to accommodate the various levels of writers we have in a given class. Those teachers who have a syllabus planned by their department must look for ways to tailor it to the needs of the students and to flesh it out with energetic assignments.

Developing this ability to plan the course but not to over-plan it (addressed in more detail in Chapters 2 and 4 of this supplement) is one step in communicating to students our awareness of their uniqueness and the potential that it brings to the classroom. It also communicates to the students that they are partners in the writing class, not objects to be talked at. In fact, we should involve students in planning the class periodically, perhaps one day every couple of weeks. We must allow students to see the possibility that their contributions to the class will result in assignments that grow out of their own work.

And we should involve students in evaluating each other's work and in collaborating on projects that will strengthen the skills of each individual. Recent research has shown the great value of peer evaluation in teaching writing (discussed in more detail in Chapter 6 in this supplement) and the benefits to students of collaborative learning (discussed in Part 2—Teaching Collaborative Writing).

Another important key to success in teaching writing is developing ways to help students see why writing is important. Certainly, we all think that we promote this awareness in our first-day-of-class speeches about the value of the course and in our interaction with these novice writers throughout the term. Often, though, we are miscommunicating. Students quickly dismiss as empty platitudes our most sincere reasons for learning to write—unless we show how those reasons relate directly to their own immediate needs and experiences (see Chapter 2 in this supplement).

We obviously want students to know that well-educated people observe conventions in writing. We can set up discussions and assignments that show students that learning to write is much more than learning rules. We can show them the intellectual energy that writing can produce. We can show them that writing is a means to knowing, that it is a tool for discovering connections between the external world and the internal self.

Discovering these connections is especially difficult for students whose native language is not English or students whose language is nonstandard. We must be sensitive and diligent in helping these students acquire new skills with language. Many composition teachers have had little or no training in teaching English as a second language (TESL) and therefore are particularly frustrated when confronted with students who must struggle to express even basic ideas in Standard Written English. But we can help these students overcome their fear and frustration. Our positive attitude and our excitement about writing will go a long way toward dismantling language barriers and setting these students at ease (see Chapters 48–55 in the handbook and Part Four of this manual for help in teaching ESL students).

Another important goal is to help our students become more critical readers of other writers' work. Students become more excited about the writing process as they comprehend the communal nature of writing. We can help these novice writers understand the value of their audience, and we can show them the important contribution they make to society as responsive, critical readers.

One path to this understanding of audience is the use of well-planned and well-supervised peer critiques. Recent research has shown the gains to be made if we increase students' understanding of audience, and it has supported the effectiveness of peer critiquing as one method for showing students the value of the audience.

Helping our students evaluate what they read also makes them better writers. Critical reading, emphasized in Chapter 4c of the handbook, requires students' attention to nuances of structure and ideas in such a way that these readers pay more attention to similar nuances—and their effects—in their own writing. Critical reading stimulates students to develop subtler topics than they likely would otherwise. And, critical reading makes students aware of the power of language.

Teaching writing effectively means emphasizing what students are doing well. It means exciting them about the possibilities—and being excited about them ourselves. As we are helping our students develop more confidence in their abilities, we must have more confidence in our own skills and professionalism. With that professionalism in mind, I hope that this supplement will stimulate some new insight, sense of purpose, and sources for energy and enthusiasm as we teach and our students learn.

WEB RESOURCES

Web Resources can be found at **www.prenhall.com/troyka** under Instructor's Resources.

SUGGESTED READING

Adler Kassner, Linda. "Structure and Possibility: New Scholarship About Students Called Basic Writers." *College English* 63, no. 2 (Nov. 2000): 229–43.

Anson, Chris M., and Hildy Miller. "Journals in Composition: An Update." "A Progress Report from the CCCC Committee on Professional Standards." *College Composition and Communication* 42 (Oct. 1991) 330–44.

Austin, Kurt. *Trends & Issues in Postsecondary English Studies.* Urbana, IL: National Council of Teachers of English, 1999.

Badger, Richard, and Goodith White. "A Process Genre Approach to Teaching Writing." *ELT Journal* 45, no. 2 (Apr. 2000): 153–60.

Berlin, James. *Writing Instruction in American Colleges* 1900–1985. Carbondale, IL: Southern Illinois University Press, 1987.

Bloom, Lynn Z., Donald A. Daiker, and Edward M. White. *Composition in the Twenty-first Century: Crisis and Change.* Carbondale, IL: Southern Illinois UP, 1997.

Bowden, Darsie. "The Limits of Containment: Text-as-Container in Composition Studies." *College Composition and Communication* 44 (Oct. 1993): 364–79.

Bullock, Richard, and John Trimbur, eds. *The Politics of Writing Instruction: Postsecondary*. Portsmouth, NH: Boynton/Cook, 1991.

Elbow, Peter. "Reflections on Academic Discourse: How It Relates to Freshmen and Colleagues." *College English* 53 (Feb. 1991): 135–55.

——. "The War Between Reading and Writing—And How to End It." *Rhetoric Review* 12, no. 1 (Fall 1993): 5–24.

France, Alan A. "Assigning Places: The Function of Introductory Composition as a Cultural Discourse." *College English* 55, no. 6 (Oct. 1993): 593–609.

Gale, Fredric G., James L. Kinneavy, and Phillip Sipiora. *Ethical Issues in College Writing*. New York: Peter Lang, 1999.

Gale, Xin, and Fredric G. Gale. *(Re)visioning Composition Textbooks: Conflicts of Culture, Ideology and Pedagogy*. Albany: State UP of New York, 1999.

Hairston, Maxine. "Diversity, Ideology, and Teaching Writing." *College Composition and Communication* 43, no. 2 (May 1992): 179–93.

Horner, Bruce. "Resisting Traditions in Composing Composition." *Journal of Advanced Composition*. 14, no. 2 (Fall 1994): 495–519.

Indrisano, Roselmina, and James R. Squire. *Perspectives on Writing: Research, Theory and Practice*. Newark, DE: International Reading Association, 2000.

Jarratt, Susan Caroline Funderburgh. *Feminism and Composition Studies: In Other Words*. New York: Modern Language Association of America, 1998.

Kennedy, Mary Lynch. *Theorizing Composition: A Critical Sourcebook of Theory and Scholarship in Contemporary Composition Studies*. Westport, CT.: Greenwood Press, 1998.

Kirsch, Gesa, and Patricia A. Sullivan, eds. *Methods and Methodology in Composition Research*. Carbondale, IL: Southern Illinois University Press, 1992.

Laurence, Patricia. "The Vanishing Site of Mina Shaughnessy's 'Error and Expectations.'" *Journal of Basic Writing* 12, no. 2 (Fall 1993): 18–28.

Lindemann, Erika. *A Rhetoric for Writing Teachers*. 3rd. ed. New York: Oxford University Press, 1995.

Lourey, Jessica. "Grease on the Keyboard: Making Composition Work in a Technical College. *Teaching English in the Two-Year College* 28, no. 2 (Dec. 2000): 175–81.

Love, Michael. *A Resource Text for College Writing*. Boston: Houghton Mifflin Custom Pub. 2000.

McComiskey, Bruce. *Teaching Composition as a Social Process*. Loga, Utah: Utah State UP, 2000.

Miller, Richard E. "Composing English Studies: Towards a Social History of the Discipline." *College Composition and Communication* 45, no. 2 (May 1994): 164–79.

Miller, Susan. *Assuming the Positions: Cultural Pedagogy and the Politics of Commonplace Writing*. Pittsburgh: UP of Pittsburgh, 1998.

Moore, Sandy, and Michael Kleine. "Toward an Ethics of Teaching Writing in a Hazardous Context—The University." *Journal of Advanced Composition* 12, no. 2 (Fall 1992): 383–94.

Morgan, Dan. "Ethical Issues Raised by Students' Personal Writing." *College English* 60 (Mar. 1998): 318–25.

Norton, L. S. "Essay Writing: What Really Counts?" *Higher Education* 20 (Dec. 1990): 411–42.

Nystrand, Martin, et al. "Where Did Composition Studies Come From? An Intellectual History." *Written Communication* 10, no. 3 (July 1993): 267–333.

Odell, Lee, ed. *Theory and Practice in the Teaching of Writing: Rethinking the Discipline*. Carbondale: Southern Illinois Press, 1993.

Penrod, Diane. *Miss Grundy Doesn't Teach Here Anymore: Popular Culture and the Composition Classroom*. Portsmouth, NH: Boynton/Cook, 1997.

Phillips, Donna Burns, et al. "'College Composition and Communication:' Chronicling a Discipline's Genesis." *College Composition and Communication* 44, no. 4 (Dec. 1993): 443–65.

Qualley, Donna J. *Turns of Thought: Teaching Composition as Reflexive Inquiry*. Portsmouth, NH: Boynton/Cook, 1997.

Renard, Lisa. "Cut and Paste 101: Plagiarism and the Net." *Educational Leadership* 57, no. 4 (Jan. 2000): 38–42.

Runciman, Lex. "Fun?" *College English* 53 (Feb. 1991): 156–63.

Saks, A. L., and Richard L. Larson. "Annotated Bibliography of Research in the Teaching of English." *Research in the Teaching of English* 28, no. 2 (May 1994): 208–23.

Schultz, Lucille M. "Elaborating on Our History: A Look at Mid-19th Century First Books of Composition." *College Composition and Communication* 45, no. 1 (Feb. 1994): 10–30.

Sommers, Nancy I. "The Need for Theory in Composition Research." *College Composition and Communication* 30 (Feb. 1979): 46–49.

Tate, Gary, and Edward P. J. Corbett, eds. *The Writing Teacher's Sourcebook.* 3rd. ed. New York: Oxford University Press, 1994.

"Teaching Writing [Symposium]." *College Teach* 39 (Spring 1991): 44–64.

Thomas, P.L. "The Struggle Itself: Teaching Writing as We Know We Should." *English Journal.* 90, no. 1 (Sept. 2000): 39–45.

Tobin, L. "Reading Students, Reading Ourselves: Revising the Teacher's Role in the Writing Class." *College English* 53 (March 91): 333–48.

Trimbur, John. "Composition and the Circulation of Writing." *College Composition and Communication* 52, no. 2 (Dec. 2000): 188–219.

Troyka, Lynn Quitman, with Gerber, Lloyd-Jones, et al. *A Checklist and Guide for Reviewing Departments of English.* New York: Modern Language Association and Associated Departments of English, 1985.

——. "Perspectives on Legacies and Literacy in the 1980s." *College Composition and Communication* 33 (Oct. 1982): 252–62. Reprinted in *Sourcebook for Basic Writing Teachers*, edited by Theresa Enos. New York: Random House, 1987.

Wallace, Ray, Alan Jackson, and Susan Lewis Wallace. *Reforming College Composition: Writing the Wrongs.* Westport, CT.: Greenwood Press, 2000.

Yagelski, Robert P. "The Ambivalence of Reflection: Critical Pedagogies, Identity, and the Writing Teacher." *College Composition and Communication* 51. no. 1 (Sept. 1999): 32–50.

CHAPTER 2
The Impossible and the Possible: Realistic Goals for Courses in Writing

Well before the bell signals the first class meeting, teachers of writing must have come to terms with goals which are realistic for a college writing course. In other words, we must understand what is possible given the constraints of time and the backgrounds and attitudes of our students. Many teachers get so caught up in trying to teach the impossible that frustration clouds their vision of the possible.

The best confidence builder—and one too often neglected by most of us—is a long, hard look at what is possible during a term. Although the following list of goals is not comprehensive, most teachers would agree that these goals are realizable for most students in a single course in composition.

1. We can help students understand that they can learn to write. Building a positive attitude is essential. We can build the kind of confidence that will ensure an interest in writing long after the students have left our classes.

2. We can help students become aware of the role of writing in their lives. It is both possible and essential to show students that even in this age so often dominated by images, writing plays a major part in everything they do—from checking the weather in the newspaper to looking at the menu in a fast-food restaurant to playing a computer video game. We can help them see the need for learning to write.

3. We can help students learn to use technology to empower them as writers. By integrating technology into our courses, we can help students see how technology offers rich possibilities for research, collaborative work, peer review, and presentation of their writing.

4. We can help students realize that writing is a tool for learning about themselves and the world. We can help students discover that a paper is taking a direction they have not planned on. From that point, we can show them that this departure from their expectation is teaching them what they are really trying to say.

5. We can help students realize that writing is a process. Many students think that writers are born being able to write and that a piece of writing springs, fully finished, from the brain of a "real" writer. We can certainly show students that all writing involves stages and that each stage can be learned. (See Troyka & Hesse, *Simon & Schuster Handbook for Writers*, Chapter 2, hereafter referred to as Troyka & Hesse.)

6. We can show students that brainstorming a topic and writing a draft of a paper can give rise to questions that lead them to new ideas and connections. (See Troyka & Hesse, Chapter 2.)

7. We can help our students see the importance of revision. We can use peer critiquing and our own comments to help students see that papers grow slowly through definite stages, each of which requires full development, with revision being perhaps the most important. We can show them that revision is more than patching up problems with usage and mending a few awkward sentences, and instead that it involves several stages of reconceiving the purpose of the paper and reviewing its effect on the audience. (See Troyka & Hesse, Chapter 2, section i.)

8. We can help students understand that a piece of writing is never finished. As a part of learning the stages that make up the process of writing, students can learn that writers finally let go of a piece of writing when they have revised it enough to satisfy the demands of the situation but that they rarely think they have written something that is perfect and defies improvement. (See Troyka & Hesse, Chapter 2, sections i, j, and k.)

9. We can help our students understand the importance of structure in writing. We can show students the relative merits of various kinds of sentences, the effectiveness of various kinds of paragraph structure, and the effectiveness of structure in an essay. Students may not be able to apply all of the principles of structure that we show them, but making them aware of structure is important and possible. (See Troyka & Hesse, especially Chapters 1, 3, 5, and 7.)

10. We can help our students understand what a paragraph is and how to write a coherent one. We can acquaint students with various methods for developing paragraphs that suit the audience and topic with which they are working. Chapter 3 of the Troyka & Hesse handbook explains many methods of paragraph development and gives interesting, easy-to-grasp examples of each. It also provides a clear explanation of how to make paragraphs coherent and unified. By teaching students how to write effective paragraphs, we can help ensure the sturdiness of the groundwork on which they will eventually build coherent, effective essays.

11. We can help students understand the importance of making clear connections between ideas. It is possible to teach students to draw logical conclusions, to make their thoughts coherent, to support their generalizations with evidence. We can teach them how to make connections among ideas in their own writing and to look for them in the writing of others. (See Troyka & Hesse, Chapters 3, 4, and 5.)

12. We can help students understand the nature and the importance of the audience. Too many students think that English papers are written only for the English teacher. In making this assumption, they do not realize that many choices they make as writers depend on defining the audience for a given piece of work. We can help students realize that as writers they belong to a community of readers and writers. In short, we can teach students that they do not write in a vacuum. (See Troyka & Hesse, Chapter 1.)

13. We can help students understand that good grammar is not the same thing as effective writing. Although good grammar helps make writing clear and more acceptable to some audiences, it is a far different thing from the process of writing. We can, and must, clarify this important point for students. Part 3 of Troyka & Hesse's handbook clearly presents basic grammar, but it does so in a positive way that should minimize students' feelings of inadequacy with grammar.

14. We can help our students understand that inflated diction does not equal sophisticated thinking. In the same way that many students equate good grammar with "good" writing, many students equate big words with elevated style and thought. We must show students that the most effective writing is that which puts clear, simple language together in a coherent and interesting way. (See Troyka & Hesse, Chapter 12.)

15. We can help students understand what an essay is. Experienced teachers know that even the brightest students have read few essays and that most students have only vague notions of what an essay really is. Students frequently call them "stories," and they think that essays, invented by English teachers, are found only in school. Helping students define the term *essay* is important, as is showing them where they can find good essays being published today.

16. We can help our students understand how to use a dictionary. Students think that all dictionaries are created equal, and they think of a dictionary as a place to look up a word to check spelling or meaning. We need to acquaint them with the aids for using the dictionary, given in each one, and we need to show them the value of the prefatory matter in the dictionary. We can help them see the value of both desk dictionaries and unabridged dictionaries. (See Troyka & Hesse handbook Chapter 12, section d.)

17. We can help students learn to use a handbook to find answers to questions they have about writing. Too often many of us assume that because we know what's in a handbook and how to find it, students will as well. We should take some time to show students how to use the book we have chosen. To a great extent, knowledge is knowing where to find out what one needs to know. Encouraging students to read Troyka & Hesse's

"Preface to Students" likely will help students feel that they are part of the book and that Troyka and Hesse have considered their needs. The easy-to-find information located before the Preface, "How to Use Your Handbook," will also help students become independent learners.

18. We can help students understand that they have a responsibility to be critical readers. Most students think that if something is published, it must be important or "good." We can help them understand how to recognize the flaws in scholarship and logic that make much published work inferior. (See Troyka & Hesse, Chapter 4.)

19. We can help students see that they live in a community of readers and writers, a community which can grow in mutual understanding and respect only through careful, sensitive reading and writing that will promote dialogue between groups of different genders, ethnic origins, ages, socioeconomic class, and geographic areas. (See Troyka & Hesse, Chapters 1 and 6.)

20. We can, and must, help students realize that writing is neither "good" nor "bad." Too often our students come to us having been labeled by themselves or by others as "good" writers or "bad" writers; but we can help them see that a better way of judging writing is to consider the effectiveness of a piece of writing in its context.

Taking stock of what we can do in a single course contributes significantly to our own sense of confidence in our ability to teach a stimulating class. My own experience has shown me clearly that students respond with more assurance and interest when they sense my confidence in achieving these goals.

WEB RESOURCES

Web Resources can be found at **www.prenhall.com/troyka** under Instructor's Resources.

SUGGESTED READING

Baines, Lawrence, Coleen Baines, and Gregory Kent Stanley. "Losing the Product in the Process." *English Journal* 88. No. 5 (May 1999): 67–72.

Bizzaro, Patrick. "What I Learned in Grad School, of Literary Training and the Theorizing of Composition." *College Composition and Communication* 50, no. 4 (June 1999): 722–42.

Bruffee, Kenneth A. "Academic Castes, Academic Authority, and the Educational Centrality of Writing." *College Composition and Communication* 50, no. 4 (June 1999): 722–42.

Connors, Robert J. "The Erasure of the Sentence." *College Composition and Communication* 52, no. 1 (Sept. 200): 96–128.

Devine, T. G. "Caveat Emptor: The Writing Process Approach to College Writing." *Journal of Developmental Education* 11 (Fall 1990): 2–4.

Dossin, Mary Mortimore. "Writing Across the Curriculum: Lessons from a Writing Teacher." *College Teaching* 45 (Winter 1997): 14–15.

Lardner, Ted. "What Works? Rethinking the Theory-Practice Relationship in Composition." *Writing Instructor* 15 (Fall 1995): 5–17.

——. "Locating the Boundaries of Composition and Creative Writing." *College Composition and Communication* 51, no. 1 (Sept. 1999): 72–77.

Mayers, Tim. "(Re)writing Craft." *College Composition and Communication* 51, no. 1 (Sept. 1999): 82–89.

Newkirk, Thomas, ed. *Nuts and Bolts: A Practical Guide to Teaching College Composition.* Portsmouth, NH: Boynton/Cook, 1993.

Reid, Joy M., and Patricia Byrd. *Grammar in the Composition Classroom.* New York: Heinle & Heinle Publishers, 1998.

Troyka, Lynn Quitman. "Closeness to Text: A Delineation of Reading Processes as They Affect Composing." in *Relating Writing and Reading in the College Years*, edited by Thomas Newkirk. Boynton/Cook, 1986.

Wallace, D. L., and J. R. Hayes. "Redefining Revision for Freshmen." *Research in the Teaching of English* 25 (Feb. 1991): 54–66.

CHAPTER 3
Using a Handbook: Why and How

Tyrant or tool, or something in between—one of these is the role that a handbook of grammar and usage generally plays in a writing course. To play a vital role in a student's experience of learning to write and a teacher's experience in teaching writing effectively, the best role for a handbook like the *Simon & Schuster Handbook for Writers* is that of tool.

Many of us have seen the handbook as tyrant. Either as students, observers of other composition teachers, or new teachers of writing, we have seen the handbook become the focus of the course. In this scenario bad grades are often used to browbeat students into virtually memorizing the handbook. The teacher equates rules with writing. Instead of concentrating on the positive features of a piece of writing, the teacher points out all the rules it has violated. Revision becomes a belabored effort to "fix" the mistakes in the paper. The product of a handbook-as-tyrant class is frustrated students who come to fear using the handbook because they think that they can never fix their writing to reflect its perfect standards. Of course, a byproduct is a frustrated teacher who works hard and cannot see why the students are not improving.

In the ideal scenario, students view the handbook as a means to effective writing. They look upon it as a tool in the same way they consider a dictionary, a notebook, or a computer disk a tool.

But, we all know that it is totally unrealistic simply to plunk copies of the handbook down on students' desks and instruct the students to use the handbooks as tools. Few students know how to use a handbook, and, given their previous experience with writing classes and handbooks, many of them do not even want to try.

Teachers must help students figure out the apparatus of the handbook to make using it second nature, and, equally important, they must help students see that being able to use the handbook well as independent learners can improve both their writing skills and their sense of self-confidence as students. Initially, at least, students probably learn together the apparatus and the confidence to work with the book on their own.

In addition to helping make students familiar with the handbook—and comfortable and confident using it—teachers are faced with important decisions about how large a role the handbook should play in the syllabus for the course. They also must consider ways in which they will use the handbook in marking students' papers.

■ THE HANDBOOK AS TEXT

Although the handbook rarely works well as a central text for a course in writing, many teachers are successful in assigning parts of it for class discussion or as the basis for written assignments. We should be open to possibilities for using it that require us to deviate from the order of information in the text; that is, we should not be afraid to mix and mingle parts of the handbook to suit our students' interests and needs.

Depending on the focus of the individual teacher's class, several sections of the *Simon & Schuster Handbook* may be used separately or together as useful information for class discussion or writing assignments. Since Chapter 4 of this supplement gives sample syllabi which include sections of the handbook, the following are only general suggestions.

1. Choose to teach a unit on language, grounding it on Chapter 12 of the handbook. Since this chapter is not made up of "rules," it offers the teacher a good beginning point for creating a positive interest in writing rather than a negative one. Most students are keenly interested in improving their vocabularies, though often for the misguided notion that big words equal important ideas. They also know very little about dictionaries and etymology. Chapter 12, "The Impact of Words," can provoke some substantial discussion, especially when coupled with a look at several kinds of dictionaries, including the *Oxford English Dictionary* (OED). Students often have lively discussions on such topics as sexist language, jargon, slang, doublespeak, and cliches. These discussions can be effective springboards into some energetic writing about language.

2. Choose to teach a unit on research and assign parts of Part 5, "Research and Writing." Or you could choose a unit on writing across the curriculum or public writing using Part Six, "Writing Across the Curriculum and Beyond," which includes chapters on writing in the disciplines, making multimedia presentations, business and professional writing, public writing, and document design. In using these chapters, emphasize that you want the students to get an overview of the range of audiences for which research is done and the common methods respected in the many communities that rely on research. Many students are unaware of how much research is done in businesses and service industries, and some good class discussions can explore the real-life uses of research. We want to teach them that research is not something that only chemists and English teachers do. Class discussions should focus on the process of research and the process of writing information found in research. Discussions can make clear to students that knowing how to do research and write about their findings is much more than knowing the proper forms of documentation to use in research papers. This kind of assignment can combat the negative experiences that many students have had with term papers, especially if they begin to see that research is an essential part of most kinds of careers and fields.

In addition, this unit offers a great opportunity to help students understand the role of computers and electronic databases in current research. Although some students will be experienced with the "information highway," even they will enjoy discussing the strengths and weaknesses of electronic searches. Less computer-literate students need to be introduced to the possibilities of electronic research. All students need help with learning to document material from electronic sources, and they need to learn what constitutes plagiarism in the world of electronic sources. The handbook's Chapter 34 ("Finding and Evaluating Sources") and Chapter 35 ("Using Sources and Avoiding Plagiarism") offer such help. (For help with integrating computers into your teaching, see Part seven of this supplement.)

3. Choose to teach a unit on argument, basing it on Chapters 4 and 5, "Thinking Critically About Ideas and Images" and "Writing Arguments." Many students believe that anything in print is useful and true, and they will respond with interest to Chapter 4, which shows why critical reading is important and how they can learn to read critically. Most of them have had little or no exposure to logic, and they will find the discussions of evaluation and reasoning informative and stimulating. Troyka & Hesse's handbook features a section in Chapter 5 (section 5h) that includes Steven Toulmin's ideas about argument. In addition, students are surrounded by visual rhetoric and will benefit from learning how to "read" visuals and understand their arguments.

This chapter can be a useful basis for assignments, both oral and written, which ask students to evaluate the arguments in books, movies, editorials, or advertisements. Once students learn about inadequate evidence and about inductive and deductive reasoning, they enjoy scrutinizing ads or letters to the editor for flaws in reasoning.

4. Choose to teach a unit on the paragraph, for which you assign Chapter 3, "Writing Paragraphs, Shaping Essays." Many teachers like to begin composition courses by having students learn to write well-unified, coherent paragraphs before they tackle a whole essay. Others like to do a unit on developing paragraphs after they have discussed the essay as a whole. In either case students can usually benefit from discussing varieties of methods for developing paragraphs. They will particularly enjoy the information in this section if they locate samples of paragraph development and critique the paragraphs of classmates. A whole class workshop using transparencies or photocopies of student paragraphs can be a useful strategy to teach paragraph development and peer-response skills.

5. Choose to teach a section on revision and assign Chapter 2, "Essential Processes for Academic Writing." Many teachers prefer to teach revision as the third major step in the process of writing, but others find that pulling revision out of the chronology and emphasizing it helps students understand that revisions are a major element of producing an effective piece of writing and that it involves far more than patchwork repairs to grammar and spelling. Often students need some time away from a piece of writing in order to re-think its content or structure. Revising an essay from a previous course or having students rewrite a piece for a new audience or purpose can be useful methods for teaching students global revision.

6. Choose to teach a unit on planning a piece of writing and assign Chapter 2, "Essential Processes for Academic Writing. This unit should bring about some lively discussion, especially if you illustrate the chapter's points by having students work in class in groups to generate ideas and shape them into manageable topics for papers or paragraphs.

Many students complain that they cannot think of anything to write about, or they turn in topics that are worn out or too large for even a multi-volume work. These students can benefit from reading this section of the text, but they will benefit much more if they are assigned activities that reinforce the skills introduced in the chapter. Unless students actually practice these skills, the information does not really register and many will revert to planning their essays as they write them.

7. Choose to do a unit on effective sentences and assign Part Three, "Writing Effectively, Writing with Style." Especially helpful for students are discoveries they make about conciseness (Chapter 11), parallelism (Chapter 10), and coordination and subordination and variety (Chapter 9).

Even students who are improving their skills at the slowest rate take pleasure in crafting effective sentences, and more proficient writers enjoy working with the possible variations of form for a single sentence.

8. Choose to teach a unit on the importance of audience and assign Chapter 1, "Understanding College and Other Writing Situations." Many teachers like to begin writing courses by introducing students to the concept of audience, but others prefer to introduce this idea after students have begun to work on paragraphs, research, or even whole essays.

Nevertheless, audience and purpose are two of the most important concepts that beginning writers need to know about, and most students do not. This chapter of the text presents information that is stimulating to students because it is largely new and nonthreatening in terms of "rules." They generally enjoy class discussions of alterations one would need to make in a piece of writing for a change in audience or purpose.

9. Choose to help students improve their ability on typical types of college writing assignments, including summaries, lab reports, critical responses, and essay exams. Using Chapter 7 ("Strategies for Writing Typical Kinds of College Papers"), you can help students, develop effective processes and organizational strategies to improve their success in these situations.

10. Choose to help students improve their writing skills by teaching a unit on "Business and Professional Writing," Chapter 43, or "Writing for the Public," Chapter 44 in the handbook. Most students are eager to learn about employment letters and résumés, and most also enjoy writing other kinds of letters and proposals. Such a unit allows us to help them see the importance of organization, precision with diction, grammar, and spelling, a clear view of purpose and audience, and attention to conventions of address and format.

In fact, business letters work better than many kinds of assignments to help students see the importance of careful planning of their message as well as careful revision and proofreading. We can help them see that personal pride in their work can be communicated in letters and other business documents. Students enjoy writing letters of complaint about real problems they have experienced with products or services, and they enjoy responding to one another's complaints. You might choose to have them write to local companies requesting information useful for research projects or samples of business documents the company routinely processes. Whatever the assignment, students usually take the business writing tasks more seriously than other writing requirements because they see an immediate value for this knowledge. For this reason, many teachers like to do some business writing early in the term to help motivate students to write and to make connections between business writing and extremely important concepts like audience and purpose, which should figure prominently in later writing assignments.

In addition, empowering students to write about public issues and concerns in such documents as letters to the editor, news releases, and statements to government officials will help equip them to be better informed and more articulate citizens likely to participate in group discussions in their own communities as well as in issues facing state and national governing and policy-making bodies. The material in Chapter 43 and Chapter 44 will help you show students how to make their writing heard in matters that affect their lives.

In a class, all of these sections of the handbook work well as text. They are not concerned with right and wrong usage and are thus nonthreatening to students. Most of these sections contain concepts which the students are only marginally knowledgeable about, if at all, and the information generally stimulates them to have a more positive attitude toward the whole process of writing. The content in these chapters can also be supplemented with Chapter 42, "Making Presentations and Using Multimedia," Chapter 45, "Document and Visual Design," and Chapter 46, "Multimodal Texts and Writing for the Web."

■ THE HANDBOOK AS AN AID IN MARKING PAPERS

Many teachers like to use a handbook as an aid in marking papers. The numbers listed inside the front cover or the symbols given at the back of the book make it easy for a teacher to indicate in an abbreviated way both what the problem is and where in the text the student can find an explanation and examples to help in the revision. Certainly the ease with which these numbers and symbols can be used makes them an attractive feature to busy teachers. For example, see the teacher's comments on Sara Cardini's second draft in Chapter 2 of the handbook. But numbers and symbols are best used in conjunction with some written comments by the teacher. Such comments help remind the student that a human being has read the paper and is interested in it. (See Chapter 7 of this supplement, for additional information on evaluation.)

The following paragraphs from students' essays show how a teacher can use these symbols and numbers along with written comments to help students understand how to revise their work and to help them feel that they can, in fact, continue to improve.

If we have given our students a preliminary introduction to the handbook during the first few days of class, they have little trouble using the symbols and numbers marked by the teacher to find the explanation they need. Having students keep an error log can heighten their awareness of mistakes they commonly make when writing and how to correct those errors.

20c   17i
Studying in the dorms is difficult, at night everyone <u>begin</u> to act silly.

17e
Questions and laughter <u>fills</u> the air. Shawn and Julie bombard Nadine

16d
and <u>I</u> with pillows or play practical jokes (on) us. The many distractions

16d
of a relaxed environment force Nadine and <u>I</u> back to our room.

27b   24d
Attempts to complete homework in the boy's friendly, noi<u>sy and</u> busy

room always fail.

—Holly Burnette

Holly,

You're off to a good start here, but can you flesh out the paragraph with more details? You'll also want to revise the mechanical problems I've marked.

Whether they choose Topps, Fleer, Donruss, or Upper Deck, millions of
11e   16r
Americans delight <u>in the collection of</u> baseball cards. For 75 cents, <u>you</u>

can buy a pack of ten cards, and if the brand is Topps a piece of gum
                                            not quite clear
will accompany the cards. Some collectors strive <u>to obtain a certain</u>

<u>team</u>, while others attempt to gain as many cards as possible. Whatever
                             awkward phrasing
the quantity, <u>the idea of the trading card still exists</u>, as the collector's

favorite pastime may be trading cards with a friend or local dealer.
see 12f   *see 11d.1*
The baseball card collector ⓒan bⓔ a <u>boy</u> in the seventh grade or ⓟossibly

a sophisticated business executive. Card collection is not restricted to

males, as girls can easily be found with their Barbies and baseball
                                            of?
cards. Clearly this American tradition truly entertains a wide <u>variety.</u>

                                            —Steve Weathers
Great topic, Steve.
Try to make the sentences more specific and clearer.

Often, in addition to marking symbols or numbers or both, teachers indicate exercises that they want the student to do to strengthen particular skills. Sometimes they have students write a revision as well as certain exercises before they meet with students about the paper. Of course writing exercises can be simply busywork unless the teacher carefully monitors the students' use of them and encourages the students to see that the exercises are not ends in themselves but means to strengthening the revision. And having students work on a revision and exercises can help students become more independent learners.

■ THE HANDBOOK AS A TOOL FOR STUDENTS

Perhaps the most important function of a handbook is as a tool for the students to use independently. But before we can expect them to use it, or even to want to, we must show them how to make the handbook work for them. One good way is to take two or three class meetings at the beginning of the term to acquaint students with the handbook's features and to give them an overview of its contents.

A simple but effective beginning, especially for weaker students, is to have them read the "To the Student" part of the Preface and write answers to the following questions (or similar ones):

1. What will Troyka & Hesse discuss in this book?
2. How many chapters does this book have?
3. In what three ways can you look something up in this book?
4. What appears on the inside back cover?
5. What does it mean when a term in the book appears in all caps?

Even though the students write out the answers, you will usually need to have them discuss their findings and do some exercises on locating material to ensure that everyone in the class has absorbed the information in the Preface. For all levels of students, discussion of the handbook seems to work better than individual written responses since students are capable of mechanically writing information without understanding or processing it.

In-class group exploration of the handbook can stimulate learners of all levels, and it can be a good icebreaker to help students get to know one another during the first few class meetings. You may wish to have each group respond to more detailed versions of the questions above, perhaps giving a couple of examples to support each answer. In addition you may wish to have students do exercises that show them how to locate kinds of information in the handbook. These kinds of exercises not only teach students to find their way around in the book, but, more importantly, they build the students' confidence in their own ability to use it.

In using these kinds of exercises, you should emphasize, however, that the point is not the answer itself but the process of learning how to use the handbook. Following are some sample exercises that you may find useful models for your own versions.

1. Suppose you want to find out when to use *who* and when to use *whom*. Where could you learn the difference? Most students would probably begin with the index to solve this problem since few of them would know that these are pronouns. When they found the *who* entry in the index, they would be referred to section 16g on pp. 341–342, "When should I use *who, whoever, whom,* or *whomever?*" where these forms are discussed in detail. Those students who knew that these were pronouns could have gone directly to the Terms Glossary and looked under *pronoun*, where they would find references to the appropriate section. Finally, those students who recognized that these are pronouns could quickly have found the reference to section 16g by looking in the inside front cover under Pronouns: Case and Reference, where section 16g is defined as *"who, whom; whoever, whomever."*

2. Suppose you are confused about the placement of quotation marks with commas. Where would you find some help? If the students first looked up *comma(s)* in the index, they would find an entry "use with quotation marks" which would direct them to pages 435–437. There they would find examples illustrating the placement of the two marks. If they first looked up *quotation marks* in the index, they would be directed to Chapter 28, pages 460–468, where section *h* discusses the conventions of using quotation marks with other punctuation. If they first looked at the inside front cover of the text, they would find *With other punctuation* as subdivision *h* of Chapter 28. Similarly, if the students first looked at the Response Symbols Chart, the symbol for "punctuation error" is *pe*, which is followed by a reference to Chapters 23–29.

3. Where can you find out how to revise your essay to rid it of sexist language? If the students looked up *sexist language, nonsexist language or gender-neutral language* in the index, they would be directed to pages 258–260 where, in Chapter 12f, they would find the section "What is gender-neutral language?" There, students will find a shaded box (Quick Reference 12.2) labeled *"How to avoid sexist language."* Although most students are not sophisticated enough to look under *pronoun* in either the index or front cover of the text, many could find *nonsexist language* by looking under "The Impact of Words" inside the front cover. The abbreviation *sxt* in the correction chart also refers students to Section 12f.

4. Your teacher has indicated that you have trouble making transitions both within your paragraphs and between paragraphs. Where can you learn how to make smooth transitions? If students looked up the word *transition* in the index, they would find both a reference to page 85 in the text as well as page 842 the Terms Glossary. Looking in the Glossary, they might notice the term *transitional expressions* directly following the transition entry. The definition of *transitional expressions* briefly explains how they function as transitional devices. Under *transitional expressions* students would also find a reference to section 3g.1, which illustrates how to use transitions both within and between paragraphs.

Here are other sample questions for this kind of exercise:

1. Where can you find out how to omit information from a quotation or to add explanatory words to it?
2. Your teacher has indicated that you frequently write dangling modifiers. Where can you find an explanation of this problem and some examples of ways to correct dangling modifiers?

3. You are writing a term paper which often quotes lines of poetry. Where can you find guidelines for conventions of quoting lines of poetry?

4. Your teacher has said that your writing is wordy. You don't quite understand the term *wordy*, and you want a further explanation of this concept and some suggestions for improvement. Where can you find them?

5. Your teacher has commented on your paper that your style is choppy and monotonous because you use too many short, simple sentences. The teacher has said that you need to subordinate more. Where can you find out what *subordination* means and how to put it into practice?

Such exercises will go a long way towards alleviating the fear and feeling of helplessness that handbooks often inspire in inexperienced writers and will help the students feel more confident that they can find in it what they need to know. After they use the handbook for a couple of weeks, most students will begin to regard it as a tool and an important reference work that they will want to keep for writing beyond the English classroom.

WEB RESOURCES

Web Resources can be found at **www.prenhall.com/troyka** under Instructor's Resources.

SUGGESTED READING

Boyd, Richard. "Mechanical Correctness and Ritual in the Late Nineteenth-Century Composition Classroom." *Rhetoric Review* 11, no. 2 (Spring 1993): 436–55.

Broad, Bob. "Pulling Your Hair Out: Crises of Standardization in Communal Writing Assessment." *Research in the Teaching of English* 35, no. 2 (Nov. 2000), 213–61.

Fredericksen, Elaine. "Letter Writing in the College Classroom." *Teaching English in the Two Year College*, 27, no. 3 (Mar. 2000): 278–84.

Glasser, Marc. "Grammar and the Teaching of Writing: Limits and Possibilities." *Journal of Technical Writing and Communication* 22, no. 4 (Winter 1993): 23–32.

Hayes, Christopher G. "A Brief Writing Assignment for Introducing Nonsexist Pronoun Usage." *Teaching English in the Two-Year College*, 28, no. 1 (Sept. 2000): 74–77.

Helton, Edwina L., and Jeff Sommers. "Repositioning Revision: A Rhetorical Approach to Grading." *Teaching English in the Two-Year College* 28, no. 2 (Dec. 2000): 157–64.

Reynolds, Patricia R. "Evaluating ESL and College Composition Texts for Teaching the Argumentative Rhetorical Form." *Journal of Reading* 36, no. 6 (March 1993): 474–80.

Shuman, R. Baird. "Grammar for Writers: How Much Is Enough?" *The Place of Grammar in Writing Instruction: Past, Present, Future.* Ed. Susan Hunter and Ray Wallace. Portsmouth, NH: Boynton/Cook, 1995.

Whichard, Nancy Wingardner, et al. "Life in the Margin: The Hidden Agenda in Commenting on Student Writing." *Journal of Teaching Writing* 11, no. 1 (Spring–Summer 1992): 51–64.

Williams, James D. *Preparing to Teach Writing.* Belmont, CA: Wadsworth, 1988. "Rule-Governed Approaches to Language and Composition." *Written Communication* 10 (October 1993): 542–68.

CHAPTER 4
The Course Syllabus: Some Models

The term *syllabus* is our own jargon for the plan or outline of the purpose, goals, and form of our course. The syllabus is meant to be a tool for teachers and students—a guide, not a remonstrance constantly reminding us that "at my back I always hear / Time's winged chariot hurrying near." The term conjures up images of shackles for some teachers and steamrollers for others. But it's a safe bet that teachers who view a syllabus in these negative ways have been victims of rigidity rather than masters of the course plan. A syllabus, an essential anchor for our teaching, is, however, relatively easy to prepare and use if we approach its construction with some guidelines and some enthusiasm.

Twenty years ago handing out a syllabus on the first day of class was the exception, not the rule. Teachers were more likely to write the names of the texts on the blackboard and make an assignment orally for the next class. Those teachers who did hand out a syllabus usually gave their students a much more succinct statement of the policies of the class than what we have come to view today as a typical syllabus.

Today the syllabus comes in various forms, but it is generally more detailed than it was even a decade ago. One form is the departmental syllabus, often devised by a committee in those departments that teach numerous sections of basic courses. But even these fairly rigid guidelines need fleshing out, and teachers must do so, on paper, before the term begins, modifying the syllabus as necessary throughout the term. Now, the syllabi of many teachers incorporate instruction about word processing, document design, online research, and other computer skills that students need to acquire before they enter the workforce or graduate school.

These changes in the nature of the syllabus and the frequency of its use have come about for several reasons. Many department chairs and deans have urged faculty to give their students fairly detailed syllabi, because having course policies and assignments in writing helps prevent misunderstandings that, in extreme cases, can result in lawsuits. Spelling out attendance policies, grading policies, the goals of the course, and the skills required of students earning credit for the course makes a kind of contract between teachers and students.

Also, in this age of accountability, students like to know what will be expected of them and that the requirements are not going to be changed drastically and arbitrarily (or, as they perceive it, whimsically). A syllabus—even a demanding one—is a security blanket of sorts.

From the teacher's point of view, however, the real advantage of having a syllabus is that it gives a game plan for the term. To be effective, such a game plan affords teachers much leeway in strategy, but at the same time it clarifies for teachers the material that they think is realistic and manageable for them to cover in that term. Teachers who begin a composition course with no syllabus often run the risk of getting to the last two weeks of the term and realizing suddenly that there's no time to do the four additional papers required by the department or that only two of the twelve goals they have set for the course have been met.

Thus, legalities and students' security aside, handing out some kind of a syllabus makes good pedagogical sense. Having chosen to give students a syllabus, however, teachers are still faced with some major decisions about the syllabus: How detailed should it be? How much should it control the class? To what extent can the teacher feel free to deviate from it?

A syllabus should include the obvious information about the course: the teacher's name, the catalogue number of the course, the classroom number, the attendance policy, the grading policy—perhaps only a brief statement about what percent of the final grade will be made up of class work, essays, exams, and so forth. In addition, the syllabus should contain a statement of the overall goals for the course. Often this statement will be one formulated by a department or freshman writing committee. Also, as part of the syllabus many teachers like to include a statement defining plagiarism and the penalties for it.

In addition to this basic information, teachers usually give an outline of the course. This outline may be as specific as a day-by-day list of assignments for the entire term, or it may be as general as a list of dates on which specific assignments are due. Students like the day-by-day list of assignments because it helps them plan their work around that demanded by other courses, but teachers find it more problematic. With a day-by-day list of assignments, teachers often find themselves behind on the second or third day so that the syllabus either will be inaccurate throughout the course or will require constant revision. This kind of syllabus leaves little room for the slowing down or speeding up that will be motivated in all classrooms by the students themselves. Teachers may begin to feel that this kind of syllabus is a set of chains.

Conversely, the syllabus that lists only the dates when major assignments are due frustrates the students somewhat because they have a hard time juggling the seemingly arbitrary assignments that the teacher sporadically makes to supplement the syllabus. More importantly, such a syllabus may also be too vague to help the teachers pace themselves.

For many, a good compromise is the kind of syllabus that breaks the course into weekly chunks and gives the goals and major assignments for the week. This kind is usually detailed enough to allow students to plan well with their other courses and to allow teachers to get through the allotted material during the term. Writing a course syllabus effectively also requires that we consider both the length of the term and the emphasis we want to impose on the material. There's really no such thing as a generic composition course: the teacher's own interests or the philosophy of the department or freshman committee dictates a particular goal or emphasis for the basic college course in composition. These goals must be considered realistically in light of the length of the term.

In composition courses, time is extremely relative; that is, the forty-five or so contact hours required for most three- or five-hour courses are not equally effective if one compares a long term to a short, compressed one. Obviously, time is required for the process of writing to take root and for the students to begin to have confidence in their ability to write. The closer together the class meetings are and the longer the class sessions are, the more difficulty students have assimilating the principles we are trying to teach them. Thus, in arranging the syllabus we should keep in mind that less work is often more learning. Of course, those teachers in departments who require an absolute number of pages or papers per term have less flexibility with this idea that less is more, though they can perhaps adjust the subjects and lengths of papers with this concept in mind. Among the many possible focuses for a basic composition course, teachers often adopt one of these five approaches:

> ➤ *the whole essay*, showing students several rhetorical modes of development (narrative, description, definition, etc.) or various purposes (informative, persuasive) or contexts (writing across the curriculum, workplace and public writing, etc.) for writing;

> ➤ *the paragraph*, working up to the whole paper at the end of the term, a method often favored particularly by those working with developmental writers;

> ➤ *research skills*, perhaps having students write papers for disciplines other than English and focusing on critical reading skills and attention to audience or developing a Web-based alternative of the traditional research paper;

> ➤ *technology and writing*, either integrating technology into the classroom or teaching the course itself online;

> *critical thinking*, empasizing critical thinking, reading, and writing skills, particularly argument, and often working with both print and visual rhetoric.

These five approaches are illustrated in the sample syllabi which follow: two fifteen-week semester samples (technology and writing and whole essay/writing across the curriculum, respectively), two ten-week quarter samples (paragraph and research skills, respectively), and one six-week summer term sample (critical thinking/argument). To approach the course in any one of these five ways, teachers will find the *Simon & Schuster Handbook for Writers* easy to use, although the book's usefulness is certainly not limited to these five approaches. In addition, help in the handbook is supported by several online resources offered by Prentice Hall.

All sample syllabi are based on the assumption that teachers are using Troyka & Hesse's *Simon & Schuster Handbook for Writers* and perhaps a reader as well. For any of the syllabi, essay assignments may be altered to include writing arguments (Chapter 5), visual rhetoric (Chapter 4), research writing (Part 5), writing about literature or other readings (Chapter 7 and Chapter 40), writing in the disciplines (Chapters 39–41), business and professional writing (Chapter 43), writing for the public (Chapter 44), collaborative writing (Chapter 6 of the handbook and Part Two of this manual), and essay exams (Chapter 7f.7). Instructors may also opt to include oral presentations (Chapter 42) or Web page design (Chapter 46) along with their writing assignments, or they may desire to emphasize grammar, punctuation, mechanics, syntax, and diction (Part 2, Part 3, Part 4, and, possibly Part 7). Any of these syllabi can be modified to fit weighted, portfolio, or contract evaluation.

■ SYLLABI FOR SEMESTER (FIFTEEN-WEEK) COURSES

The two syllabi here focus on technology and writing and on writing across the curriculum, respectively. The first syllabus, which focuses on technology and writing, may be used in a computer-assested classroom or may be taught partially or fully as an online course. This syllabus assumes the use of portfolio evaluation and includes collaborative writing and presentation projects, but can easily be altered to focus solely on essay writing or writing in the disciplines using weighted or contract grading.

The second syllabus for a course focused on essay writing emphasizes esssay writing and writing across the curriculum. This syllabus may be adapted to fit a learning community, a course which links or integrates courses from two or more disciplines. If the composition class was linked to a psychology class, for example, the instructor may prefer to focus the entire course on writing in the social sciences. Incorporating collaborative writing, whether in the form of an essay, a multimedia presentation, or Web page design, is another effective way to generate interest and develop a sense of community in the classroom.

✓ **Emphasis on Technology and Writing**

WEEK ONE

Goals:	Learn how to use the handbook
	Learn about the importance of audience and purpose
	Learn to summarize
	Learn to read critically
	Learn about developing electronic portfolios (Chapter 47, particulary Chapter 47.f; instructors, see Part Three, "Using Portfolios for Learning and Assessment," in *Strategies and Resources for Teaching Writing*)
Review:	E-mail and Internet use, including "netiquette" (Ch. 43d.2)
Assignments:	Read and analyze blogs, websites, and assigned readings
	Summarize two readings or blogs
	E-mail instructor (introduction)
	View sample electronic portfolios
	Read Chs. 1 and 4 in handbook

WEEK TWO

Goals:	Learn about the writing process
	Learn how to plan an essay
	Learn to find and evaluate sources
	Learn about writing to inform
Review:	Summary (7f.1), purpose (1c)
Assignments:	Online discussion of readings or blogs
	Brainstorm topic for essay #1 (informative essay with sources)
	Research and evaluate sources

Summarize one article related to essay #1 topic

Read Chs. 2 and 34 in handbook

WEEK THREE

Goals: Learn to write a thesis

Learn to create an outline

Learn about developing paragraphs

Learn to paraphrase, quote, and cite sources

Review: MLA documentation (Ch. 36); thesis statements, outlines, drafting (Ch. 2)

Assignments: Continue research

Continue online discussion (readings and/or research and/or class topics)

Read and discuss features of sample informative essays

Write a paragraph (definition, exemplifcation, or other relevant rhetorical mode) related to essay #1 topic, which integrates one paraphrase and one quote (both attributed and cited) from source material

Develop a thesis and rough outline for essay #1

Read Chs. 3 and 35 in handbook

WEEK FOUR

Goals: Learn about introduction and conclusion paragraphs

Learn to develop a Works Cited page

Learn to draft and revise an essay

Review: Ch. 2 (drafting and revising) and collecting/developing materials for electronic portfolios; fragments (Ch. 19) and comma splices and run-ons (Ch. 20)

Assignments: Develop introduction and conclusion paragraphs for essay #1

Write first draft of essay #1

Create a Works Cited page for essay #1

Peer response (in-class or online) and revision of essay #1, including Writer's Memo (see Ch. 43e for memo format)

Submit essay to instructor for feedback via e-mail or via an online peer review site

WEEK FIVE

Goals: Learn to edit and proofread essays

Learn the features of argument writing

Learn types of persuasive appeals

Learn to choose a topic and create a claim for an argument

Review: Pronoun Case and Reference (Ch. 16) and Agreement (Ch. 17); review Ch. 34 (finding and evaluating sources)

Assignments: Revise, edit, and proofread essay #1; use computer tools to aid editing and proofreading

Read and analyze sample arguments, including editorials or blogs; continue online discussion of readings

Read Ch. 5 in handbook; review Chs. 4 and 34

Write a letter to a public official which presents an argument about an issue that concerns you (and/or publish to a "letter to the editor" on a class online discussion forum)

Use pre-writing strategies to develop a topic and claim (thesis) for essay #2 (a research-based argument connected to informative essay topic)

WEEK SIX

Goal: Learn to structure and develop an argument essay

Learn to synthesize source material

Review: Paraphrasing, summarizing, quoting, and citing (Ch. 35); Ch. 2 (planning and shaping)

Assignments: Research and evaluate sources for essay #2

Develop a rough outline of essay #2

Read and analyze sample arguments; continue online discussion of readings

Develop a support paragraph that synthesizes information from two sources and correctly paraphrases or quotes from and cites those sources

WEEK EIGHT

Goal: Learn to revise an argument essay

Learn to critically analyze images

Review: Use of quotation marks, parentheses, brackets, and the ellipsis (Part 4, "Using Punctuation and Mechanics"); electronic portfolio development

Assignments: Peer response and revision of essay #2 (in-class or online), including Writer's Memo

Revise, edit, and proofread essay #2

Submit essay to instructor for feedback via e-mail or via an online peer review site

View and analyze visual images from textbook and/or online

WEEK NINE

Goals: Learn to write an analysis essay

Learn about visual rhetoric

Review: The Impact of Words (Ch. 12)

Assignments: Revise, edit, and proofread essay #2 based on teacher feedback

Review Ch. 4; Read Ch. 7f in handbook

Practice analyzing images, visual arguments; continue online discussion

Select an image and develop a plan for analysis essay (essay #3)

Plan and begin drafting essay #3

WEEK TEN

Goals: Learn to revise, edit, and proofread an analysis essay

Learn about collaborative research and writing

Review: Sentence Variety and Style (Ch. 9)

Assignments: Peer response and revision of essay #3 (in-class or online), including Writer's Memo

Revise, edit, and proofread essay #3

Submit essay to instructor for feedback via e-mail or via an online peer review site

Read Ch. 6 (collaborative writing)

Form collaborative groups and brainstorm topic ideas for essay #4, which includes an oral presentation and/or Web writing component

WEEK ELEVEN

Goals: Learn to work in groups

Learn about research writing

Review: Parallelism (Ch. 10); group dynamics (see Part Two of *Strategies and Resources for Teaching Writing*); electronic portfolio development

Assignments: Revise, edit, and proofread essay #3 based on teacher feedback

Read Chs. 32 and 33

In class and/or in online discussion, select topic and begin researching for essay #4 (collaborative research-based essay); plan subtopics and group member responsibilities

WEEK TWELVE

Goals: Learn about document design

Learn to organize and synthesize group's research and writing

Review: Shifting and Mixed Sentences (Ch. 22)

Assignments: Read Ch. 45 in handbook

View and analyze various documents and discuss effectiveness of design for intended audience and purpose

Develop a rough outline for Essay #4 and begin drafting

Meet with each group individually to discuss essay plans and group process

Week Thirteen

Goals: Learn to draft a collaborative research paper

Learn to develop a Web page or oral presentation

Review: Critically analyzing images (Ch. 4) and Document Design (Ch. 45)

Assignments: Read Ch. 42 or 46 in the handbook

Draft collaborative research-based essay (essay #4), including appropriate graphics or other images

Peer response and revision of essay #4

Plan and prepare for Web page project or oral presentation using multimedia

Week Fourteen

Goals: Learn to collaboratively revise, edit, and proofread

Learn to develop reflective pieces for electronic portfolio

Review: Adjectives and Adverbs (Ch. 18) and Misplaced and Dangling Modifiers (Ch. 21); electronic portfolio development

Assignments: Polish final essays for electronic portfolio

Draft portfolio cover letter, reflecting on learning and achievements over semester (see 43f for business letter format)

Complete Web page project or oral presentations

Read assigned material for final essay exam

Week Fifteen

Goals: Present final Web page project or oral presentations

Complete and submit final portfolios

Complete final essay exam

Review: Essay exam-taking strategies; portfolio requirements

✓ **Emphasis on Writing Across the Curriculum**

WEEK ONE

Goals: Learn how to use the handbook

Learn about writing across the curriculum

Learn rhetoric strategies for paragraph development

Review: Fragments (Ch. 19) and Comma Splices and Run-ons (Ch. 20)

Assignments: Read Chs. 1, 3, and 39 in handbook

Read paragraphs or essays using various rhetoric modes of development

Develop narrative paragraph about personal writing history and/or college or career goals

Develop exemplification and compare and contrast paragraphs discussing writing in the disciplines

WEEK TWO

Goals: Learn about writing in the natural sciences

Learn critical reading strategies

Learn about the writing process

Review: Sentence Variety and Style (Ch. 9)

Assignments: Read Ch. 4 (focusing on critical reading and summary and synthesis), Ch. 2, Ch. 7f.1 (summary), and Ch. 41 in handbook

Read, analyze, and summarize science reports

Develop a definition, description, and/or process paragraph(s) based on a scientific concept

Develop a paragraph describing personal writing process

WEEK THREE

Goals: Learn about writing in the humanities

Learn the difference between summary and response writing

Review: Agreement (Ch. 17) and Pronoun Case and Reference (Ch. 16)

Assignments: Read Chs. 7f and 40 in handbook

Read, discuss, and analyze short stories and poems or plays in reader

Write a brief summary and a personal response to two of the assigned readings

WEEK FOUR

Goals: Learn about literary analysis and interpretation

Learn how to generate topic ideas

Review: Literary terms/devices and strategies for writing about literature

Assignments: Review Ch. 2 and Ch. 40 in handbook

Read, discuss, and analyze short stories and poems in reader

Read sample literary analysis essay and interpretation essay

Begin developing essay #1 topic (literary analysis or interpretation essay)

WEEK FIVE

Goals: Learn how to write an effective thesis statement

Learn how to organize and draft a literary analysis or interpretation essay

Learn how to quote and cite passages from a literary work using MLA documentation

Review: Adjective and Adverbs (Ch. 18) and Misplaced and Dangling Modifiers (Ch. 21)

Assignments: Review Chs. 2 and 40 in handbook

Practice paraphrasing, quoting, and citing using MLA Documentation (Ch. 36)

Develop a thesis for literary analysis or interpretation essay

Plan a literary analysis or interpretation essay and begin drafting essay #1

WEEK SIX

Goals: Learn to write introduction and conclusion paragraphs

Learn to give effective feedback on peer's essays

Learn to use comments to revise, edit, and proofread essay

Learn to develop an MLA Works Cited page

Review: Quotation mark and ellipses use; citing sources; Ch. 3, "Writing Paragraphs, Shaping Essays"

Assignments: Review Ch. 2 and Ch. 6 in handbook

Develop an introduction and conclusion paragraph for literary analysis or interpretation essay

Create a Works Cited page for essay #1

Peer review and revise essay

Submit revised essay for teacher evaluation

WEEK SEVEN

Goals: Learn about writing in the social sciences

Learn to find and evaluate sources

Review: Shifting and Mixed Sentences (Ch. 22) and Parallelism (Ch. 10)

Assignments: Review Chs. 34 and 41 in handbook

Read sample articles from the social sciences (i.e., research reports, case studies)

Begin researching a social issue (essay #2); evaluate sources

Summarize 3 – 4 articles from research

WEEK EIGHT

Goals: Learn to synthesize sources

Learn about using APA documentation

Review: Summary and synthesis (Ch. 7); thesis and outline development (Ch. 2); using sources and avoiding plagiarism (Ch. 35)

Assignments: Review Ch. 37, APA Documentation; practice in-text and reference page documentation

Continue research on social issue (to sythesize for essay #2); summarize articles in journal

Read sample synthesis essays

Write a paragraph which synthesizes two or more sources of information about your selected social issue (using APA documentation)

Develop a thesis and plan for essay #2 (synthesis of research on a social issue)

WEEK NINE

Goals: Learn to draft and revise a synthesis essay in the social sciences

Review: Review Ch. 2 (drafting and revising) and Ch. 3 (writing paragraphs)

Assignments: Draft synthesis essay (essay #2)

Develop APA References list for essay #2

Peer review and revision of esssay #2

Submit essay #2 for teacher evaluation

Introduce writing in your major/career assignment (essay #3)

WEEK TEN

Goals: Learn about primary and secondary research

Learn to interview and gather information from interviewed sources

Learn about the types of writing and features of writing in one's major or career

Review: Ch. 39 (comparing the disciplines)

Assignments: Develop interview questions to learn about writing in one's major or career; students also may wish to explore other questions about expectations in and preparation for this major or career

Students will arrange and conduct at least one interview with a professor in student's major and/or a prefessional in student's career of interest; student also may wish to interview one or more upper-division students or interns in his or her field of interest

Research secondary sources to learn more about required course work, experiences, and skills in student's field of interest

WEEK ELEVEN

Goals: Learn to develop an oral presentation using multimedia

Learn elements of effective document design

Learn to draft an essay or creative piece, such as a brochure, related to writing in student's major or future career

Review: Sentence Variety and Style (Ch. 9) and Style and Tone in Writing (Ch. 8)

Assignments: Plan and draft an essay or creative piece using primary and secondary research

Read Chs. 42 and 45 in handbook

Begin developing oral presentation to accompany essay #3 (writing in the disciplines)

WEEK TWELVE

Goal: Learn about writing in various careers and majors

Review: Punctuation (Part 4), especially comma use (Ch. 24)

Assignments: Peer review and revision of essay #3

Present oral presentation using multimedia

Submit essay #3 to instructor for evaluation

WEEK THIRTEEN

Goal: Learn to write for public and the workplace

Review: Conciseness (Ch. 11)

Assignments: Read Ch. 44 in handbook

Read and analyze business and public communications

Develop a résumé and job application letter

WEEK FOURTEEN

Goal: Learn about writing arguments

Review: The Impact of Words (Ch. 12)

Assignments: Read Ch. 5 in handbook

Read, discuss, and analyze various arguments in public writing (i.e., news editorials)

Develop a letter to a community, college, or state official arguing an issue that concerns you

WEEK FIFTEEN

Goal: Review the achievements of the term and note areas which still need work

Assignments: Revise, edit, and proofread business and public writing pieces

In-class write reflecting on learning and achievements during semester

■ SYLLABI FOR QUARTER (TEN-WEEK) COURSES

Even though the quarter-length term offers the same number of contact hours with the students as the semester system, some teachers find that for students to master the principles of writing covered in the course, they should do fewer papers with more time between or write shorter papers. Because of these individual preferences, the models that follow may be adjusted for more or fewer papers than are suggested. Or instructors may choose to incorporate alternative writing assignments, such as Web pages, business and public writing, or timed writing. And like those for the semester-length term, these syllabi also can make use of a reader in addition to the handbook, though teachers may adjust them to use only the handbook. Individual teachers may choose to incorporate more or less grammar and usage review.

✓ *Emphasis on Research Skills*

In this syllabus, students' research skills are developed and assessed using a variety of methods besides research-based essays, including summaries, working bibliographies, an annotated bibliography, outlines with notecards, and an oral presentation. This course can easily be adapted to incorporate a single, extended research paper or several shorter essays that incorporate research or to develop a Web-based research project. Additionally, this syllabus can be altered to introduce students to disciplinary differences in research and documentation; it may be effective to introduce writing across the curriculum early in the term and to encourage students to select topics and use documentation styles in their "major" or relevant to their current course work. Another alternative may be to tie students' research work to their future careers, allowing them to research their interests and to explore the types of writing they will be required to do in the workplace.

WEEK ONE

Goals:	Learn how to use the handbook
	Learn about the importance of situation, audience, and purpose
	Learn to summarize information
	Learn to think and read critically
Review:	Sentences, run-ons, comma splices, and fragments (Chs. 14, 19, and 20)
Assignments:	Read Chs. 1 and 4 in the handbook
	Practice critical reading skills on articles
	Summarize and annotate assigned readings
	Write formal summaries of two assigned articles
	In-class, document articles using MLA or APA format

WEEK TWO

Goals:	Learn how to use library and Internet for research
	Learn how to find a writing topic
Review:	Sentence Variety and Style (Ch. 9)
Assignments:	Read Chs. 2, 32, and 34 in handbook
	Use pre-writing strategies to find a research topic for research-based essay (synthesis of arguments on a current issue)
	Develop a preliminary topic proposal (using memo format—see Ch. 43e)
	Begin "Scavenger Hunt" bibliography: find 8 - 10 different types of sources (including library, Internet, and

other types of research) related to selected topic and cite them correctly using MLA or APA documentation

WEEK THREE

Goals: Learn to document sources on a Works Cited (or References) page

Learn to critically evaluate sources

Review: MLA and APA Documentation (Chs. 36 – 37)

Assignments: Finish "Scavenger Hunt" bibliography (cited correctly using MLA or APA documentation)

Develop a working bibliography (using *relevant* sources from "scavenger hunt" bibliography as well as newly researched sources), citing sources correctly using MLA or APA format

Evaluate sources, determining which are credible and relevant to topic (Review Ch. 34)

Summarize four relevant sources

WEEK FOUR

Goals: Learn to paraphrase, quote, and cite in-text

Learn to create a thesis and outline

Learn to take content notes

Review: Conventions of quoting (Ch. 28)

Assignments: Read Ch. 35 in handbook; review Ch. 2

Using relevant source material, practice paraphrasing, quoting, and citing in-text

Develop a thesis and rough outline for research-based synthesis essay

Create two or more notecards for each topic on rough outline (minimum eight notecards)

WEEK FIVE

Goals: Learn to draft a research-based essay

Learn to develop paragraphs, particularly introduction and conclusion paragraphs

Learn to revise and edit research-based essay

Review: Shfting and Mixed Sentences (Ch. 22) and documentation

Assignments: Read student sample research essay(s)

Read Ch. 3 and Ch. 33 in handbook

Draft research-based synthesis essay

Peer response and revision of synthesis essay

WEEK SIX

Goals: Learn to read and analyze written arguments

Learn to develop a topic and research plan for a research-based argument essay

Review: Research writing as process (Ch. 33) and finding and evaluating sources (Ch. 34)

Assignments: Submit research-based synthesis essay for teacher evaluation

Read Ch. 5 in handbook

Read and analyze written arguments using Toulmin analysis

Develop a preliminary argument-based research topic proposal and research plan

Begin developing a working bibliography

Annotate two sources related to proposed topic (one pro and one con)

WEEK SEVEN

Goal: Learn to create an annotated bibliography

Review: Conciseness (Ch. 11), Parallelism (Ch. 10), and Writing Paragraphs (Ch. 3)

Assignments: Continue to research, evaluate, read, and annotate sources

Create an annotated bibliography (minimum 10 credible, relevant sources)

WEEK EIGHT

Goals:	Learn to develop a thesis statement and outline for an argumentative research paper
	Learn to use refutation
Review:	Style and Tone in Writing (Ch. 8), Variety and Style (Ch. 9) and The Impact of Words (Ch. 12)
Assignments:	Select development method(s) for argument and create a preliminary outline
	Create two or more notecards for each section/item on preliminary outline (minimum eight notecards)
	Develop a rebuttal paragraph

WEEK NINE

Goals:	Learn to draft a research-based argument essay
	Learn to use peer response to revise research-based argument essay
	Learn principles of document design
Review:	Writing process, paraphrasing, quoting, synthesizing, and citing sources
Assignments:	Read Ch. 45 in handbook
	Draft research-based argument, incorporating at least one graphic in paper
	Peer response and revision of research-based argument

WEEK TEN

Goals:	Learn to develop an oral presentation (argument)
	Review the achievements of the term, and note areas which still need work
Assignments:	Develop oral presentation based on research-based argument
	Submit research-based argument for teacher evaluation
	Write a brief essay about what you have learned about doing research and its connection to writing
	Final exam: oral presentation

✓ *Emphasis on Paragraphs*

The sample syllabus below, which emphasizes paragraph development, assumes students are enrolled in a developmental writing course. The syllabus shows students how to develop paragraphs and later essays using rhetorical modes, such as narration, description, classification, compare and contrast, cause and effect, definition, and process. This sample syllabus can easily be adapted to accomodate Portfolio Evaluation (see Part One, Ch. 7 of this instructor's manual).

This syllabus begins with narration and description, not necessarily because they are easier than some other types of development (as some teachers argue), but because students feel more comfortable writing narrations and descriptions. As students first begin to study the writing process, these more accessible types of development ease them into writing papers that are more analytical and for many students more difficult. Later in the term, students are introduced to basic research skills; however, this introduction may not be necessary, or it may be necessary to introduce research skills earlier in the quarter, depending on what skills students will need to bring into the next course in their writing sequence.

This syllabus also assumes that some of the work will be done in class, especially review of mechanics and grammar. Some teachers will spend more time with this than others. Although the syllabus suggests that students will review particular grammar topics each week, it is generally more effective to tailor grammar instruction to the students' strengths and weaknesses (perhaps based on some sort of diagnostic performed at the beginning of the quarter). There may be topics that the whole class needs to review, but often instruction and practice will need to be more individualized. The "editing log" listed below tries to accomplish this, allowing students to record and correct their particular errors. This log could be developed into a personal grammar workbook, which includes both editing log entries and individualized grammar activities.

WEEK ONE

Goals: Learn how to use the handbook

Learn what a paragraph is

Learn about ways to develop paragraphs (focus on narrative and descriptive)

Learn pre-writing strategies

Review:	Grammar diagnostic; if needed, Ch. 14—Parts of Speech and Sentence Structures, and/or Ch. 48—Writing in U.S. Colleges
Assignments:	Use prewriting strategies to develop narrative and descriptive paragraphs
	Write 1 - 2 narrative paragraph(s) and 1 - 2 descriptive paragraph(s)
	Read Chs. 1, 2, and 3 (i) in the handbook
	Read sample narrative and descriptive paragraphs or essays from reader
	In-class, handbook activity/overview

WEEK TWO

Goals:	Learn how to write effective topic sentences
	Learn additional ways to develop paragraphs (definition, classification, and exemplification)
	Learn about paragraph unity and coherence
Review:	Fragments (Ch. 19) and, if needed, Handling Sentence-Level Issues in English (Ch. 49)
Assignments:	Write definition, classification, and exemplification process paragraphs with effective topic sentences
	Read Ch. 3 (b, e, f, g, i) and review pre-writing strategies (Ch. 2) in the handbook
	Read and analyze examples of definition, classification, and exemplification paragraphs or essays in reader
	Introduction to editing log (each week students list, label, correct, and explain 1 – 2 errors made in their writing)

WEEK THREE

Goals:	Learn additional ways to develop paragraphs (process and compare and contrast)
	Learn to revise
Review:	Comma Splices and Run-on Sentences (Ch. 20)
Assignments:	Write a descriptive paragraph and classification paragraph

Review Ch. 2 in the handbook

Revise two of the paragraphs previously written in course (intro. to peer response)

Read and analyze examples of process and compare/contrast paragraphs or essays in the reader

Keep an editing log

WEEK FOUR

Goals:	Learn critical reading skills
	Learn to summarize and analyze readings
	Learn to revise and edit
Review:	Pronoun Case and Reference (Ch. 16)
Assignments:	Write summary and analysis paragraphs
	Revise two of the paragraphs previously written in course (peer and/or teacher feedback)
	Read Chs. 4 and 7f in the handbook
	Read and analyze essays in the reader
	Practice summary and critical reading skills in-class
	Keep an editing log

WEEK FIVE

Goals:	Learn what an essay is
	Learn to select an essay topic
	Learn to develop a thesis statement
	Learn to develop an outline
	Learn to develop an informative essay (process)
Review:	Agreement (Ch. 17)
Assignments:	Revise summary and analysis paragraphs
	Generate a topic for a process essay
	Develop a plan for process essay
	Develop a thesis statement and rough outline for process essay
	Finish reading/review Ch. 2 in the handbook

Read and analyze sample process essays (either from reader or student samples)

Keep an editing log

WEEK SIX

Goals: Learn to develop special paragraphs (introduction and conclusion)

Learn to use peer feedback to revise an essay

Review: Shifting and Mixed Sentences (Ch. 22)

Assignments: Read Ch. 3 c and k and Ch. 6 c and review Chs. 2 and 3 in the handbook

Develop an introduction and conclusion paragraphs for process essay

Draft process essay

Participate in peer response and revise and edit essay based on peer feedback

Keep an editing log

WEEK SEVEN

Goals: Learn to plan a compare and contrast essay

Learn to find sources for compare and contrast essay

Learn to paraphrase, quote, and cite source material

Review: Punctuation: commas, apostrophes, quotation marks (Chs. 24, 27, and 28); MLA Documentation (Ch. 36)

Assignments: Submit process essay for evaluation

Submit editing log for evaluation

Select topic for compare and contrast essay

Develop a thesis for compare and contrast essay

Develop a plan for compare and contrast essay

Research for compare and contrast essay (two sources)

Read Chs. 34 and 35 in the the handbook

Read and analyze student samples of compare and contrast essays

In-class practice on paraphrasing, quoting, and citing sources

WEEK EIGHT

Goals: Learn to develop a Works Cited page

Learn to organize and develop a compare and contrast essay (integrating source material)

Review: Sentences and Sentence Types (Ch. 14 k and q) and Sentence Variety and Style (Ch. 9)

Assignments: Develop an MLA Works Cited page for compare and contrast essay (Ch. 36)

Develop an outline and rough draft of compare and contrast essay

Peer response and revision of compare and contrast essay

Keep an editing log

WEEK NINE

Goals: Learn to write an argument (letter to editor)

Learn to select a topic and organize an argumentative piece

Learn to read and analyze written arguments

Review: Conciseness (Ch. 11)

Assignments: Read Ch. 5 in the handbook

Read and analyze arguments in reader and in local newspaper

Use pre-writing strategies to develop a topic for letter to editor

Develop thesis and rough outline for letter to editor

WEEK TEN

Goal: Reflect on learning and achievements in course

Assignments: Peer response and revision of letter to editor

"Publish" letters to editor on interactive online discussion site

Read, analyze, and respond to peers' letters

Write a reflective essay discussing achievement in editing (see editing log), reading, writing, and critical thinking throughout the quarter

If needed, final exam (essay exam and/or editing exam)

■ SYLLABUS FOR SUMMER SCHOOL (SIX-WEEK) COURSES

Planning courses for such intensive terms as summer school requires great care. Classes in these sessions, normally about six weeks, are generally scheduled daily for about two hours, a long enough period for the teacher to allow in-class work on papers. A big advantage of the short term is that teachers can observe students while they write and help them in the process, lending immediacy to the process. A second advantage, shared by the quarter-length term, is the continuity of class meetings, which usually occur daily.

Along with the more constant teacher-student contact that this schedule provides comes the down side—the much more intensive pace. Teachers must decide if they can have students do numerous short papers (one or two per week) or a few long ones. Those whose departments demand the same number of papers for summer school as for a regular term have little choice but to require shorter ones, usually with less revision. Those with more control over the syllabus may choose fewer papers; the sample below includes three, or about one every other week. In any case, teachers need to pace themselves carefully.

The following syllabus emphasizes critical thinking and is designed for a course in writing arguments. Like the other sample syllabi here, this one assumes the use of a reader. Teachers who wish to emphasize paragraphs, research skills, technology, essays (and types of development) and/or writing across the curriculum may adapt the previous models to accommodate the shorter term.

✓ *Emphasizing Critical Thinking and Argument*

WEEK ONE

Goals: Learn how to use the handbook

Learn about thinking, reading, and writing critically

Learn to summarize and synthesize sources

	Learn how to plan an essay and write a rough draft
Review:	Research strategies (Ch. 32), Finding and Evaluating Sources (Ch. 34)
Assignments:	Read Chs. 1, 2, and 4 in handbook

Read, summarize, analyze, and evaluate arguments from reader

Use pre-writing strategies to select a topic for essay #1, a synthesis of arguments or perspectives on a contemporary social issue

Develop a thesis and outline for essay #1

Research and evaluate sources to use in essay #1 (minimum six sources)

WEEK TWO

Goals:	Learn to paraphrase, quote, and cite source material in-text and on a Works Cited page
	Learn how to revise and edit an essay
Review:	MLA Documentation (Ch. 36)
Assignments:	Practice paraphrasing, quoting, and citing from essay #1 source material

Develop a synthesis paragraph using (and citing) two or more sources related to essay #1

Read sample synthesis essays in reader

Draft synthesis essay; including a Works Cited page, of at least six sources

Peer response and revision/editing of essay #1; submit for teacher evaluation

Read Ch. 7f and 35 in handbook

WEEK THREE

Goals:	Learn about writing to argue (Toulmin, logical fallacies, etc.)
	Learn how to develop a claim and structure and support a position argument (Classical argument)
Review:	Paraphrasing, summarizing, quoting, and citing
Assignments:	Read Ch. 5 in handbook; review Ch. 4

Read and analyze (using Toulmin's method and ethical, logial, and emotional appeals; also, logical fallacies) arguments, both visual and print, from reader

Practice refuting arguments in readings

Develop a claim and rough outline for essay #2 (a position on issue researched in essay #1)

Find and evaluate additional sources for essay #2

Begin drafting essay #2

WEEK FOUR

Goals:	Learn how to write introduction, conclusion, and transition paragraphs
	Learn how to revise and edit an argument essay
Review:	Sentences, comma splices, run-ons, fragments (Chs. 14, 19, and 20), and Sentence Variety and Style (Ch. 9)
Assignments:	Read Ch. 3 in handbook
	Finish drafting essay #2, including introduction and conclusion paragraphs and Works Cited page
	Peer response and revision/editing of essay #2; submit for evaluation
	Read and analyze sample critical reviews and other evaluations in reader

WEEK FIVE

Goals:	Learn how to evaluate a product or performance based on criteria
	Learn how to write an evaluation (or critical review) essay
Review:	Agreement, pronoun case and reference, shifting and mixed sentences (Chs. 16, 17, and 22)
Assignments:	Read Ch. 7 and/or Ch. 40 in handbook and analyze sample reviews and evaluations from reader and from class research
	Use prewriting strategies to find a topic for essay #3, an evaluation of a product or performance

Do necessary background "research" for essay #3 (attend play or other type of performance, visit a restaurant, read a book, etc.)

Develop a plan—thesis, criteria, outline—for essay #3

WEEK SIX

Goals: Review the achievements of the term and note areas which still need work

Learn how to write essay exams

Assignments: Draft, revise, and edit essay #3; submit for evaluation

Read Ch. 7f.7 in handbook; review Ch. 4

Prepare for essay exam (final)—analysis/evaluation of visual argument

All teachers eventually come up with combinations of mechanics, grammar, rhetoric, and research that work well together in any given class. Therefore, these models are offered only as guidelines until the teacher's own creativity with using the handbook takes over.

WEB RESOURCES

Web Resources can be found at **www.prenhall.com/troyka**.

SUGGESTED READING

Baecker, Diann L. "Uncovering the Rhetoric of the Syllabus: The Case of the Missing I." *College Teaching* 46.2 (Spring 1998): 58–62.

Dahlin, Amber. "A Student-Written Syllabus for Second-Semester English." *Teaching English in the Two-Year College* 21 (Feb. 1994): 27–32.

Devine, Thomas G. " Caveat Emptor: The Writing Process Approach to College Writing." *Journal of Developmental Education* 14 (Fall 1990): 2–4.

Figg, Kristen M. "Handbook Use in College English I: Classroom Practices and Student Responses." *Teaching English in the Two-Year College* 19 (Oct. 1992): 185–91.

Fleming, David. "Rhetoric as a Course of Study." *College English* 61.2 (1998): 169–91.

Gold, R. M. "How the Freshman Essay Anthology Subverts the Aims of the Traditional Composition Course." *Teaching English in the Two-Year College* 18 (Dec. 1991): 261–65.

Krest, Margie, and Daria O. Carle. "Teaching Scientific Writing: A Model for Integrating Research, Writing, and Critical Thinking." *The American Biology Teacher* 61.3 (1999): 223–27.

Kroll, Keith. "A Profile of Community College English Faculty and Curriculum." *Community College Review* 22 (Winter 1994): 37–54.

Lindemann, Erika. "Three Views of English 101." *College English* 57 (March 1995): 287–301.

Martinsen, Amy. "The Tower of Babel and the Teaching of Grammar: Writing Instruction for a New Century." *English Journal* 90.1 (2000): 122–26.

Nilson, Linda Burzotta. *Teaching at Its Best: A Research-Based Resource for College Teachers.* [n.p.]: Anker Publishing, 1998.

Quigley, Dan. "The Evolution of an Online Syllabus." *Computers and Composition* 11.2 (1994): 165–72.

Salvatori, Mariolina. "Conversations with Texts: Reading in the Teaching of Composition." *College English* 58 (April 1996): 440–54.

CHAPTER 5

Teacher Feedback:
Methods to Improve Student Writing

Commenting on Drafts

One of the most common methods that teachers use to offer students feedback on their writing is handwritten comments. When giving students feedback on their work, we must use strategies that will help students, not demoralize them. These methods include such decisions as the color of ink we use and the tone of our remarks, as the following suggestions show:

1. CHANGE INK. Many teachers have found that as simple a change as switching from red ink to pencil or blue ink has a positive effect on the students' attitudes. No one denies the authority of red ink, but the students are more likely to see pencil comments as less threatening. By choosing another color, the teacher in effect says that he or she is just another critical reader in a world of readers.

2. CHANGE TONE. The old saying that "you can catch more flies with honey than with vinegar" applies significantly to grading papers. Students who are bombarded with "don't do this" and "don't do that" soon give up altogether. Naturally we cannot say that a poor piece of work is great just to make students feel good, but students' improvement is directly related to how we tell them the work is poor.

Throughout the paper as we are marking ineffective features of the writing, we should also take the few seconds needed to write in the margin "I like this image," "These details really help make your point," or "Your transition is especially skillful between these two paragraphs." More important, we should begin the first part of a final note with comments about the strengths of the paper. Then we can comment on the parts that need work, but we should end with an additional positive comment. All of us like to be complimented, and students especially respond well to compliments. By beginning and ending our notes with positive statements, we show students that we're not in the business of simply hunting for errors but that we also notice what they do well.

As the term goes on, these comments should, if possible, emphasize the improvement we are seeing regarding particular features of the students' writing. And even when we're hard pressed to find new elements to compliment, we can always end with a statement like, "I'm really looking forward to seeing your revision of this piece. You've got some strong ideas here that I know will come together well in your final draft." If the students believe that we are genuinely interested in what they are saying, they will work hard to come up to our expectations as far as mechanics are concerned.

3. CHANGE PRIORITIES. Don't mark everything that's wrong all at once. Doing so overwhelms learners. It stands to reason that if we mark all the errors and stylistic problems in a piece of writing—especially in red ink—the student who looks at this sea of red ink is likely to give up in the face of his or her hopeless inadequacy. If we want students to improve and learn to revise, we should keep our commentary focused on a few areas that are most in need of change.

Those teachers who are selective about the errors they mark each time vary with regard to the criteria for marking papers in a given week. Some mark only the most serious mechanical errors early in the term (comma splices, fragments, subject-verb disagreements, and run-together sentences) and comment only on major problems in content and style (adequate transition within and between paragraphs, enough evidence and detail, clear thesis and topic sentences, for example). Others mark only matters of content and organization first, inspiring students to think clearly about the subject, and gradually mark mechanics as the term proceeds. Some teachers mark matters of content and organization first as well as whatever mechanics they review during the period in which the students are working on the essay (usually these teachers, too, begin reviewing the most serious mechanical problems first). As the term goes on and students gain confidence in their ability to express their ideas in coherent paragraphs that support a clearly stated thesis, teachers have more success with criticizing problems of style (wordiness, adequate subordination, inconsistency of diction, and ineffective sentence structure).

Some teachers think it is dishonest to leave errors unmarked. They argue that by doing so, we only mislead the students into thinking that they are much better writers than they in fact are. Other teachers—and these seem more successful, in the long run—believe that it's what the students know at the end of the course that matters and that keeping them involved in improving and enthusiastic about their writing is ultimately more important than absolute tyranny in marking errors.

Some teachers find that students respond especially well to written comments if the students have communicated to the teacher the degree of detail with which they wish the teacher to mark the essay. Agreeing with the teacher about this helps create a sense of shared responsibility for the grading that can make students more responsive to the comments the teacher does make.

Although handwritten comments are the most common method of teacher feedback, some teachers prefer variations of this method. A colleague of mine, a former writing center consultant, prefers to audiotape his comments to students. Doing this allows him to explain himself in more detail and monitor the tone of his comments. Other teachers prefer to type or e-mail global comments to students, which prevents them from taking over the authority of students' drafts by making the changes for the students. Some teachers develop checklists or other types of evaluation rubrics that enable them to cut down on time spent crafting comments while still providing students with direction for revision.

Conferences: Student and Teacher One-to-One

Some of the most valuable time that we spend with students is time we spend in conference, one-on-one, in our offices. Conferences can give us the opportunity to make students more confident of their ability to write and can give us the opportunity to nurse along the weak writers who, without our interest, would simply give up. Conferences are the times when we try to overcome the inequities inherent in teaching writing to a group of students with different abilities, problems, and levels of commitment.

One of the important early realizations that we writing teachers come to is that if we have twenty-two students in a class, for all practical purposes we are teaching twenty-two different courses. Each student's problems are so individual that some of them cannot be addressed satisfactorily in class. Thus, the conference becomes useful as a means of dealing with concerns that lie outside the interests of the class as a whole. All students need the extra attention to individual problems that conferences offer, but the strong students and the weak ones particularly benefit from this attention to their needs, which normally are not addressed when circumstances force us to teach more to the average students.

Student-teacher conferences not only enable teachers to respond individually to students, they also allow teachers to learn about the effectiveness of their instruction. The conference can teach us what we are not clarifying in the classroom and what concerns and needs among students we should respond to in our assignments.

But how do we get the students into our offices willingly for help? How do we use this valuable time to the best advantage to achieve both our goals and those of the students?

Many departments stipulate that instructors must devote a given number of hours per week to office hours, and teachers in such departments dutifully post the hours when they will be available to students. Students do not, however, always come. Thus the teacher sits in the office waiting for students who often want help but are too frightened of the teacher or formality of office suites to seek it. Unfortunately, many students have grown up with the notion that it is a sign of weakness to ask a teacher for help, and too many of them have been told that the big bad college teacher is interested not in helping students, but flunking them.

One good solution to the problem of getting students into the office is simply to require each student to sign up for a ten-minute get-acquainted conference during the first week of school. Yes, that is heavy traffic for the teacher, but it is time well spent. During such a visit the teacher might ask the students to explain their experiences with writing in high school and their current feelings about their writing. Students usually begin to relax in this kind of conference, and they seem to appreciate the new teacher's interest in their past. Teachers who have large classes may find it helpful to take notes immediately following the conference so that they will be able to recall the meeting when the student comes in again.

In addition to showing students that we don't maim and torture them in our offices but are, instead, interested in them, these short, early-in-the-term conferences show them that we are available in our offices to help them continue to learn about writing. These mandatory get-acquainted conferences show them where our offices are and emphasize that we expect them to come there regularly. The conferences also help the students see that being a member of a community means taking responsibility for getting help with their work.

Even with these early required conferences, many students still will not come regularly when they need help, and some won't come at all until they've received a low grade or two. Therefore, some instructors schedule optional or mandatory conferences a few times during the term to go over problems that students have had up to that point. Other teachers may schedule conferences with students as a means of giving feedback on their drafts. Although the conferences are time consuming, many teachers find they take less time and are more effective than writing comments on their drafts. Multi-student conferences enable teachers to focus on a problem common to those students. These group conferences often help students more than the teacher alone can—the interaction with other students can help make the student more independent and more excited about writing. Some teachers, however, simply do not have the luxury of this choice because the available time for conferences is severely curtailed by other responsibilities and by having too many students in writing classes. Thus teachers must decide for themselves if they want to do more than extend an invitation for students to come in during office hours.

Even before we decide how to use conferences most efficiently, we must consider what to do about the outpouring of personal problems that frequently occurs in conferences about writing. Because students in composition classes often share information about their personal lives in their essays, even in non-narrative essays, it stands to reason that they will talk with us about their personal lives. After all, we are already submerged in their personal lives by virtue of having read their essays. For many of us this kind of personal sharing is one of the allures of teaching: We want to know that we are dealing with human beings. On the other hand, teachers who hear about students' personal lives can find themselves in serious dilemmas about how to proceed with a student and sometimes how to evaluate a student's work.

Most of us can deal effectively, if not painlessly, with certain kinds of personal problems, for example, problems of the heart. We have learned simply to listen and not to offer advice. And we've learned to steel ourselves against the appeals to pity. What we have a harder time with are students who come ostensibly to talk with us about a paper but who really come because they need help with a serious problem: parents who are getting a divorce, siblings or friends who have betrayed them, friendships that depend on drugs, sexual abuse by family or other adults, and serious financial threats, even homelessness.

What do we do in the face of these serious issues? They are not remotely related to comma splices and paragraph coherence, yet we cannot teach students who are threatened by problems of such magnitude. Since we have read our students' papers about what they think and feel, students recognize that we know them better than most teachers do—and even, perhaps, better than most adults do—and they may seek us out as confidants and counselors.

But we must remember that we are not trained counselors, and we must therefore resist the temptation to offer advice. We may give the wrong advice, seriously wrong. Of course, few teachers want to turn their backs on students who really need help. What we must do is get the right kind of help for them insofar as we are able to do so.

We might, for example, suggest that the student see a trained counselor in the counseling center. Most colleges have such personnel, but often students (and many faculty) do not know about them, or they believe that these counselors are for "mentally ill" people, not someone with problems like theirs. Often a student who is reluctant to seek such help beforehand will go if a teacher he or she respects suggests it. The teacher may even intervene to the extent of calling to make the appointment while the student is there. Such action conveys the teacher's concern. Students don't usually think the teacher is trying to get rid of them or sidestep the problem if the teacher has listened carefully to the student and has explained that this problem warrants a kind of advice that the teacher is not trained to give.

Sometimes several sessions in which the teacher only listens and reacts sympathetically help the student think through the problem. In serious cases, when the student refuses to seek counseling, a concerned teacher may want to call the staff therapist or the dean, or the department head or a dorm counselor and alert him or her to the student's problem—preserving confidentiality, of course.

At times, teachers must decide if what a student is telling them is really a crisis or is a ploy to win sympathy and easier grades or exemptions from deadlines. Dealing with the genuine malingerer may require some sympathy, but usually we help this kind of student more by showing firmness in requiring them to meet deadlines and practice responsible behavior. Some students must be shown that they are responsible for the consequences or their actions or inaction. The best technique for dealing with these types of students, however, is to make writing so stimulating and so dynamic that they will want to do the assignments. One of the ways to interest the lagging student is to have a conference in which the teacher really excites him or her about writing. Such conferences should also reinforce and intensify the interest of the hard-working, responsible student.

To work well, a conference must put students at ease, not on the defensive. We should greet students pleasantly and ask how they are doing generally. If the students have requested the conference, we should invite them to voice the concerns that prompted the conference. Often these will be specific questions about a specific paper. We can answer these questions fully—but we should do so only with the student's help; that is, we ought to question students about how they would go about solving the problem they've brought to us, but we must question them in a nonthreatening, supportive way. These questions help us understand where communication in the classroom is breaking down, and they help teach the student more about independent problem solving.

More often, however, the conference is prompted not by specific questions about a particular assignment but by the student's vague feelings that he or she is failing, is lost, is depressed about his or her progress, or just discouraged. These kinds of conferences require more skill than those prompted by specific questions.

First, we should try to get the students to articulate insofar as possible how they are feeling about the process of writing and why they feel this way. Typically they say that no matter what they write, teachers don't like it and it's no good, or they say that they just can't think of anything to say and they feel stupid, or they say that they've never been any good at writing before and they don't sense that it's getting any better now.

Then we can ask them to explain how they go about the process of writing: how long they spend brainstorming, how long they spend drafting a paper, what forms their revision and proofreading take. We want to try to show them, of course, the direct correlation between their work habits and their attitudes. In most cases students who are discouraged are not spending enough time or they are badly misusing the time they spend writing.

When students come in frustrated or discouraged about an assignment, we want to spend the conference talking with the students in such a way that they will feel proud of the achievements they have made in the paper up to this point so they will feel confident in their ability to revise the paper and excited about doing so. To this sense of achievement we can add a sense of the independence they will have in learning to use the handbook to help answer questions as they write.

To foster this positive response, we want to reinforce orally the compliments we originally wrote in the margins of the paper. Instead of bowling the students over with negative comments about their inadequacies, we want to emphasize what they have done well. We can, for example, compliment them on choosing a uniquely interesting topic and focusing it well, or we can talk about particular images and phrasing that are especially evocative and original. Perhaps we can pull out a particular paragraph that has exceptionally good coherence and unity and structure, or we can comment on the excellent sentence variety in a place or two. (Of course, sometimes these strengths in the writing have come about accidentally, but our comments make the students aware of what they are doing well so that they will continue to do it, whether or not it has been an accident this time.)

Once we have made the students feel good about their achievements, we can explain what they need to do to strengthen the paper. If they believe that we like it up to this point and that the paper is worth working on—that they in fact have an interested reader—they will be eager for our suggestions for improvement. Even so, these suggestions should not be a list of errors. As much as possible, we should ask the students to explain what they think they should do to strengthen a particular passage, the organization, or the examples. Our gentle questioning makes the students feel more in control of their writing and helps them become more independent thinkers.

Often the students' questions should be the focus of the conference with the teacher doing little more than listening and asking other questions. The Socratic method works well with many students. Sometimes the right question opens the student's imagination or memory so that he or she goes away from the meeting eager to get the new ideas down in writing. The judicious question helps teachers avoid talking too much and inadvertently dictating the paper. Questions also work well when teachers see several students at once.

Whatever problems students bring to our offices can usually be handled best by beginning with positive assumptions about their ability to write and their interest in writing. No matter how positive we may be, however, students who have just received a paper with a low grade generally are anything but positive. Thus, it is a good idea to tell them that we are happy to make appointments—but not on the day we return papers. We should tell them that we expect them to go home and look at our written comments and look up the references to the handbook so that our conference with them will be really productive. Certainly if students have taken their papers home and spent some time trying to figure out what the problems are and how they can be solved, they are more likely to have useful questions when we do have our conference.

Although a few students may resist our efforts in conferences to help them improve, most will appreciate the time we spend with them and will use our guidance to think in positive ways about their writing. It's human nature to enjoy personal attention, and most students thrive on our interest in their lives and their writing—and especially the intersection of the two.

SUGGESTED READING

Flynn, Thomas, and Mary King, eds. *Dynamics of the Writing Conference: Social and Cognitive Interaction.* Urbana, IL: National Council of Teachers of English, 1993.

Hacker, Tim. "The Effect of Teacher Conferences on Peer Response Discourse." *Teaching English in the Two-Year College* 23 (May 1996): 112-26.

Kuriloff, Pesche E. "Reaffirming the Writing Conference: A Tool for Writing Teachers across the Curriculum." *Journal of Teaching Writing* 10, no. 1 (Spring/Summer 1991): 45–57.

Morse, Philip S. "The Writing Teacher as Helping Agent: Communicating Effectively in the Conferencing Process." *Journal of Classroom Interaction* 29.1 (1994): 9-15.

Newkirk, Thomas. "The Writing Conference as Performance." *Research in the Teaching of English* 29 (May 1995): 193-215.

Patthey Chavez, G. Genevieve, and Dana R. Ferris. "Writing and the Weaving of Multi-voiced Texts in College Composition." *Research in the Teaching of English* 31 (Feb. 1997): 51-90.

CHAPTER 6
Peer-Response: Opinions That Matter

Many teachers today recognize that their own painstaking comments, made with measured tone and affirmative intention, have much less impact on students' writing than even the most superficial and offhand comments by their peers. Increasingly teachers have worked diligently to harness the power of peer feedback and to shape it to suit their pedagogical aims. The result of this experimentation is the realization that generally the kind of evaluation most helpful to students combines carefully directed peer-response and carefully thought out paper evaluation by the teacher.

Many teachers use peer critique as a way of "cleaning up" a draft before it receives teacher evaluation. Whether or not peer-response achieves this goal, it can be an integral part of student learning. Peer-response gives students the chance to share their ideas with one another. Many students use peer-response sessions as a means of clarifying the assignment or the teacher's expectations. In peer-response sessions, students have the opportunity to be critical readers—to read for understanding and to respond to what they have read. By reading the work of others, students see different models or approaches that can be used to communicate a message. Ultimately, peer-response sessions give students an opportunity to test the clarity and effectiveness of their message on a real audience.

Peer evaluation, if well directed by the teacher, can rival—if not surpass—the teacher's criticism in terms of impact on student writers. The teacher's control of peer evaluation and careful direction to students about the goals of it are critical. If teachers do not give students specific goals, the criticism that results is likely to be vague and impressionistic and not worth the time devoted to it. Some help with these guidelines is to be found in section 6c of the *Simon & Schuster Handbook*. Following these or similar guidelines can produce surprisingly fruitful results that will excite students about the possibilities inherent in their work. Such critiques work so well perhaps because students believe that their classmates understand their vision better than we do or—heaven help us!—that their classmates' eyes are less clouded by matters of grammar and style and are thus more capable of keen insight. When classmates tell a student that the thesis is fuzzy or that they don't understand why four different topics are included in a single paragraph, the student usually believes the criticism and revises accordingly. Often an identical criticism from the teacher wins a shrug and a puzzled look that forecast a hit-or-miss, unenthusiastic revision.

But how do we get good responses from students? And how often in a term and at what stages in the composition process should we use peer-response?

As with most techniques in teaching, we do not want to use critiquing by classmates to the point that it becomes trite, predictable, and dull. Varying the frequency and complexity of this kind of evaluation helps maintain the students' interest and helps make critiquing an activity that the students look forward to participating in each time.

Peer-response can be employed usefully at any point in the development of an essay. But before we use this tool, we need to establish some ground rules. We need to remind students that what is being evaluated is the piece of writing, not the individual who wrote it. We need to remind them that both taking and giving negative criticism are hard but that honest comments are essential. We need to remind students that the word criticism implies much more than "bad" or "wrong"; it also implies "good" and "effective." Most students believe criticism is a pejorative term. We must show them that all effective feedback points out strengths and discusses weaknesses of a piece of work best in the context of the potential of the piece of writing. In other words, students should point out the weaknesses in the writing by making positive statements about the effectiveness that will result from revision.

Once students understand what it means to give feedback to their peers, they are ready to practice. One good exercise in critiquing is to have them comment only on one section of an essay—an introduction or one body paragraph. To begin, the teacher might hand each student's paper to another student in the class, having requested the students' permission to share their work. Some teachers find that students are less inhibited by peer critiquing if they do not know the name of the author whose work they are reading, and others believe that students should have the courage of their convictions and directly address the students whose work they are critiquing. I have found that having students address one another by name in the written reviews makes them somewhat more serious and constructive in their approach.

Once each student has a classmate's paragraph, the students need to be given specific directions for responding. You might do this by listing questions on the board or on a handout. Some teachers make up forms for this kind of exercise. And, it might even be useful to have students help compile a list of the elements they think they need help with. For this particular exercise in analyzing strengths and weaknesses of only the introduction or a body paragraph, the following questions might be asked:

1. What ideas are particularly effective and interesting?
2. What seems to be the purpose of this paragraph? What is the writer trying to accomplish?
3. What seems to be the main point of this paragraph? Where is it located?
4. Do you need additional support or background information to understand the paragraph's topic sentence or thesis?
5. Do you have trouble understanding how the writer gets from one idea to the next? Are the transitions smooth?
6. Which sentences are particularly effective? Which words, phrases, or sentences do you find especially strong? Which details do you especially like?
7. Are there places where the writer needs to be more specific and less abstract?
8. Who seems to be the audience for this essay? How do you know? What words or phrases has the writer used which suggest the audience?
9. Do you see any grammatical or punctuation problems which weaken the credibility of the paragraph?
10. What specific suggestions can you make to this author to help him or her strengthen this introduction?

Students need ample time to read the paragraphs more than once and to write full answers to these questions. They should begin their written responses with a salutation—"Dear Sally"—and at the end of their comments they ought to sign their names. Using names reminds the students that they are talking to a human being who has feelings. Students generally are not embarrassed to have their work read by classmates or to give honest criticism if teachers explain that the students are a community who can teach one another the way more experienced writers do in workshops. If teachers appeal to students in a professional way, students usually respond enthusiastically.

If time allows, you may wish to have students critique two papers in the same session. Doing so gives each writer two sets of suggestions, suggesting to him or her that as brief a piece of writing as an introduction can impress readers in different ways, often widely different. Having two or three responses to the introduction can also help students begin to understand the concept of audience. And using only part of an essay for a critique provides a quicker way of helping the students begin to think critically about the writing process.

Once students understand the response process, many teachers choose to put students into peer-response groups. These groups may be configured in a variety of ways, but generally groups larger than four will have difficulty giving all members feedback in an hour-long class period. Some teachers allow students to select their own peer groups. Other teachers assign peer groups to ensure groups are diverse yet compatible and to include writers of varying strengths and weaknesses. Many teachers keep the same peer groups throughout the term while others prefer to change groups for each peer-response session. Having the same peer groups can improve students' confidence in one another, but switching peer groups enables students to receive different perspectives on their writing.

Teachers may choose to use peer-response at different stages of writing process. But no matter what stage of the essay's development is evaluated, the process should be more or less the same: the teacher should give specific questions for the readers to answer, and students should be given ample time both for reading the paper several times and for writing their responses. To this end, many teachers utilize question sheets or checklists to guide student feedback. As writers become more proficient, teachers may require them to bring in their own questions and concerns to be addressed in their peer groups.

Teachers can choose which method of feedback—oral or written—works best for their class. Some teachers prefer to have students read their work aloud to their peer group. Reading aloud encourages questions and conversation and allows the writer to clarify points for the group. Through conversation, students often work together to solve problems in the writer's draft. However, if writers do not take notes on these conversations, they may forget important details about what was discussed. Many instructors prefer to have students write comments on their classmates' draft. Written comments are easier for the writer to refer back to when he or she is ready to revise the essay. The instructor also can monitor written comments to ensure all students are making an effort to give constructive feedback to each other. As with teacher comments, students' writing may be illegible or their comments may be hard to understand.

Some teachers like to sit in on peer-response groups and monitor their feedback, but others think that students perceive the teacher's interference as threatening or as somehow diluting the impact of their peers' thoughts. Monitoring the first critiques, however, helps teachers spot the students who need help learning how to respond to a piece of writing. If your campus has sufficient resources, writing center consultant or peer tutors can be used to help facilitate peer-response groups in a classroom. Often teachers can help students improve at giving and using feedback by asking them to complete journal entries or writer's memos after a peer-response session. Students can summarize what kind of advice is being offered in their peer group and negotiate how to use it, and teachers can see which groups need additional support or training to be successful evaluators.

Teachers who prefer not to give class time for peer feedback may opt to have students take drafts home to critique or to e-mail drafts to one another. Although students are certainly capable of taking others' papers home to critique them, the process often does not work as well at home as it does in the classroom. Students like the instant feedback in the classroom critiques. Divorced from the presence of their classmates and the energy of the class, they may be less willing to take the time required to do a careful evaluation. It is also more difficult to monitor the quality of feedback students give outside the classroom setting. To improve students' performance on out-of-class responses, many teachers will have students practice giving feedback in the classroom first or will pair take-home peer-responses with in-class sessions.

In some programs teachers operate their classrooms like real writers' workshops, at least for one or two class meetings a week. During the workshop sessions students are asked to present their own papers to the class for discussion. A fifty-minute period allows for about two such presentations per session. For such classes the students who will present their work are responsible for bringing enough copies of their paper so that each member of the class will have one. Some teachers prefer to have the papers distributed several days before the discussion, and others prefer that the students read the papers a couple of times just before the discussion.

Sitting or standing in front of the class, the student whose paper is up for discussion explains what the purpose of the paper is and its intended audience. The student also tells the class the specific problems encountered in writing the essay, explaining as clearly as possible why these trouble spots seemed to present problems. Then the student opens up class discussion of his or her essay.

Like other kinds of peer-response, this process can benefit students in several ways. But this kind of face-to-face discussion also requires good preparation. Many of us have had the experience of trying to lead a class discussion in which an apathetic class participated only through groans and the occasional monosyllabic response to a question designed to evoke a lively conversation. Students who are told simply to discuss an essay written by a classmate will respond in a similarly apathetic way, particularly if they think that grammar and usage are the focus of the discussion. They must be prepared with a vocabulary of critical terms, and they must be taught what kinds of features to notice in an essay. And, as in written critiques, they need to be shown how to make suggestions for improvement that will sound positive and affirmative, not negative and hurtful. This vocabulary and preparation may be provided in a handout of basic critical terms and a teacher's demonstration of a critique.

Some teachers using the workshop method have found that they must pull back from the group (literally pull their chairs away from the circle so as to be unobtrusive) and not speak at all until the end of the class, even when long pauses tempt them to rush in and explain the weaknesses and strengths of the paper under discussion. If the students know that the teacher is observing, not participating, they are far more likely to take control of the discussion.

Teachers who want to reap some of the benefits of the workshop method without taking so much class time may try in-class criticism of single paragraphs, perhaps taken anonymously from one or two papers in the process of revision by class members. Even a brief exercise like this helps acquaint students with the vocabulary they need as writers and thinkers, and it helps reassure weak writers, who may be reluctant to speak, that their unspoken ideas are the same as those articulated by stronger writers in the class who do not mind speaking out.

Peer-response reinforces the important concept that writing involves not only the writer but also the reader. And it makes students aware, as they likely have never been before, that the ultimate reader is no longer the English teacher. The teacher's written comments on the paper and the grade can help the student improve, but comments by peers contribute substantially to students' learning about their own writing and that of others.

WEB RESOURCES

Web Resources can be found at **www.prenhall.com/troyka** under Instructor's Resources.

SUGGESTED READING

Barron, Ronald. "What I Wish I Had Known About Peer-Response Groups but Didn't." *English Journal* 80.5 (Sept. 1991): 24–34.

Berliner, David, and Ursula Casanova. "The Case for Peer Tutoring." *Instructor* 99 (April 1990): 16–18.

Broglie, Mary. "Who Says So? Ownership, Authorship, and Privacy in Process Writing Classrooms: Privacy Issues Regarding Peer-Revision Workshops." *English Journal* 86 (Oct. 1997): 19–23.

Chapman, Orville L., and Michael A. Fiore. "Calibrated Peer Review." *Journal of Interactive Instruction Development* 12.3 (Winter 2000): 11–15.

Harris, Helen J. "Slice and Dice: Response Groups as Writing Processors." *English Journal* 81.2 (Feb. 1992): 51–54.

Hughes, J.A. "It Really Works: Encouraging Revision Using Peer Writing Tutors." *English Journal* 80 (Sept. 1991): 41–42.

Leverenz, Carrie Shively. "Peer Response in the Multicultural Classroom: Dissensus—A Dream (Deferred)." *Journal of Advanced Composition* 14.1 (Winter 1994): 167–86.

Liftig, R.A. "Feeling Good About Student Writing: Validation in Peer Evaluation." *English Journal* 79 (Feb.1990): 62–65.

McKendy, T. F. "Legitimizing Peer Response: A Recycling Project for Placement Essays." *College Composition and Communication* 41 (Feb1990): 89–91.

Sengupta, Sima. "Peer Evaluation: 'I Am Not the Teacher.'" *ELT Journal* 52 (Jan. 1998): 19–28.

Topping, Keith J. "Peer Assessment Between Students in Colleges and Universities." *Review of Educational Research* 68.3 (Fall 1998): 249–76.

CHAPTER 7

Evaluation by the Teacher: Using Grading to Help Students Develop their Writing

Evaluation of writing presents many challenges which quite naturally give pause to the new teacher sharpening up the red pencil to pass judgment on the first set of papers. But even experienced teachers fret over obvious inconsistencies among philosophies of grading and inconsistencies between theory and application. Evaluation of writing is possibly the single most difficult task required of us, yet it may well be the most important part of our job insofar as helping individual students.

Careful evaluation has the potential not only to improve students' writing dramatically but also to boost students' confidence in themselves as important members of a community of writers. As teachers, certainly we have the power to use grades to browbeat students—to show them every flaw in their mechanics and every crack in their logic. But, more important, we have the power to use evaluation to foster students' interest in writing, to help them develop a sense of confidence in their own ideas and their ability to express those ideas, to awaken their excitement as they discover the satisfaction of finally being able to say what they mean—and be understood by others. Whether we influence our students negatively or positively largely depends on the way in which we go about grading their papers.

It's no wonder our students sometimes think their grades result from luck or the teacher's mood. Far too many teachers view grading as a chore defined by vague concepts or harsh, absolute categorization of errors. In some departments grading policies are spelled out in a sort of "theme penalty sheet" so that the student earns grade X if he or she avoids certain kinds of errors. This kind of absolute, negative grading teaches the students only that they know how to write well if they succeed in avoiding problems in grammar and punctuation. Surely this kind of misconception is not what we wish to teach. Good writing is much more than avoiding mechanical problems, and our methods of grading need to make this point loudly and clearly.

Even before we begin to think about grading individual papers, however, we must decide how to consider the whole body of work a student does during the term. Three of the most current and common ways are using portfolios, using a contract system, and weighting each assignment.

■ PORTFOLIO ASSESSMENT

Using portfolios to determine a student's final grade in the course is an increasingly popular assessment method. Although some teachers find that, initially, at least, portfolio grading takes more time than other methods of assessment, many agree that in the long run this technique is worth their attention because it gives students the kind of individual assessment that such a personal skill as writing requires. Instead of squeezing each student into standardized notions of time required for a paper and number of revisions needed, this method comes closest of all forms of evaluation to personalizing grading. Therefore, it offers rich rewards to both students and teachers alike when they see that grading is part of a dialogue that helps each student work at an individual pace to overcome individual problems and feel a sense of accomplishment at having done so.

Teachers who want to use this kind of assessment, however, should have a clear strategy of what the portfolio will contain, when and how often they will grade it, and what the grades will mean. Some teachers want to have all assignments in the final portfolio and will ask students to "showcase" particular pieces that highlight their strengths. Others select certain essays as required pieces and allow students choices about other items to include in their portfolios. Still other teachers set a number of papers or pages the student must include in the portfolio and allow the students to choose its content. I prefer to allow students to choose, because they know which papers are working well for them in terms of interest and revision. Of course, it is important to have enough variety in the required assignments to ensure that many types of writing skills are finally graded, not just the one type that the student may have always been good at. Students who are allowed some choice about what will be assessed for their final grade seem to feel more invested in the course and to take the grading more seriously.

When grading student work, most teachers use portfolios as a means of giving feedback while postponing the assignment of letter grades until the end of the course. Students usually do not like waiting until the end of a term to get some grades. They would rather be reassured several times during the term that the grades have some connection to what they perceive of as the work they are doing. To address this concern, some teachers opt to grade portfolios at midterm or perhaps even two or three times during the term, announcing the dates on the syllabus so that students may plan their work from the first day. Such scheduling also teaches students to be responsible about deadlines and commitments. Teachers may also choose to use ratings, such as "Excellent," "Satisfactory," or "Needs Revision," or grading rubrics on essays to communicate a students' progress during the term while still allowing the student time to make improvements on their work.

One problem teachers find with portfolio grading is that consistency from student to student is more difficult to maintain in terms of the equation between letter grade and quality of work. Many portfolio-graders are influenced by improvement and effort, especially because students who revise over and over usually believe they are improving and that this improvement deserves better grades. Of course, not every student who revises improves the paper, and not all assignments are equally appealing to all students. Thus, teachers should clarify for themselves and for their students at the outset what standards they will apply, how much they will reward effort and improvement, and how closely they will monitor consistency in grading overall.

■ CONTRACT GRADING

Some teachers like to use contracts with their students, but these contracts take many forms. Some teachers make contracts for each grade, contracts that spell out precisely what proficiency level a student must reach and the amount of work which will show that level in order to receive a specific letter grade for the term.

Other teachers like to use contracts to allow students to choose how they want certain assignments weighted. For example, in a course which requires six essays, a journal, ten paragraphs, and an essay test, the teacher might allow students to decide what percentage of the final grade (perhaps within a range) would be from the essays, what percentage from the journal, and so on. The teacher might even allow students to weight each essay a different percentage.

The major advantage of contracts is that they allow students to enter into dialogue about grading and to feel that they have had a say about something important to them. Contracts also allow students to learn the responsibility of sticking to commitments once they are made.

The disadvantages may discourage some teachers from using the technique, but they become relatively minor once a teacher has tried this method once and learned from the experience. The major problem is the time-consuming bookkeeping that must keep track of the value of each assignment for each student, all assignments possibly having a different weight. However, a computer program or handwritten spreadsheet will reduce the confusion. Another problem for some teachers is the time and tact necessary for dealing with those students who, having signed the contract during the first few days of class, want to change it at one time or another during the term, once the student sees how the grades are going. I recommend not opening the Pandora's Box of altering contracts. Students can learn from the process of contracts that they must make decisions and abide by them. On the other hand, some teachers think that students are justified in requesting a change or two during the term, because they believe that students don't always know at the beginning where their strengths and weaknesses lie. Whether a teacher decides to alter contracts or not, he or she must have made that decision and explained it clearly to the class at the beginning of the term.

■ WEIGHTED GRADING

Many teachers believe that they should decide the relative value of assignments, because, they argue, students don't really know enough about the course's goals to be able to make or enter into those decisions. Therefore, they assign a certain percentage toward the final grade to each assignment or group of like assignments.

This traditional method, probably the most common kind of grading in college writing courses, can, however, be more or less effective, depending on the teachers' methods of weighting assignments and factoring in revision. In order to reward improvement, it makes sense to weight the earlier assignments as much less than later ones and to allow revision a high percentage.

No matter how lenient or harsh our letter grades are—and there is a good deal of leeway here—we must seek ways of grading that will help students. Chapter five details specific suggestions for commenting on students' work during the writing process. As composition instructors, we can expect to spend a great deal of time offering students feedback on their work. The amount and type of feedback we give should depend on what we expect students to do with it. When commenting on drafts we expect students to revise and resubmit, we should offer detailed feedback about what the student is doing well and how the student can improve. Comments that accompany grades often serve a different purpose: justifying the letter grade we gave it. As such, the focus is less on what to change on this particular draft and more on what the student can do to improve his or her writing on future drafts.

Once we decide how to comment on student work, we still have to make the difficult decision about what letter grade to assign the essay. As with other matters of grading, this decision is sometimes made largely by departmental consensus on what kinds of achievements merit certain letter grades. In some departments this consensus can take the form of the rigid "theme penalty sheet," which dooms papers with certain errors to the grade of *F* or *D*. Fortunately, in most cases departmental consensus is meant as a guideline for the teacher, not as an absolute set of criteria.

Though standards vary from school to school with regard to some features of writing, in general the following standards seem to be generally acceptable guidelines. Some teachers find that handing these kinds of guidelines to their students makes grading seem less arbitrary to students.

A—Most teachers recognize as an *A* paper one which has a spark of true originality. It has few if any mechanical errors, and it has clear organization, smooth transitions, exceptional detail, consistent diction and tone, and sophisticated sentence structure. Its thesis and evidence are specific and intriguing, not dull and predictable.

B—A *B* paper is one in which the writer organizes the material into coherent, well-unified paragraphs which have clear topic sentences. The writer does not violate the tone by shifting levels of diction, nor does the writer make serious or numerous mechanical errors. The evidence is fairly detailed, and the sentences are somewhat varied in terms of structure and length. The thesis, while perhaps not as insightful or original as in an *A* paper, is nevertheless neither dull nor obvious.

C—In a *C* paper teachers find evidence that the student is learning. *C* is not a negative grade: it demonstrates competence. Students often think that this grade means "mediocre" or "unsatisfactory," but with our positive comments about what they have done well in the paper, we can help students take pride in the considerable accomplishment that goes into the paper which earns a *C*.

A *C* paper communicates, but often not as clearly or specifically as we would like. Its thesis may need to be narrowed, and the paper often needs more detail and evidence. The paper may need better transitions both within and between paragraphs, and some paragraphs may need better topic sentences. A *C* paper is generally less fluid than more highly ranked papers; it may be wordy or have inadequate subordination and illogical coordination. Its sentences are often monotonous in terms of structure and length. The paper may shift tone and levels of language. Usually a *C* paper has several serious grammatical or mechanical errors.

D—A *D* paper generally has serious problems with both content and conventions, problems which hinder communication. A *D* paper usually has numerous mechanical errors, including some problems in sentence boundaries (comma splices, fragments, run-together sentences) that make the ideas unclear. Usually it lacks a clear thesis and clear organization, and its language is often much too general and dull. It offers no real evidence to support its points. Its sentences may be wordy and unvaried in terms of length and structure. This kind of paper often shifts levels of language and tone. A *D* paper can, however, be relatively free of mechanical errors but have so many serious problems with content and organization that it seems unfocused and even garbled.

F—An *F* paper is one which has no clear thesis, no clear organization, little specific detail, and many mechanical errors, especially problems with sentence boundaries (comma splices, fragments, and run-together sentences). This kind of paper usually has problems with diction and wordiness, and its sentences are unvaried in terms of structure and length. The writer often coordinates ideas which do not belong together. Paragraphs lack coherence and unity.

Some teachers like to give split grades, that is, one grade for content and one for mechanics. Although this kind of grading reduces the complaints from students about not getting enough credit for their good ideas, it also suggests that mechanics are separate from effective writing and perhaps that they are less important. As teachers we know the extent to which writing loses credibility in our culture when it does not follow the conventions. Thus, it seems misleading to separate the grade in this way and, as a result, foster the notion that the conventions are not part of the content.

Many teachers worry about discouraging students with low grades. Some avoid putting grades on the papers until late in the term when presumably students have learned what it takes to write an effective paper. Some teachers use evaluation rubrics or checklists that provide students with information about their strengths and weaknesses without assigning the essay a grade. A colleague of mine devised a system in which she marks essays "Excellent," "Satisfactory," or "Needs Revision" to encourage students who perform poorly to continue revising. Another method teachers use is to give grades from the beginning but stipulate that students must continue to revise papers until they are of at least *C* quality. And within reason, some teachers manipulate grades so that the standards for grading get slightly harder as the term progresses: a *C* early in the term is weaker than a *C* later in the term.

As they mark papers, most teachers find it convenient to use a numerical chart or symbols referring to sections in the handbook. These numbers or symbols make it easy for the teacher to direct the student to the appropriate rule or explanation he or she needs in order to revise well. The *Simon & Schuster Handbook for Writers* contains both a chart of symbols and a numerical chart. In addition to using these numbers or symbols, most teachers like also to write some comments in the margins, particularly comments about whatever skill or concept the class is working on that week or about the most serious problems. Certainly teachers should also use these marginal comments to compliment students on mastering particular skills.

Following are two copies of a student's paper, one overmarked and too harshly graded and the other less heavily marked and more affirmative. (This comparison-and-contrast paper was the fourth essay in a one-term composition course, preceded by a narrative essay, a cause-and-effect essay, and a classification.) Both copies are marked with numbers and symbols from the *Simon & Schuster Handbook*. The second example is the kind of grading that seems to be most helpful in terms of inspiring students to care about revising and continuing to learn about writing. It asks the student questions rather than dictating changes, and the tone of the marginal comments is friendly, not sarcastic and insulting to the student.

Overmarked

Sinatra Versus Vandross

Power surges into the radio. The music blares from the speakers with

intensity. But what really is music? Music has many definitions according

this is not at all clear

All of them? That must be tough.

to each individual's taste. <u>Multitudes of singers</u> strive to fulfill these

You're getting less and less clear

different definitions to achieve success. Both Frank Sinatra and Luther

Vandross fulfill two of these contrary definitions of music. On the surface it

16n, 16p

appears as though th<u>ey a</u>re inherently dissimilar, but upon closer

evaluation they share certain specific details in common. Comparing the

emotional quality of their music, the importance placed on lyrics, and their

24d   *wordy*

use of rhythm ⌒ can reveal that even ~~the most~~ diametrically opposed singers

share important similarities.

if it's background music,
it <u>has</u> been utilized

For both Sinatra and Vandross, the ~~utilized~~ background music indicates

their different styles of music. Vandross's style best fits into the category of

soul music. Vandross does not sing straight soul; however, he takes certain

elements from jazz. In some forms of jazz, instrumentation takes a

What are you comparing and contrasting in this ¶? I don't understand what you mean.

secondary role as the voice develops into the key element. Vandross uses

this element to accent his voice to become the most important element in his

sp

music. Sinatra, unlike Vandross, gears his music toward older (genenrations.)

His music relates back to the big band era as he uses the violin and brass

sections of the band in many songs. The violin and the piano play an impor-

tant part in the majority of his love songs while the brass section communi-

cates the stalwart feeling in others. The large band helps to make his music

more diverse as his voice cannot produce much variety. The band plays

equal to what?

<u>an equal role</u> in complimenting Sinatra's voice yet not overpowering it.

For both Sinatra and Vandross, the emotion communicated through

wordy!

their songs plays a vital role. The majority of Vandross's music deals with

11

sexual ~~connotation of~~ love. This does not mean that he directly sings of awkward diction – 12d

sexual <u>confrontation</u>, but rather his singing brings physical stirring within

the listener. His voice makes the listener appreciate the emotion he or she

feels. Vandross also communicates loneliness and solitude in songs dealing

with the loss of love. Through Vandross's voice, the listener has the

capacity to feel the loneliness and pain associated with losing a special

transition – 3g

love. Vandross has the ability to relate love to other topics as well. In the

song "A House is Not a Home," Vandross uses this theme to present the idea

of what a real home should entail. He combines love with the idea of a home

and makes a point of the importance of having a home with love present

This ¶ is too long

¶

within. For Sinatra as well, the theme of love appears in many songs. In

16n

Sinatra's songs, however, <u>he</u> emphasizes more emotional and innocent love.

hyphen

Songs like "Tell Her" sing of a never ending love that needs to be renewed

17o

two words

everyday by telling that special person that they are loved. Indirect

reference to sexual love commonly occurs but only using subtle under-

tones. Sinatra also has the ability to relate love to inanimate objects.

Several of his most famous songs are about cities like New York and Los

Angeles and how he finds them special or unique. More frequently Sinatra's

songs deal with lost love and reminiscing over past loves. Instead of making

the listener feel sorry for his condition like Vandross, he imparts a message

of stalwartness to hold on to hope for the future. The song "That's Life" is

word choice? 12d

expressly <u>donated</u> to this idea. This message of hope gives Sinatra a more

optimistic message than Vandross. But on the same idea, Vandross can be

confusing

considered a more realistic singer. Sometimes a listener may not want to

hear about the defiance of love's importance which Sinatra sings about. In

this case they listen to Vandross who makes the listener come to grips with

sexist! 12f, 17s   16o

you're awfully absolute here

his true feelings. Sinatra cannot do <u>this</u> as his voice does not allow him to

is this really what you mean?

relate the pain associated with lost love on a realistic level. Vandross lets

21a

the listener relate to the <u>pain he or she feels through the song and his voice.</u>

To achieve the intended emotion in their songs, both Vandross and
16o
Sinatra utilize strikingly different methods. For Vandross, this is done

through his remarkable vocal ability. One can understand the emotion he
21a
he's trying to   tries to convey by just listening to his voice. He can attain any range of
convey by   16o
listening?   notes which gives his music flavor and uniqueness. He uses this indirect

method of convey the desired emotion to the listener. Sinatra, on the other

hand, depends on his lyrics and not on vocal ability. To express himself,

Sinatra tells an emotional story through his songs. To receive the full effect
21d   *awk*
of this emotion, the complete song must be listened to. Like in a fairy tale,

the complete story makes it magical and not just the individual parts. The

lyrics play such an important role in songs such as "The September of My

Years" that the sadness of growing old would not be understood had the
                                        wordy   *awk*
lyrics not been listened to completely. Taking songs where both Sinatra and

Vandross sang the words "I love you" reveals striking contrasts in how

each conveys emotion. For Sinatra, the surrounding lyrics give these words

meaning. Taken in context, they derive their meaning. Vandross, on the

other hand, can make a person weep by saying these words. The listener is
                                   wrong preposition
able to understand whether Vandross is reminiscing of a past love, has just
dangling modifier   21a
lost a love, or is currently in love, by singing just these three words. His

vocal ability gives him this talent.

When people listen to music, no two people hear exactly the same

thing. Singers like Frank Sinatra and Luther Vandross each fit different

definitions of music. The rhythms they use and the way they convey
                     wordy
their ideas may be different, yet they still share important similarities.
                        ▼   17o   24b   *sp*
Each imparts love as their main theme for music and they also utilize
                          don't split infinitive   12d
appropriate background music to properly accent their different vocal

abilities. For both Sinatra and Vandross they utilize every aspect of their
wordy ⟨
        music to accent the strengths and reduce the weaknesses of their music.

Even though on the surface two singers may appear to be totally contrary to each other like Sinatra and Vandross, even the most opposite singers share important similarities.

Steve, you've got the beginning of a paper here—but this needs much more work to get it up to an acceptable level. — D

More Affirmatively Marked

Sinatra Versus Vandross

Can you be more precise here? How do these ideas relate to what you're exploring in this paper?

Power surges into the radio. The music blares from the speakers with intensity. But what really is music? Music has many definitions according to each individual's taste. Multitudes of singers strive to fulfill thee different definitions to achieve success. Both Frank Sinatra and Luther Vandross fulfill two of these contrary definitions of music. On the surface it appears as though they are inherently dissimilar, but upon closer

16n, 16p

This is a good idea, but you need to focus a bit more clearly

evaluation they share certain specific details in common. Comparing the emotional quality of their music, the importance placed on lyrics, and their use of rhythm, can reveal that even the most diametrically opposed singers share important similarities.

Steve, you've got the idea of comparison and contrast, but you are looking at different kinds of things in this ¶. You need to look again.

For both Sinatra and Vandross, the utilized background music indicates their different styles of music. Vandross's style best fits into the category of soul music. Vandross does not sing straight soul; however, he takes certain elements from jazz. In some forms of jazz, instrumentation takes a secondary role as the voice develops into the key element. Vandross uses this element to accent his voice to become the most important element in his music. Sinatra, unlike Vandross, gears his music toward

sp

older genenrations. His music relates back to the big band era as he uses

very interesting!

the violin and brass sections of the band in many songs. The violin and the piano play an important part in the majority of his love songs while the brass section communicates the stalwart feeling in others. The large band helps to make his music more diverse as his voice cannot produce much

equal to what?

variety. The band plays an equal role in complimenting Sinatra's voice yet not overpowering it.

For both Sinatra and Vandross, the emotion communicated through

wordy
see 16

their songs plays a vital role. The majority of Vandross's music deals with a

sexual connotation of love. This does not mean that he directly sings of

word chioce? 12d

sexual <u>confrontation</u>, but rather his singing brings physical stirring within

the listener. His voice makes the listener appreciate the emotion he or she

feels. Vandross also communicates loneliness and solitude in songs dealing

with the loss of love. Through Vandross's voice, the listener has the

capacity to feel the loneliness and pain associated with losing a special

transition – 3g

Can you subdivide this ¶ to make more well focused points?

love. Vandross has the ability to relate love to other topics as well. In the

song "A House is Not a Home," Vandross uses this theme to present the idea

of what a real home should entail. He combines love with the idea of a home

and makes a point of the importance of having a home with love present

within. For Sinatra as well, the theme of love appears in many songs. In

Sinatra's songs, however, he emphasizes more emotional and innocent love.

Songs like "Tell Her" sing of a never ending love that needs to be renewed

You have given some good examples and details—can you give even more?

everyday by telling that special person that they are loved. Indirect

reference to sexual love commonly occurs but only using subtle under-

tones. Sinatra also has the ability to relate love to inanimate objects.

Several of his most famous songs are about cities like New York and Los

Angeles and how he finds them special or unique. More frequently Sinatra's

songs deal with lost love and reminiscing over past loves. Instead of making

the listener feel sorry for his condition like Vandross, he imparts a message

of stalwartness to hold on to hope for the future. The song "That's Life" is

12d

expressly <u>donated</u> to this idea. This message of hope gives Sinatra a more

can you make this more precise?

optimistic message than Vandross. But on the same idea, Vandross can be

considered a more realistic singer. Sometimes a listener may not want to

hear about the defiance of love's importance which Sinatra sings about. In

this case they listen to Vandross who makes the listener come to grips with

can you make this less absolute?

12f   *16o*

<u>his</u> true feelings. Sinatra cannot do <u>this</u> as his voice does not allow him to

relate the pain associated with lost love on a realistic level. Vandross lets
21a – misplaced modifier
the listener relate to the pain he or she feels (through) the song and his voice.

To achieve the intended emotion in their songs, both Vandross and

good topic
sentence
                                 16o
Sinatra utilize strikingly different methods. For Vandross, this is done

through his remarkable vocal ability. One can understand the emotion he
                            21a
tries to convey by just listening to his voice. He can attain any range of
         16o
notes which gives his music flavor and uniqueness. He uses this indirect

method to convey the desired emotion to the listener. Sinatra, on the other

hand, depends on his lyrics and not on vocal ability. To express himself,

Sinatra tells an emotional story through his songs. To receive the full effect
21d
of this emotion, the complete song must be listened to. Like in a fairy tale,

the complete story makes it magical and not just the individual parts. The

lyrics play such an important role in songs such as "The September of My

Years" that the sadness of growing old would not be understood had the
                                    awkward, wordy – see 11
lyrics not been listened to completely. Taking songs where both Sinatra and

Vandross sang the words "I love you" reveals striking contrasts in how

each conveys emotion. For Sinatra, the surrounding lyrics give these words

meaning. Taken in context, they derive their meaning. Vandross, on the

other hand, can make a person weep by saying these words. The listener is
                                    wrong preposition
able to understand whether Vandross is reminiscing of a past love, has just
                                21a
lost a love, or is currently in love, by singing just these three words. His

vocal ability gives him this talent.

When people listen to music, no two people hear exactly the same

thing. Singers like Frank Sinatra and Luther Vandross each fit different

definitions of music. The rhythms they use and the way they convey
                11
their ideas may be different, yet they still share important similarities.
                             ▼ 17o
Each imparts love as their main theme for music and they also atilize

12d

appropriate background music to properly accent their <u>differing</u> vocal

wordy
11

abilities. For both Sinatra and Vandross they utilize every aspect of their

music to accent the strengths and reduce the weaknesses of their music.

Even though on the surface two singers may appear to be totally contrary

to each other like Sinatra and Vandross, even the most opposite singers

share important similarities.

Steve, Sinatra-lover that I am, I'm intrigued with your topic. You have some great ideas to support your comparison and contrast. In a few places you need to focus your ideas more precisely, and some mechanical problems weakened the paper. On the whole, though, you're off to a great start.

I'm looking forward to the next draft! — D

WEB RESOURCES

Web Resources can be found at **www.prenhall.com/troyka** under Instructor's Resources.

SUGGESTED READING

Addison, Joanne, and Rick Van De Weghe. "Portfolio-based Assessment and Professional Development." *English Education* 32.1 (Oct. 1999): 16–33.

Anderson, Larry, et al. "Reader-Response Theory and Instructor's Holistic Evaluating in and out of Their Fields." *Teaching English in the Two-Year College* 21.1 (Feb. 1994): 53–62.

Baker, N.W. "The Effect of Portfolio-Based Instruction on Composition Students' Final Examination Scores, Course Grades, and Attitudes toward Writing." *Research in the Teaching of English* 27 (May 1993): 155–74.

Belanoff, Pat, and Marcia Dickson, eds. *Portfolios: Process and Product.* Portsmouth, NH: Boynton/Cook, 1991.

Bloom, Lynn Z. "Why I (Used to) Hate to Give Grades." *College Composition and Communication* 48 (Oct. 1997): 360–71.

Broad, Bob. "Pulling Your Hair Out: Crises of Standardization in Communal Writing Assessment." *Research in the Teaching of English* 35.2 (Nov. 2000): 213–60.

Bullock, Richard. "Spreading the Word . . . and Possibly Regretting It: Current Writing about Portfolios." *Journal of Teaching Writing* 12.1 (1993): 105–13.

Caulk, Nat. "Comparing Teacher and Student Responses to Written Work." *TESOL Quarterly* 28 (Spring 1994): 181–88.

Chandler, Jean. "Positive Control." *College Composition and Communication* 48 (May 1997): 273–74.

Christensen, N.E "Avoidance Pedagogy in Freshman English." *Teaching English in the Two-Year College* 18 (May 1991): 133–36.

Christian, Barbara. "Freshman Composition Portfolios in a Small College." *Teaching English in the Two-Year College* 20.4 (Dec. 1993): 289–97.

Connors, Robert, and Andrea A. Lunsford. "Teachers' Rhetorical Comments on Student Papers." *College Composition and Communication* 44.2 (May 1993): 200–23.

Duke, C. R., and R. R. Sanchez, "Giving Students Control over Writing Assessment." *English Journal* 83 (April 1994): 47–53.

Elbow, Peter. "Ranking, Evaluation, and Liking: Sorting Out Three Forms of Judgment." *College English* 55.2 (Feb. 1993): 187–206.

Haswell, Richard, and Susan Wyche Smith. "Adventuring into Writing Assessment." *College Composition and Communication* 45.2 (May 1994): 220–36.

Helton, Edwina L., and Jeff Sommers. "Repositioning Revision: A Rhetorical Approach to Grading." *Teaching English in the Two-Year College* 28.2 (Dec. 2000): 157–64.

Hillenbrand, Lisa. "Assessment of ESL Students in Mainstream College Composition." *Teaching English in the Two-Year College* 21.2 (May 1994): 125–29.

Hodges, Elizabeth. "The Unheard Voices of Our Responses to Students' Writing." *Journal of Teaching Writing* 21.2 (1992): 203–18.

Jones, Brett D. "Computer-Rated Essays in the English Composition Classroom." *Journal of Educational Computing Research* 20.2 (1999) 169–87.

Knudson, Ruth E. "College Students' Writing: An Assessment of Competence." *The Journal of Educational Research* 92.1 (Sept./Oct. 1998): 13–19.

Metzger, Elizabeth, and Lizbeth Bryant. "Portfolio Assessment: Pedagogy, Power, and the Student." *Teaching English in the Two-Year College* 20.4 (Dec. 4 1993): 279–88.

Norton, L. S. "Essay Writing: What Really Counts?" *Higher Education* 20 (Dec. 1990): 411–42.

O'Neill, Peggy. "From the Writing Process to the Responding Sequence: Incorporating Self-Assessment and Reflection in the Classroom." *Teaching English in the Two-Year College* 26.1 (Sept. 1998): 61–70.

Peckham, Irvin. "Beyond Grades." *Composition Studies Freshman English News* 21.2 (Fall 1993): 16–31.

Purves, Alan C. "Reflections on Research and Assessment in Written Composition." *Research in the Teaching of English* 26.1 (Feb. 1992): 108–22.

Reeves, Thomas C. "Alternative Assessment Approaches for Online Learning Environments in Higher Education." *Journal of Educational Computing Research* 23.1 (2000): 101–11.

Roemer, Marjorie, Lucille M. Schultz, and Russel K. Durst. "Portfolios and the Process of Change." *College Composition and Communication* 42 (1991): 455–69.

Slevin, James F. "Engaging Intellectual Work: The Faculty's Role in Assessment." *College English* 63.3 (Jan. 2001): 288–305.

Smith, Mark Edward. "Using Markings to Respond to Writing." *English Journal.* 86 (Feb. 1997): 79–80.

Smith, Summer. "The Genre of the End Comment: Conventions in Teacher Responses to Student Writing." *College Composition and Communication* 48 (May 1997): 249–68.

Speck, Bruce W. "Grading Students' Classroom Writing: Issues and Strategies." *ASHE ERIC Higher Education Reports* 27.3 (2000): 1–98.

Sperling, Melanie. "Constructing the Perspective of Teacher-as-Grader: A Framework for Studying Response to Student Writing."

Sweeney, Marilyn Ruth. "Relating Revision Skills to Teacher Commentary." *Teaching English in the Two-Year College* 27.2 (Dec. 1999): 213–18.

White, E.M. "Language and Reality in Writing Assessment." *College Composition and Communication* 41 (May 1990): 187–200.

——. "The Opening of the Modern Era of Writing Assessment." *College English* 63.3 (Jan. 2001): 306–20.

Valentino, Marilyn J. "Responding When a Life Depends on It: What to Write in the Margins When Students Self-Disclose." *Teaching English in the Two-Year College* 23 (Dec. 1996): 274–83.

CHAPTER 8
Some Ideas for Assignments and Classroom Activities

Before we meet our students the first day of class, we need to have analyzed the skills we want to teach them and formulated some assignments and classroom activities which will help them develop those skills. Certainly making a syllabus (see Chapter 4 in this supplement) helps us come to terms with how much we can realistically expect to teach and the order in which we should introduce the skills we want our students to master. But carefully planning our assignments and use of time in the classroom can further ensure that we meet our goals.

For most of us, the list of basic skills we want our students to have when they leave us includes:

1. Writing as a process.
2. Clear, varied, and concise sentences in terms of diction and phrasing.
3. Coherent organization of paragraphs and essays.
4. Transition between and within paragraphs.
5. Different methods for developing paragraphs and essays and the ability to make the appropriate choice of methods for a given purpose and audience.
6. Focused topics and narrow theses.
7. Critical thinking, the ability to detect weaknesses and strengths in the arguments of others and to support their own arguments with appropriate evidence.
8. Basic use of the library and other resources for research.
9. Up-to-date documentation.
10. Conventional mechanics.

Certainly other, more sophisticated skills would be expected of accelerated students, but these are the basic skills for most students in their first college writing course. Our task is to design assignments and activities that will teach and reinforce these skills.

Before students write anything, they need to begin thinking in terms of the purpose of what they are writing. Are they writing to inform their audience or to persuade their readers? Many teachers prefer to begin the course by having students discuss both audience and purpose and their interrelatedness. (See Troyka & Hesse, Chapter 1.) An obvious but effective way to generate meaningful discussion of audience and purpose is to have students bring to class samples of various kinds of writing. Teachers may direct these choices or simply ask students to bring two different kinds of writing to class for discussion. Interesting discussions can result from students' assessments of the purpose and audience for writing such as letters to the editor in a newspaper or magazine, advertising copy, the preface to a book, directions for assembling a toy or an appliance, a poem or a piece of fiction, a sales letter, an article in a teen magazine, an article in a technical journal, and so on. Class discussion of audience can include speculation about the educational level, gender, race, age, and perhaps even the social and economic levels of the intended readers for these various pieces.

An effective exercise to follow up this discussion is to have students choose one piece of writing that they have brought into class and to have them rewrite it, or part of it if it is long, for a different kind of audience. For example, a student might choose to rewrite an article about general nutrition that is aimed at retired Americans so that it would appeal to teens. In struggling to rewrite the article, the student would have to grapple with important choices of vocabulary level, sentence structure, and tone.

Many teachers are finding that letter-writing and journal-writing can help students understand audience and purpose. A good way to help students learn to be comfortable in the class at the beginning of the term is to pair each student with one or two others and have the students write letters to one another following specified instructions that will help you achieve your purpose. For example, you might ask the students to write about what points in the class discussion confused him or her and speculate on the causes of the confusion. Similarly, using a journal for a group of five or six students for the entire term might afford the students to learn something about audience and purpose if you specify the kinds of issues and topics the group is to address each week. I have found that these work best if I grade only for the ideas and only mark major mechanical errors. Students naturally enjoy writing to their peers and reading what their classmates think, and we should design assignments that take advantage of this kind of writing that seems more like pleasure than work.

Another effective exercise, especially useful early in the term, is to ask students to write a paragraph that gives directions to a carefully specified audience (a babysitter, a mechanic, a parent, etc.), directions which explain how to do something, and then ask them to rewrite the directions for a totally different, perhaps more general audience. You may even ask students to write an analysis of the kinds of changes they made and the reasons for them.

This same kind of exercise works well in helping students understand purpose. Too often students have the mistaken impression that certain kinds of topics are informative—always—and that other kinds of topics are persuasive—always. Students usually gain valuable insight if we have them write a paragraph or brief essay which is informative in its purpose and then have them rewrite it to make it persuasive. A written analysis of the changes students made in this revision may also help them see the critical importance of determining purpose before they write.

In the handbook, Chapters 39–41 and Chapters 43–44, students can look at the differences in communication between the disciplines or in real-world communication and how the different audiences and purposes change the style and content of the communication. Students can explore how different disciplines talk about similar topics or issues. Students can also see how their communication changes when they move from the private writing (letter writing, e-mails, journals) to public writing (résumés, reports, business letters).

Some teachers ask students to identify the purpose and intended audience as part of the students' plan for the essay. They may even ask the students to explain how their choice of purpose and audience will affect other choices they must make as writers—choices of vocabulary level, tone, sentence structure, paragraph structure, and so on. Other teachers ask students to write the intended audience and the purpose in the upper corner of the first page of the essay. Even this simple act emphasizes to the students the importance of these decisions.

Title Sinatra Versus Vandross   January 30, 2002   Steven Feyl

Comparison-and-Contrast Essay   Dr. Julian, English 11K

    <u>Audience</u>: This essay is written for a friend on my hall, Eric Fuller. At the beginning of the year we had extensive conversations about each other's taste in music.
    <u>Purpose</u>: The purpose of this essay is to take an unbiased position on the topic to show Eric that even in our different opinions about music, there also are similarities.
    <u>Thesis</u>: Comparing the emotional quality of their music, the importance placed on lyrics, and their use of rhythm can reveal that even the most diametrically opposed singers share important similarities.
    <u>Difficulties in writing the essay</u>: The chief difficulty in this essay came with research. I know a lot about Frank Sinatra but relatively little about Luther Vandross. Eric Fuller gave me help with this as he gave me one of Vandross's tapes and directions about what to look for in his music. Grammatically, linking verbs still gave me the most trouble. I also had trouble making the essay flow together with proper transitions.

An example of a cover sheet which identifies audience and purpose is this title page for the essay given in Chapter 5 of this supplement:

No matter what method of organization a teacher chooses for the writing course, some attention to purpose and audience are essential early in the term.

Some teachers prefer to organize their course by theme. They may ask students to write several papers on a subject of general interest to the students. Organizing the course by topic provides teachers an ongoing opportunity to have students explore differences in purpose and audience.

Using this approach, the teacher might ask students to write an informative essay on a topic which the students have specialized knowledge of, rock music or clothing fads, for example. The students would tailor the essay to whatever audience they chose. Then the teacher might have the students expand the essay into a research project and change the audience significantly. Next the teacher might have the students make the paper persuasive, for a totally different audience than that of the first two essays. Other variations are possible and instructive. Combining this topical approach with a rhetorical approach also works well for some instructors.

Many teachers prefer to organize their course by rhetorical type. In this organizational plan the teacher's most important decisions are choosing the order in which to present the types of development and making appropriate assignments for each.

Beginning with narrative and descriptive writing puts students at ease because these kinds of development draw on the students' own experiences and feelings. Although some students have a hard time finding something to say even about themselves, most students can write a personal narrative more easily than an essay developed by other methods. Beginning with personal narrative helps weak writers who are intimidated by the writing process. Because they are writing about something they know well, they do not have to struggle with both form and content at once, at least not to the degree that later papers will require.

A good beginning assignment is a topic like "Until I experienced X, I had never understood Y." If the event (X) being described is limited to something which happened in a couple of hours, the student has a manageable narrative chunk to control in the essay. A useful exercise is to have each student write three versions of this topic sentence, each version completing the blanks with a different experience. Then teachers—or classmates—can choose the topic that will lend itself best to an interesting narration.

While the students are working on this essay, however, the teacher can teach several skills at once. As students begin to brainstorm in an effort to narrow their topics, they should discuss the purpose of the essay and the intended audience. On all outlines and drafts of the paper, students should write the intended audience in the corner as well as the level of formality dictated by that choice. Thus when classmates critique the essay, they can comment on whether or not the writer is considering the needs of the audience that he or she has chosen.

In addition to audience and purpose, a narrative essay as a first essay is a good place to begin teaching various related kinds of paragraph development. In class students can practice developing paragraphs by chronology. We can show them the differences between chronological narrative paragraphs, chronological process paragraphs, and chronological climactic paragraphs.

A narrative essay also gives us the opportunity to talk about topic sentences in narrative and descriptive writing—to say that they are not always stated but that they can be. A useful classroom exercise is to take a hypothetical version of the topic they are working on and have the class break the narration down into segments that could become paragraphs. They then can write topic sentences for each segment. The class can do this assignment independently and then discuss their versions, or the class can collaborate on an outline and topic sentences for the sample topic, with the teacher writing their suggestions on the board.

The narrative essay is also a good place to begin a discussion of descriptive detail. It's a good time to make the point that no piece of writing is entirely narrative or descriptive or expository or argumentative but that we classify according to the dominant mode. We can ask them to imagine the lack of interest they would create in a version of "Little Red Riding Hood" if they were allowed to tell only what happened and not to describe the big, bad wolf or the dark forest.

In discussing the relationship between narration and description, we can begin to emphasize the need for specific, original detail in writing, a point that we need to make over and over during the course. One good way to help students think about detail is to do a classroom exercise in which each student must write five sentences about the classroom, one sentence evoking each of the senses (taste, touch, smell, hearing, and sight). After students share their sentences, it's fun to have them do sentences again, this time making similes and metaphors. Exercises requiring all the senses help them realize that good description means doing more than simply saying how something looks. Having done this exercise, we can even insist that the narrative essay have sentences evoking each of the senses at least once. Such an arbitrary, artificial exercise impresses upon students the need to create for their reader the world which is part of narration.

Moving from narrative writing to the descriptive essay, we can show students that although descriptive essays often relate events, their primary goal is to convey a sense of place and mood. A good topic is something like "Why *X*-place makes me feel *Y*-emotion." Some teachers like to have students describe a place on campus, looking for the unusual features that make it unique. Having students write an in-class description of the classroom or of a common place can make it easy for the teacher to talk about cliches and the need for fresh, specific detail.

Good choices for the third paper are comparison-and-contrast writing or classification. Both are a little harder for the students than narrative and descriptive writing because they require some analysis, but they are less difficult at this point than, say, cause and effect or definition or argument.

Compare-and-contrast is a type of development that most students have been taught in high school; thus they are usually receptive to learning a more sophisticated version of it. This type of development offers a lot of flexibility with regard to the kind of topic, depending on what skills we want to teach along with it.

We can appeal to the interests of the class with this kind of essay, by having art students, for example, compare and contrast paintings or statues by the same artist, or engineering students compare and contrast methods for solving some kind of problem. Obviously, teachers who are using a reader can easily have students compare and contrast essays with regard to content or style. Most students enjoy comparing a movie with its sequel or a book with the movie made from it, and they enjoy comparing television shows or magazine ads or fast-food restaurants— any topic, in fact, which draws on what they experience.

A topic which works well for the teacher who is interested in teaching stylistic elements early in the course is to have students compare and contrast the styles of two movie reviews. This assignment can teach several important skills: it can teach students how to use the library to find movie reviews, it can teach them about conventions of quoting, paraphrasing, and summarizing, and it can teach them about elements of style.

Teachers can also couple comparison-and-contrast writing with definition. A good assignment is to have students compare and contrast definitions of the same word in several dictionaries. This assignment helps acquaint students with various kinds of dictionaries. Now that students use computers which have spell-checks and thesauruses, it's more important than ever that we help them understand how to use a dictionary and why they should want to. Many students are unaware of the differences between abridged and unabridged dictionaries, and few of them have had any experience with the *OED*. Thus a comparison of a couple of dictionaries or definitions teaches much more than the method of comparison and contrast.

Classification works well after comparison and contrast because the idea of comparison and contrast is implicit in classification. Certainly topics like "types of horror movies" or "types of golf swings" work well, but students also enjoy classifying groups of people. If we allow them to write on such topics as "types of drivers" or "types of basketball fans," we can teach them about the dangers of stereotyping and the need for qualifying our generalizations.

Since the organization of a classification essay is implied by the topic, the time we normally would have to devote to explaining structure—obviously important with comparison and contrast, for example—can be devoted to work on transition between and within paragraphs and varieties of introductions and conclusions. This assignment also gives students further practice in using effective descriptive detail.

Equally useful because of its relatively simple organization is the process essay. This kind of essay provides a perfect way to teach attention to audience. We can have students explain a process in the second person and have them rewrite it into the third person. We can have them assume that the audience is somewhat familiar with the process or is not familiar with it at all and do a version suitable in each case. Particularly useful for weak writers, process writing can really boost the understanding of transitions and assumptions made by the writer.

As a prelude to argumentation, many teachers find it helpful to do a definition essay. Students believe that if they don't know the meaning of a word, they should simply look it up in a dictionary. To correct this misconception, we must show them that disagreement about definitions of abstract terms is at the root of many issues. We can ask them, in fact, to find editorials to share in class that argue about terms like *pornography* or *freedom* or *democracy* or *liberal* without defining the terms.

Before we ask students to write a definition of one of these kinds of terms, though, having students write paragraph-length definitions of a slang term or newly coined term like *yuppie* or *airhead* can teach them about the subtleties of definition. Within this paragraph they can practice citing the dictionary meaning (more practice in quoting accurately) and expanding it by giving examples, defining in terms of negatives, comparing the term with terms closely related to it, exploring the source of the quality or thing, explaining how our culture generally defines the term, and stating, finally, their personal definition.

As an essay assignment, we can have the students choose from a list of abstract terms like *pornography, art, fun,* or *selfishness,* or we can give them more practice with comparison-and-contrast writing by having them compare and contrast often-confused terms like *right* and *privilege, selfishness* and *self-esteem,* or *hero* and *celebrity.* In making these kinds of assignments, we want to emphasize that in argumentative writing, careful writers define their terms early in their arguments and do not shift the meaning of these terms. Some careful attention to audience and purpose in definition is also important.

Argumentative writing requires a lot of preparation by the teacher, but it allows us much flexibility in teaching some secondary skills. Many teachers prefer to teach argument only in the context of a research project since students usually know too little about most issues to argue their positions without research. But whatever kind of argument topic we decide to assign, we need to do some preliminary work with the class to discuss the difference between inductive and deductive reasoning, kinds of acceptable evidence, fallacious thinking, and definition of terms.

Summary skills fit well into a unit on argumentative writing. Writing summaries requires students to have a clear understanding of what they are reading. Summary writing also serves to develop paraphrasing skills. Before students critique the arguments of others or develop positions of their own, they should be able to accurately summarize what they have read.

Far too many students believe that if something is printed it is good and true, and, therefore, one of our first chores is to explain that all sources and all arguments are not equal. We must communicate that the quality of a writer's argument reveals much about the usefulness of the information he or she presents.

One good way to begin teaching students about the relative merits of arguments is to bring in to class some letters to the editor from the local newspaper. These nearly always contain fallacies, often memorable ones. After going through the basic kinds of fallacies, we can ask students to look for further printed examples of fallacious thinking. This assignment also reinforces the importance of attention to audience and purpose.

A useful kind of essay to have the students write at this point is a cause-and-effect essay that will require some research. This assignment allows us the opportunity to teach students to distinguish between sufficient and contributory causes, and it is a good opportunity to emphasize the dangers of hasty generalization.

Students can also learn much about argument by writing critiques of arguments. A good exercise that can be done in two stages to teach the difference between summary and evaluation involves such a critique. We can give students a set of brief newspaper arguments as the raw materials for a couple of essays—the point/counterpoint arguments that appear daily on the editorial page of *USA Today* work well for this. In the first of these essays, we may choose to teach the students to summarize the main points each writer makes and point out the fallacies and other weaknesses in each argument. The students should also consider the audience and purpose each writer seems to intend. With this assignment students practice comparison-and-contrast technique, and they must come up with a thesis that is nonevaluative. They must also continue to develop their ability to quote accurately and to handle quotations gracefully. Once they have done the essay summarizing the arguments of the two editorials, students should then be assigned a paper evaluating the arguments and persuading readers that one is a better argument than the other.

Assigning a full-fledged argument paper requires some careful thought by teachers. If we want to offer students a useful alternative to the traditional, argumentative, library paper, we can have them do some research of a primary nature. A useful topic is to have students tackle some school issue, interviewing appropriate authorities, polling students with their own questionnaire, and observing and analyzing the problem. Then they can support their findings with secondary material.

Similarly, students can do an interesting argumentative paper by investigating a particular kind of job or career and arguing its strengths and weaknesses. To do this essay, they might shadow someone who has that kind of job, interview others who are in the profession, and read about that field, including government predictions about the profession.

These kinds of assignments are useful not only because they teach argumentative skills but also because they help make the point that the kinds of writing and research students are doing do not end with graduation but that research, argument, and the writing process are important to us all throughout our lives.

Similarly, in assigning more traditional library projects, we ought to encourage our students to write about other disciplines. We should help them see writing as a life skill, not something one does for English teachers. Forcing students to write a paper on Keats's poetry simply because they are registered in an English class is folly: Our own partiality to Keats's poems should not blind us to the fact that students will pursue writing projects with real enthusiasm only when they are interested in the topic. Encouraging a biology major to write about the greenhouse effect will help him or her learn more about the writing process—and its continuing role in our lives—than forcing down another paper on *Hamlet* or Greek mythology. Presumably a few of our students will propose literary topics.

Whether or not we choose to organize our course by rhetorical type, these assignments can be modified to suit classes organized in other ways, for example, those emphasizing research skills, language, or paragraph development and sentence structure. And in addition to using rhetorical types for essays, they can be applied to paragraphs to strengthen the skills the students are learning, and some work with sentences also helps both stylistic and grammatical problems as well as punctuation.

One useful method of reviewing mechanics is to present "Oops!" sentences to the class each week, that is, a list of sentences we take from their own papers to illustrate problems with mechanics that the class as a whole is having. These are particularly good supplements to the handbook because, unlike the handbook, they present several problems at once. Students seem to enjoy going over these sentences because they are "real" in a way that the handbook's exercises are not.

Whatever method of organization teachers choose, the best teachers are always looking for new assignments and new ways to improve those they've found to be helpful. We need to keep files of particularly effective and ineffective sentences, paragraphs, and essays. We need to collect effective and ineffective arguments. We need to pay attention to our students' interests, always thinking how we can merge their interests with our goals.

WEB RESOURCES

Web Resources can be found at **www.prenhall.com/troyka** under Instructor's Resources.

SUGGESTED READING

Bizzell, Patricia. "Contact Zones and English Studies." *College English* 56. 2. (Feb. 1994): 163–69.

Berzenyi, Christyne A. "How to Conduct a Course-Based Computer Chat Room: Enabling a Space for Active Learning." *Teaching English in the Two-Year College* 28.2 (Dec. 2000): 165–74.

Black, Rhonda S., Thomas W. Sileo, and Mary Anne Prater. "Learning Journals, Self-Reflection, and University Students' Changing Perceptions." *Action in Teacher Education* 21.4 (Winter 2000): 71–89.

Capossela, T.L. "Students as Sociolinguists: Getting Real Research from Freshmen Writers." *College Composition and Communication* 42 (Feb. 1991): 75–79.

Fick, V.G. "A History-Based Research Paper Course." *Teaching English in the Two-Year College* 17 (Feb. 1990): 34–35.

Friedman, Eric D., Lisa Haefele, and K.M. Keating. "An Electronic Discussion List in an Undergraduate Writing Course." *Computers and Education* 24 (Apr. 1995): 191–201.

Gillis, Candida. "Writing Partners: Expanding the Audiences for Student Writing." *English Journal* 83. 3 (March 1994): 64–67.

Gordon, Heather G. "Using a Reading Experience Journal." *Teaching English in the Two-Year College* 28.1 (Sept. 2000): 41–43.

Hourigan, M.M. "Poststructural Theory and Writing Assessment: 'Heady, Esoteric Theory' Revisited." *Teaching English in the Two-Year College* 18 (Oct. 1991): 191–95.

Lent, Robin. "'I Can Relate to That . . .': Reading and Responding in the Writing Classroom." *College Composition and Communication* 44. 2 (May 1993): 232–40.

Moxley, Joseph M. "Reinventing the Wheel or Teaching the Basics: College Writers' Knowledge of Argumentation." *Composition Studies Freshman English News* 21. 2 (Fall 1993): 3–15.

Pullman, George L. "Rhetoric and Hermeneutics: Composition, Invention, and Literature." *Journal of Advanced Composition* 14 no. 2 (Fall 1994): 389–412.

Rankin, Walter. "The Cyberjournal: Developing Writing, Researching, and Editing Skills Through E-mail and World Wide Web." *Educational Technology* 37 (July/Aug 1997): 29–31.

Raymond, R.C. "Personal and Public Voices: Bridging the Gap from Composition to Comp 102." *Teaching English in the Two-Year College* 17 (Dec. 1990): 273–82.

Roemer, M.G., et al. "Portfolios and the Process of Change." *College Composition and Communication* 42 (Dec. 1991): 455–69.

Sipe, Rebecca Bowers. "Virtually Being There: Creating Authentic Experiences Through Interactive Exchanges" *English Journal* 90.2 (Nov. 2000): 104–11.

Spivey, N.N. "The Shaping of Meaning: Options in Writing the Comparison." *Research in the Teaching of English* 25 (Dec. 1991): 390–418.

Sullivan, Patrick. "Using the Internet to Teach Composition." *Teaching English in the Two-Year College* 28.1 (Sept. 2000): 21–31.

Swartzendruber-Putnam, Dawn. "Written Reflection: Creating Better Thinkers, Better Writers." *English Journal* 90.1 (Sept. 2000): 88–93.

Tucker, Lois P. "Liberating Students Through Reader-Response Pedagogy in the Introductory Literature Course." *Teaching English in the Two-Year College* 28.2 (Dec. 2000): 199–206.

Wallace, D.L., and J.R. Hayes. "Redefining Revision for Freshmen." *Research in the Teaching of English* 25 (Feb. 1991): 54–66.

Whitaker, Elaine E., and Elaine N. Hill. "Virtual Voices in 'Letters Across Cultures.' " *Computers and Composition* 15.3 (1998): 331–46.

Appendix
Further Suggestions for Reading

No matter how hectic the pace in our classes, we must—as professionals—try to keep up with the scholarship in our field. In the last twenty years much useful information about the theory of teaching composition has appeared, information that can enrich our teaching significantly if we can eke out the time to delve into the theoretical underpinnings of what we do. Recent scholarship has also made available a wealth of practical and theoretical books and articles of a more general nature that those appended to chapters.

Adams, P. D. "Basic Writing Reconsidered." *Journal of Basic Writing* 12 (Spring 1993): 22–36.

Arnold, Jane. "Keeping Language Journals in English Composition." *Teaching English in the Two-Year College* 26.1 (Sept. 1998): 71–74.

Carrell, P. L., and L. B. Monroe. "Learning Styles and Composition." *Modern Language Journal* 77 (Summer 1993): 148–62.

Cope, Bill, and Mary Kalantzis, eds. *The Powers of Literacy: A Genre Approach to Teaching Writing.* Pittsburgh: UP of Pittsburgh, 1993.

Branch, Kirk. "From the Margins at the Center: Literacy, Authority, and the Great Divide." *College Composition and Communication* 50.2 (Dec. 1998): 206–31.

Duesterberg, Luann M. "Theorizing Race in the Context of Learning to Teach." *Teachers College Record* 100.4 (Summer 1999): 751–75.

Dwyer, Herbert J., and Howard J. Sullivan. "Student Preferences for Teacher and Computer Composition." *The Journal of Educational Research* 86 (Jan/Feb 1993): 137–41.

Feris, Dana R. "Student Reactions to Teacher Response in Multiple-draft Composition Classrooms." *TESOL Quarterly* 29 (Spring 1995): 33–53.

Fischer, Elizabeth A. "Prescriptions for Curing English Teacher Split Personality Disorder." *English Journal* 89.4 (Mar 2000): 40–45.

Fox, Thomas. "Repositioning the Profession: Teaching Writing to African American Students." *Journal of Advanced Composition* 12. 2 (Fall 1992): 179–93.

Hawhee, Debra. "Composition History and the Harbrace College Handbook." *College Composition and Communication* 50.3 (Feb. 1999): 504–23.

Heilker, Paul. "Nothing Personal: Twenty-Five Forays into the Personal in (My) Composition Pedagogy." *Writing Instructor* 12. 2 (Winter 1993): 55–65.

Hindman, Jane E. "Reinventing the University: Finding the Place for Basic Writers." *Journal of Basic Writing* 12.2 (Fall 1993): 55–76.

Johns, A.M. "Written Argumentation for Real Audiences: Suggestions for Teacher Research and Classroom Practice." *TESOL Quarterly* 27 (Spring 1993): 75–90.

Jordan Henley, and Barry M. Maid. "Tutoring in Cyberspace: Student Impact and College/University Collaboration." *Computers and Composition* 12.2 (1995): 211–18.

Keyser, Marcia W., and Laura R. Lucio. "Adding a Library Instruction Unit to an Established Course." *Research Strategies* 16.3 (1998): 221–29.

Lacina-Gifford, Lorna J., and Neelam Kher-Drulabhji. "Preparing to Teach a Class by Internet." *College Teaching* 44 (Summer 1996): 94–95.

Lindemann, Erika. *A Rhetoric for Writing Teachers.* 3rd ed. New York: Oxford, 1995.

Mirskin, Jerry. "Writing as a Process of Valuing." *College Composition and Communication* 46 (Oct. 1995): 387–410.

Murphy, James J., ed. *A Short History of Writing Instruction from Ancient Greece to Twentieth-Century America.* Davis, CA: Hermagoras, 1990.

Nelson, Jennie. "Reading Classrooms as Text: Exploring Student Writers' Interpretive Practices." *College Composition and Communication* 46 (Oct. 1995): 411–29.

Oblinger, Diana, and Sean C. Rush. *The Future Compatible Campus: Planning, Designing, and Implementing Information Technology in the Academy.* Anker Publishing, 1998.

Radencich, Marguerite C., Kathy Echardt, and Rebecca Rasch. "University Course-Based Practitioner Research: Four Studies on Journal Writing Contextualize the Process." *Research in the Teaching of English* 32 (Feb. 1998): 79–112.

Scott, J. Blake. "The Literacy Narrative as Production Pedagogy in the Composition Classroom." *Teaching English in the Two-Year College* 24 (May 1997): 108–17.

Shafer, Gregory. "Composition for the Twenty-First Century." *English Journal* 90.1 (Sept. 2000): 29–33.

Spack, Ruth. "The (in)visibility of the Person(al) in Academe." *College English* 59 (Jan 1997): 9–31.

Troyka, Lynn Quitman. "The Phenomenon of Impact: The CUNY Writing Assessment Test." *Writing Program Administration* 8 (Fall-Winter 1984): 27–36.

Whitaker, E.E. "A Pedagogy to Address Plagiarism." *College Composition and Communication* 44 (December 1993): 509–14.

Wilson, Smokey. "When Computers Come to English Class." *Teaching English in the Two-Year College* 27.4 (May 2000): 387–99.

PART TWO:

Collaborative Writing
by Patricia Kelvin and Scott A. Leonard,
Youngstown State University

■ TEACHING COLLABORATIVE WRITING

This is a manual for practitioners, for the hard-working teacher striving to give students an understanding of rhetoric and the writing process. Whether you have been teaching composition for years and are ready to try something new or you are new to the teaching of writing, we hope this manual can refresh and renew your sense of excitement about teaching. The student comments you will read in this chapter are quoted (with the names changed) directly from the "process logs of memos" that we ask each student to keep for their own, as well as our, evaluation. You will also find some collaborative assignments that have worked in our classrooms. Some of the ideas presented here may work for you in your environment while others will not. But they should be a springboard from which you can dive into your own pool of ideas. While we have mentioned some of the best-known scholars working in the field of collaborative learning and writing throughout our text, we have compiled a more extensive bibliographic essay at the end for those who would like to read further on the subject.

Collaborative writing can be an extremely rewarding experience for both teacher and student. When things work well, students gain confidence in their ability to write and to work with a team. The teacher will feel energized working with a class of active, enthusiastic learners. What could be better than a writing pedagogy that encourages students to discuss every dimension of writing from topic selection to word choice? What more can the writing teacher want than a way to encourage students to view effective writing as a process within their conscious control? Collaboratively written papers, like single-authored texts, go through a series of drafts. But, unlike single-authored texts, collaborative papers will actively integrate concepts of audience, tone, planning and purpose into the writing process because at every step students must explain to one another what they think the paper needs and why.

■ WHY TEACH STUDENTS TO WRITE TOGETHER?

Collaborative Learning Is Helpful to Students

The basic premise of what John Trimbur, Kenneth Bruffee, and others have called **collaborative learning** is that peer influence is a "powerful educative force" (Bruffee 638). It is the conversation of students working together that disseminates information more surely and erects conceptual scaffolding more efficiently. In the context of the group, the internalized conversation of human thought becomes the externalized authority of the collective. The pedagogy that has developed from these assumptions has transformed both classroom architecture and the teacher's role. Those accustomed to a teacher-directed lecture or discussion classroom might wonder whether organizing students in small groups to discuss course content can lead to anything but idle chat. But those who have assigned small group exercises that give students hands-on practice in generating paper topics, or in appropriately punctuating works-cited entries, or in identifying the cohesive devices that published writers employ, know the power of collaborative learning. Providing students with opportunities to talk and work together in small groups allows them to remember and exchange points of view about what they read for class, to develop concepts more extensively than they could on their own, and for weaker students to learn from their stronger peers. Indeed, collaborative learning is excellent pedagogy because it organizes and focuses the natural human impulse to create knowledge through small-group discussion even as it fosters learning by doing. Those instructors who use response groups in their classes already know the value of collaborative learning. Collaborative writing takes the process even further.

Collaborative Writing Is Good Pedagogy

Asking students to write together takes advantage of the substantial benefits derivable from collaborative learning. Student groups of two or more authors working on a single document are able to combine their individual strengths, tackle large and complex projects, share information, challenge each other to think longer and harder about the demands of a writing situation, and model for one another the learnable skills of writing. In groups, students can also divide the work of reading, writing, organizing, and editing.

For almost a decade now, we have observed that writing collaboratively impels students to think about the learning process in ways that individuals writing alone might not. Because writing groups must negotiate everything from meeting times to paper organization to word choice, the individuals within those groups must explain what they think will work for a paper and why—a phenomenon that makes every aspect of text production an occasion for discussion, questioning, and information-sharing. In addition, because students must arrange work time in advance, they tend to procrastinate less and work with a specific sense of what they want or need to accomplish at a given time. Thus, most students, having a limited time to work on a project each week, will begin to see their project as a series of tasks, and pace their work rather than do everything they have time for the night before it is due.

Moreover, our students have often told us that they enjoy the experience of writing and researching together. One student remarked that it felt good having "someone to talk to about [a] project—about how to do it and what to say." The collaborative writing classroom frequently buzzes with energetic conversation, joking, and the excitement of discovering just the right words for a complex idea. But even when all is quiet, or when the conversation is not so jovial, students derive many benefits from the experience. For example, our students frequently report experiencing what cognitive psychologists have called *decentering* effects. As one young woman put it, "working with others in this quarter has really opened my eyes to different perspectives on how to write and on life in general." Other students confirm what many researchers have long suggested: Collaboration is good for students because it allows them to pool their resources. "Jim was our researcher," reported Allison in her process log, "while Kim's editing skills really helped us out at the end."

Collaboration Is Typical Work after College

Learning and writing together is more than just good pedagogy; it is the ideal preparation for our students' careers after college. Lunsford and Ede (1990), after surveying seven professional organizations, report that approximately half of all writing in the workplace is, broadly defined, collaborative. Newspaper editorial boards, for example, routinely engage in "peer response" critique and in group brainstorming when determining the position their paper will take on a given issue. Such technical fields as computer science, engineering, or pharmaceuticals consider the planning and writing and editing of multi-author documents standard procedure. Small groups of workers in such nontechnical fields as insurance, psychology, and social work also share the work of creating a wide variety of written products. When Patal from public relations, Chen from economics, and Jastrow from product pricing sit down to draft a corporate report, they pool their expertise to accomplish that task. Writing teachers whose pedagogical goals include helping students prepare for careers are better served by incorporating practice in writing together rather than by teaching only as though they subscribed to the Romantic ideal of the inspired poet-prophet, alone in his or her garret, struggling to put sublime visions to paper. After all, even poet-prophets like Wordsworth and Shelley benefited greatly from sharing ideas and manuscript copy with their friends.

Collaboration Affords Several Advantages

Students can undertake more complex projects when they write together than when they work alone. As writing instructors, we like the fact that, even in a ten-week quarter, collaborative writing projects can be considerably larger in scope than traditional single-writer assignments. Not only can group members divide the workload but they can also tackle several tasks simultaneously. As Jeanine wrote in her process log:

> After leaving your office, we decided how to split up the work. I had a wedding to attend this weekend and Randy had to work the Memorial [Golf] Tournament. Our time was very tight as the end drew near. (So melodramatic!) [*sic*] For a remedy to this problem, Randy and I thought it would be a good idea for three of us to work on the ethics paper while the others worked on the revision to our earlier paper.

Students writing together can emphasize their strengths rather than their individual weaknesses. Unlike many individual projects in which students' deficiencies stand out, group projects allow students to contribute what they are best at while at the same time learning, from their peers, ways to improve areas in which they are weak. As Jenny wrote in her post-paper analysis memo,

> It took a long time to decide how we were going to do this paper because each of us had different ideas, and we really didn't want to let them go. But finally we decided that Glenn was faster in the library and so he would do the research. I would do the writing, [and] Mel would be the technical expert—he got everything into the computer. We actually got a draft done two days early and we all worked on the revision. I surprised myself by coming up with some better ideas for digging up the research and I had to admit that Mel and Glenn improved the way I'd worded the draft.

Collaboration also encourages social interaction and promotes understanding of and respect for others. We find that collaborative learning and writing provide students with a sense of community so often missing in large general-education classes. Most of our students begin the term as strangers, but often become friends as well as coworkers. Dan and Frank were Air Force officers in training, majoring in engineering. Eliza, the third member of their group, was a Singaporean national in Hotel Management. She wrote,

> I do enjoy being in the group and I thank you ... for putting me in this group. It amazes all three of us that we did not have any major disagreements with one another. . . . For this meeting I brought some "hot roasted peas"—a Chinese delicacy for them to taste and they really enjoy it. [*sic*] They are good friends and colleagues to work with.

In addition, collaborative assignments promote originality because each group's approach to an assignment will be as unique as the group that generates it. While we did not begin teaching our students to write collaboratively as a way of discouraging recycled papers from other classes or generic "frat file" themes, we have since discovered that having our students work in groups has virtually eliminated plagiarism. We are continually encouraged to find that students working in groups work harder at topic selection because they must arrive at an approach on which everyone is willing to work.

■ CREATING A COLLABORATIVE CLASSROOM

Reshape the Classroom Landscape

Have you ever wanted to re-create a room? Your garden? Yourself? Creating a collaborative classroom gives you that personal and professional opportunity—imagine sowing an annual garden where you once had only perennials. Like the carefully planted linear rows of the traditional formal garden, the traditional classroom features rows of desks that face the front of the room where the instructor directs classroom activities. By contrast, the collaborative classroom is more like a country garden where the aesthetic is not rigidly constrained but is allowed to flower randomly and exuberantly. Desks are no longer always and only arranged in rows but can be clustered around the room to allow student groups space to talk among themselves. The collaborative classroom is an active and noisy place rather than a quiet and passive one. But the alternative to orderly formality is not unproductive chaos; rather, the noise you hear is the sound of knowledge being created.

Teaching in the collaborative classroom, then, works better with desks that can be moved. Ideally, the collaborative classroom will have round tables and moveable chairs, an arrangement that allows students to work together or singly and to have room enough to spread out and share their in-class assignments, research materials, and drafts. (After all, how many resources can be laid out on the typical student desk?) Interactive Web space, such as those found in WebCT or Blackboard, can enhance collaborative classrooms by creating a virtual meeting place outside the classroom. The overall effect of these classroom changes is to direct students' attention away from the teacher and toward themselves and their peers.

Rethink the Role of the Writing Teacher

The traditional model of the teacher posits one who directs, plans, assigns, grades, controls, and judges, and positions the instructor at the center of activity as *the* decision maker, *the* authority, *the* expert. Obviously, most of us excelled in traditional classrooms, even if some did not thrive in such learning environments. But if the goal of our instruction is to equip students with a working knowledge of sound rhetorical principles and compositional strategies in the surest and most efficient way possible, it should not matter to us whether we drive the car or lay the road. The role of the teacher in a collaborative classroom is considerably different from that conceived in the traditional model. In the collaborative model, the teacher provides the theatre and drafts the script, but the students take center stage. Standing in the wings, the teacher of collaborative writing facilitates, encourages, advises, and nurtures students who can learn by doing in a semi-structured environment.

Does the teacher of collaboration simply walk away from her students and leave all learning entirely in their hands? Emphatically no. While some theoretical positions assert the importance of decentering authority in the collaborative classroom, complete decentering is impossible. So long as a teacher's assessments of papers are the most authoritative response they get, and so long as he or she retains the power to assign permanent grades, the instructor has all the power that matters to most students.

Rather than looking to an impending Students' Paradise where all traces of hierarchical teacher-student power relations have been erased, we prefer to think of the teacher in the collaborative classroom as *sharing* power and using her or his authority to motivate students and to construct a learning environment that will encourage students to grow as thinkers and as writers. In our own teaching practice, we generally find ourselves playing one (or more) of three roles: the reassuring listener (counselor); the dispenser of information and clarifier of assignments (teacher); and the mediator of disagreements (referee). The teacher may well have the ultimate institutional authority, but he or she can also work *with* students on invention and organizational strategies in nondirective ways, negotiating evaluative standards that recognize students' own measures of success.

Encourage Students to Take Responsibility for Learning

The most exciting and professionally liberating part of teaching collaborative writing is that we stop managing and directing the flow of information and conversation in our classrooms and start creating a dynamic learning space in which *students* take the responsibility for learning. In the collaborative learning environment, the teacher moves away from the chalkboard or the overhead projector and organizes students into groups that work together on the many aspects of the writing process. Suddenly, students must be responsible to one another. Teacher-centered classrooms place the onus on the instructor to present information that we hope our students will absorb, albeit passively. But in a classroom where students work in small groups requiring them to create solutions to the problems they identify, the burden for learning is instead placed on the learners.

■ TEACHING COLLABORATION: CONCEPTUAL VOCABULARY AND GROUP BEHAVIORS

Remind Students as They Work Together that Collaborative Groups are Groups of People

While it may sound obvious, one must always remember that, like the individuals who compose them, collaborative groups are unique and human. Students differ in degree of motivation, type of learning style, and overall skill level. Accepting these differences and adjusting one's expectations appropriately will decrease the instructor's frustration. Equally obvious and important to remember is the fact that collaborative writing groups are social in nature. Some students (and some writing teachers) worry that joking around, passing campus gossip, or sharing information about friends and family is counterproductive. However, seemingly off-task chat is not only normal to collaborative groups, it is absolutely necessary. People who have developed a friendly working relationship can be candid with one another. It is very hard to tell a stranger that his or her ideas or writing need work. Therefore, the writing teacher should encourage social interaction within groups but prepare them beforehand for the adjustments that individuals will need to make in order to work successfully with others.

We teach our students the following "Ten Commandments" of working together:

i. COMMIT YOURSELF TO THE SUCCESS OF THE GROUP. When it is just you, you can decide whether or not you want to work hard on a project or come to class. But you do not have that luxury when you work with a group. When you miss class or a group meeting, you owe your group the courtesy of a phone call. And you should make up any time lost to the group.

ii. REMEMBER THAT EACH MEMBER OF YOUR GROUP IS AN INDIVIDUAL. Getting to know each other's strengths, capabilities, and personalities will help your group immensely.

iii. RESPECT THE DIVERSITY OF ABILITIES AND BACKGROUNDS IN YOUR GROUP. These differences may be, at times, frustrating, but diversity is actually the greatest benefit of working in a group.

iv. ASSUME A DIFFERENT IDENTITY WHEN YOU WORK IN A GROUP. Your identity as a member of a group differs from that of the solitary scholar. When your groups writes or speaks, it is "we" and "us," not "me" and "I."

v. ALLOW PLENTY OF TIME FOR COLLABORATIVE WORK. It takes longer to work with someone else than it does to work individually—but the product is invariably stronger. Give your group time for spontaneous, informal talk; many times, this is where the best ideas come from.

vi. ACCEPT SOME CONFLICT. More creative solutions are found with some conflict than without it. However, focus your disagreements on ways of approaching a task and arriving at a satisfactory solution and not on individual personalities or abilities.

vii. DISCUSS CONCERNS AND FRUSTRATIONS OPENLY WITH EACH OTHER. It is best to work problems out as they occur rather than to allow them to fester, unattended, until a crisis brings them out. If members' work habits or attendance bother you, tell them so in a nonthreatening way.

viii. MAKE IT A GROUP PROJECT TO FIND A SOLUTION TO GROUP PROBLEMS. If the group cannot find a solution, talk to the instructor immediately.

ix. LISTEN TO EACH OTHER AND ASK CLARIFYING QUESTIONS. Many problems are simply matters of poor communication.

x. COMPROMISE. Face it, you simply will not get your own way all the time.

Teach Group Roles

The traditional top-down management model of group behavior designates one person the leader and all other group members as followers. Typically, the leader solicits information from the followers, decides what the group should do, and organizes the rest of the group to implement the plan. However, the top-down management approach is rarely successful in the classroom because not all self-appointed (or even elected) leaders have true leadership qualities, and not all followers are completely sanguine about their subservient roles. Furthermore, in the collaborative writing classroom, the top-down management model often inhibits members of a student group from making rhetorical and compositional decisions. In a writing course, everyone needs to learn how to organize, to choose an appropriate topic, and to develop a workable approach to a task. Consequently the instructor in the collaborative writing classroom should work hard to assure that responsibility for projects is equally shared. More often than not, when someone "takes charge" a general breakdown in communication and motivation results. For that matter, vote-taking and a "majority rules" approach to decision making can cause disaffected group members to drop out of the process. *Everyone* has to buy into the topic and the process, or it is no longer a group effort.

Appropriate behaviors for successful group work can be learned. They should not be regarded as intrinsic personal qualities, despite conventional practice. Rather, behaviors should be thought of as contributing to the group's success or detracting from it. First, we teach students to identify and practice a wide range of positive and negative roles that a member of a group might play. We stress that these roles are not permanent, but will vary *during* a group meeting as well as from day to day.

Early studies by social scientists (notably Benne and Sheats) have identified three kinds of behaviors associated with group member performance: group-building roles, group-maintenance roles, and group-blocking roles. We have modified their lists of roles to apply to the writing classroom.

Group Building Roles

THE INITIATOR
➤ suggests new or different ideas for discussion
➤ proposes new or different approaches to the group's process (for problem solving or for writing)

THE ELABORATOR
➤ elaborates or builds on suggestions made by others
➤ gives relevant examples

THE TESTER
➤ restates problem
➤ evaluates the group's progress toward completing assignments
➤ looks for holes in the plan
➤ pulls together or reviews the discussion

THE TASK-DESIGNER
➤ raises questions about member preferences for styles of working
➤ suggests the tasks that the group will need to accomplish its goals

THE RESPONDER
➤ evaluates written work with suggestions for revision

Group Maintenance Roles

THE FACILITATOR
➤ makes sure all group members have a chance to speak
➤ supports the contributions of others

THE VIBES-WATCHER
➤ focuses on the group's process
➤ mediates differences of opinion
➤ reconciles points of view
➤ calls for a break if discussion gets too warm

THE TIMEKEEPER
➤ focuses on task completion
➤ maintains the forward progress of the meeting
➤ when necessary, shifts the group's work back to accomplishing its stated goals

Group Blocking Roles

THE AGGRESSOR
➤ deflates status of others in group
➤ disagrees with others aggressively
➤ criticizes others in group

THE BLOCKER
- stubbornly disagrees with and rejects others' views
- cites unrelated personal experiences
- returns to topics already resolved

THE WITHDRAWER
- will not participate
- daydreams during group meetings
- carries on private conversation within group
- is a self-appointed taker of notes

THE RECOGNITION SEEKER
- tries to show his or her importance through boasting and excessive talking
- is overly conscious of his or her status

THE TOPIC JUMPER
- continually changes the subject

THE CONTROL FREAK
- tries to take over the meeting
- tries to assert authority
- tries to manipulate the group

THE LOBBYIST
- tries to get the group to work on his or her own special interests

THE CLASS CLOWN
- wastes the group's time by constantly showing off and telling funny stories
- acts with nonchalance or cynicism

THE BOOR
- talks endlessly and irrelevantly about his or her own feelings or experiences

THE DEVIL'S ADVOCATE
- when he or she is more devil than advocate

Giving students the conceptual vocabulary necessary to identify and discuss both positive and negative group roles is essential for healthy collaboration. We provide the "Ten Commandments" and the Roles List as handouts. For students to try out these behaviors, we conduct the following role-playing exercise early in the term.

We print out several copies of the Roles List, cut them apart, and number enough roles to place at least one builder, one maintainer, and one blocker in groups of three to five. (Say, we have a class of twenty-four. We number building roles from one through eight, maintaining roles from one through eight, and blocking roles from one through eight. We will, of course, repeat some roles.) Students draw a slip of paper with a role on it and look for the others in the class who share the same number (all the *ones* work together, all the *twos*, etc.).

Telling the students not to reveal their roles, we offer them a humorous prompt for discussion (such as coming up with a nonviolent sport to replace football; developing unusual ways to use the library after hours for fund-raising, and the like). We give them five to ten minutes to talk about the prompt while playing their assigned roles. We then repeat the exercise with new groups, sometimes enlarging the groups to expand the numbers of roles.

Afterwards, we ask the class to discuss what happened. They find not only that they can recognize the behaviors but that they can assume unfamiliar roles. They also learn how disruptive a blocker can be and how little progress takes place when no one assumes a group-building role. While we reiterate the need for everyone to work on group-building behaviors, we suggest that for each meeting, one member take on the facilitator's role, one the vibes-watcher's, and one the timekeeper's. Rotating these tasks from meeting to meeting helps group cohesiveness and minimizes antagonism.

Other Useful Group Behaviors

We have found that groups manage their time better if they set goals for each meeting—preferably at the end of the previous meeting. Our more successful groups usually agree to an agenda in advance of a meeting and then the timekeeper checks that the previously established goals have been met before the group plans its agenda for the next meeting. When groups discover that they have diverged substantially from the agenda, they can take that occasion to review the group's goals and discuss whether adjustments are necessary.

During all group meetings, everyone should take notes. Too frequently, one of the group's female members is directly or indirectly assigned "secretarial" duty. Alternatively, one person offers to take notes in order to control decision making. We require everyone to record the group's activities and decisions. At the end of each meeting, group members compare notes to assure that they all agree on what happens next. To encourage everyone to take responsibility for keeping track of what is going on, what got said, what got done, and when the group will meet next and why, we usually assign a post-paper memo or journal in which students are asked to report what happened at all group meetings. This memo serves as more than a diary; it also provides an ideal occasion for students to reflect upon the writing process, group interaction, and the ways in which their project evolved from topic selection to final draft.

About Conflict

A number of researchers distinguish between procedural, affective, and substantive conflicts (particularly Putnam, 1986, and Burnett, 1993) as important sources of both positive and negative friction among group members. If the collaborative project is to move forward, substantive conflict, which comprises negotiations about the scope of the project, the nature of the problem, possible solutions, and the form and content of the written product, must occur. Frequently, though, students confuse this vital form of conflict with its destructive counterfeits, affective conflict and procedural conflict. Affective conflict occurs not at the level of ideas, but between individuals who are either pitted against one another in a bid for control of the group or who simply rub each other the wrong way. While teaching consensual group behaviors can minimize conflict arising from a naked power grab, it is virtually impossible to mitigate personality conflicts short of reassigning one or more members of a group. Procedural conflict issues from misunderstandings over who is responsible for what or what the group's next move should be. Discussions emanating from procedural conflict can be quite productive if everyone has an equal say. Groups that work to mitigate against affective conflict usually emerge from the process stronger and with a clearer sense of direction.

Substantive conflict originates in a group's discussion of the form and content of its essay. This form of conflict—even if it is quite spirited—can be the most productive of all. Students who argue with one another for or against the inclusion of illustrative examples, the positioning of information within an essay, and which issues to cover or to exclude are not necessarily fighting. Rather, they are learning about how to write effectively by testing ideas out on their peers. Obviously, group-maintenance roles are extremely important in preventing substantive conflict from degenerating into counterproductive interpersonal exchanges. The communications expert needs to insure that everyone has a chance to voice an opinion and the nurturer needs to draw attention to the strengths in everyone's ideas. Writing instructors should actively encourage lively debate among coworkers who know that they are being heard and appreciated for what they bring to the group.

Responding to Peers in the Collaborative Group

The value of the peer response group is well established in composition pedagogy, and some even consider the peer response group as synonymous with the collaborative writing group. However, the work of the collaborative writing group goes beyond responding to the single-authored drafts of fellow students. In the collaborative group, students develop topics and approaches to writing as well as doing the writing itself. Peer response is a continuous action. Collaborative groups integrate the benefits of peer response into a group's writing process. Students cowriting a document must explain specifically to one another what features of a draft require revision and why.

Responding to and Revising Each Other's Work

We have found that the following advice makes a good handout to guide individual responders and collaborating writer/readers:

➤ Feel free to evaluate and make changes to each other's work.

➤ Remember that it is very difficult for people to relinquish ownership over anything they have written. Here are some suggestions for making this process easier:

　➤ As a writer, try to create an objective attitude toward your work. People are responding to the words on the page, not to you as a person.

　➤ As a reader/responder/reviser, the best rule is *The Golden Rule*: "Treat others as you would like to be treated." A little sensitivity will go a long way in dealing with your peers' writing.

　➤ If you recommend changes in something someone else has written, be sure to explain to the writer how and why you changed it. If you do not, you risk alienating that person from your team.

Collaborative groups, like individual writers, can lose sight of the way their writing reads to others. When entire groups exchange papers for response, they will develop a greater sense of writing for a "real" audience if they know that others will be responding to their work. Those who are teaching more than one composition class might exchange papers across classes, which usually minimizes the "kid glove" attitudes with which some students appraise the work of their classmates.

Groups can also form a revision collective with members developing specific areas of expertise for a given assignment. For example, the members of each group can divide the *Handbook*'s revision checklists (section 2u) so that all questions are addressed. As an added advantage, having beginning responders work through scripted response sheets like these will help them avoid engaging in either unnecessarily harsh critique ("What a dumb idea!") or unhelpful vague praise ("Sounds great to me!"). On responding days, teachers should direct the focus of comments. It is not appropriate for students to pinpoint typos and usage errors in the first draft when they should be addressing such crucial global issues as organization, point of view, and sufficiency of included information. By the second or third draft, students can pay attention to usage, word choice, and transitions. As a means of building your students' repertoire of response techniques, you can—after some preliminary explanation—ask them to build their own lists of issues they should check for at each stage of the drafting process.

■ ASSIGNING GROUPS

Assigning Groups Is Too Important to Trust to Luck

Although group assignment has received little research attention, teacher lore reveals a number of methods by which students are grouped: dividing students alphabetically; pulling names from a hat; counting students off by threes, fours, or fives; requesting student preferences; classifying students by academic major; or assuring a strong and weak writer in each group, to name a few. These more-or-less random methods can be very useful for breaking the ice (see below), however, when assigning groups for major projects we consciously try to put students together in ways that will assure the highest possible level of group success—both academically and interpersonally. In class on the first day of the term, we sample writing abilities by asking students to write us letters in which they discuss:

> ➤ their reason(s) for being in the class and their expectations from it,
> ➤ their level of motivation for the class,

➤ their previous experience with writing, and,

➤ their career expectations.

A week later, we ask students to write a more formal memo to us telling us what to know before placing them in groups, paying particular attention to (a) work and academic schedules, work habits and style (e.g., driven vs. laid-back), (b) previous experience with groups and attitudes about groupwork, (c) other relevant personal data (e.g., whether students think themselves shy or likely to dominate a conversation), and (d) any preferences they might have for working or not working with particular students in the class. After students prepare an initial draft of these memos, we require private conferences which give us a chance to discuss their writing and the information in the memos, and also to let us get to know them better.

In addition, during the first two weeks of class, we introduce small group activities and role-playing exercises for students to learn successful collaboration techniques. These in-class activities also provide opportunities for us to observe how students work together—who is quiet, who is assertive, who stays on task, who gets sidetracked, and so forth. Toward the end of the second week, we assign groups of two to five members according to the following priorities:

➤ Student schedules should permit at least two hours other than class time per week in which all can meet. Often this consideration supersedes all others. After all, students must be able to work *together* on shared work. Even if groups were to meet in class only, students could work toward the group's goals by completing individual responsibilities outside class and then merging their work during class time. Sometimes students may choose to "meet" online; however, this strategy also requires a time commitment outside of class time.

➤ Students should be similarly motivated. Hard workers with high grade motivation should not be placed with those who cannot or will not spend adequate time for the class or who are simply passing. Many theorists believe that strong students should be identified and placed with weak students to encourage peer mentoring. While we find the idea philosophically noble, we have repeatedly found that differing motivation levels create the most significant roadblocks on the journey to success. Highly motivated weak students have the potential to do well and learn a great deal on their own whereas unmotivated students of whatever ability level are the source of most student complaints about collaboration.

➤ Students are not placed with those they had asked not to work with—generally a result of their having worked together in a prior class. If possible, students are placed with students they do ask to work with.

➤ Students with special needs (e.g., nonnative speakers, returning older students, shy students, minority students) are placed with those that intuition suggests might be more accepting of them.

In general, we find that large groups (four to six members) work best for in-class discussion-oriented activities whereas small groups (two or three members) work best for multi-draft writing assignments. Because writing with others—especially at first—generates numerous procedural questions, we "roam" the classroom spending time with each group listening and/or participating as needed. We also require each group to attend a private faculty-office conference for each major assignment. Most groups, however, ask for more than one conference.

Determining Group Longevity

In our ten-week quarters, there is barely enough time for students to get to know each other, let alone to build the comfort and trust necessary to create effective working relationships. Thus, barring catastrophes, we prefer to keep student groups together for the length of the term. Some teachers vary group membership so that students can benefit from exposure to a range of work styles and personality types. However, we have found that such logistical considerations as time availability outside of class usually make a general reshuffling of writing groups unworkable. To give our students the benefits of working with a wide variety of others, we "scatter" the members of collaborative writing groups when we work on in-class group nonwriting activities.

What to Do about Ungroupable Students

We always emphasize the necessity of collaborative work and outline in our syllabi, and, during the first class meeting, the unique demands it will place on students (e.g., responsibility to others, required work outside of class, the understanding that writing takes longer with a group than writing solo). Even so, we have occasionally found students for whom working in collaborative groups outside of class poses an exceptional burden. We remember, for example, one student who, in addition to a seventeen-quarter hour academic load, spent four to five hours of road work a day training for an Olympic bicycling event. He could spare only one hour, one day a week, to work with his group. Obviously, a student who cannot meet with others outside the classroom will be unable to contribute fully to his or her group. In this particular case—and the principle applies more widely—the student was allowed to undertake individualized, scaled-down versions of the class's writing projects and thus to fulfill the course requirements.

More frequently, we have encountered students who perform so poorly that they pose a significant liability for their groups. We have had students who seemed almost pathologically driven to subvert the group's efforts through habitual tardiness, failure to complete promised tasks, or by being chronically critical or obstinate. Usually we resolve these difficulties by allowing the problematic student to work alone, so the cooperative students are not penalized or forced to carry the entire workload. Altering evaluation strategies is another method for dealing with difficult group members. In some cases, having separate grades for group process and product may be effective in enabling all to receive the evaluation they deserve. One of my colleagues has had students evaluate themselves and their group members, including self-reporting the percentage of work or support they each contributed toward the final project. Final project grades were then adjusted accordingly to reward those who contributed most or penalize those who did not do their fair share.

Developing Group Ground Rules

Urge each group to develop its own drafting process. Some groups are happier if each member drafts a separate section of the document which the group will merge later as a complete draft. Other groups prefer to have each member draft the entire document, with the group picking and choosing the best parts of each. Still other groups prefer to huddle around a single computer and write the entire document together from scratch. Groups whose members have a hefty campus commute appreciate the ability to conduct at least some of their work independently or by telephone, e-mail, or online conferencing. We have even had groups who faxed sections of their papers to each other. Troyka & Hesse's handbook offers guidelines for collaborative writing in section 2x.

In any case, student groups should develop their own work styles, determine their internal management rules, and allocate tasks however they see fit. The instructor can monitor these arrangements by asking students to keep a detailed, confidential log of each group meeting—both in and out of class. The quality of these logs varies of course: high-achieving students might write pages; low-achieving students might write but a few paragraphs, generally focusing on tasks rather than ideas or behaviors.

■ AIMING THE GROUPS TOWARD SUCCESS

Success in the Collaborative Writing Classroom

No matter how many drafts a group project undergoes, at some point the text must be evaluated. But what measures of success are appropriate to a collaborative project? In the traditional writing classroom, the answer is straightforward enough. If a text is logically organized, well articulated, presented from an interesting point of view, and more or less free of mechanical errors, it can be considered a success. In the collaborative writing classroom, the issue of what constitutes a "good paper" is more complicated. Naturally, a final draft of a collaborative project featuring the above hallmarks of a well-written paper is—at least at the discursive level—successful, but in the collaborative classroom one teaches both how to write and how to work well with others. For this reason, we consider both pedagogical emphases during grading. Some groups collaborate very well together, but for a variety of reasons produce a less than perfect product. Other groups produce an excellent product, but do so by subverting the aims of collaboration. Because we believe the goal of the collaborative writing classroom is to teach both collaboration and writing, then success can only be defined as a combination of good collaboration and a well-written document. Thus, while grading, we consider a student text "good" only when produced by a truly collaborative group.

Obviously, our increasingly grade-conscious students want to know what, exactly, an "A" paper is—especially when they learn that "good collaboration" is a class requirement. We include our students in the process of defining an excellent collaborative paper by asking them to create a list of discursive features and group behaviors that distinguish an "A" paper. First the small groups draw up their lists, and then prioritize them. The class discussion that follows can provide an excellent occasion to talk about what makes a piece of writing interesting to a reader and what kinds of group behavior constitute good collaboration. As groups report what they came up with, we write their ideas on the board and by the end of class have a list of criteria that the students agree should apply to the final evaluation of their writing. This exercise is important not only because it allows collaborative groups input into the grading process, but also because students remind one another of the criteria for a good paper and good collaborative techniques as they work together.

Introduce Collaborative Work Sequentially

An informal survey of collaborative assignments in the writing class indicates that they generally fall into four broad categories:

➣ **Brief assignments,** perhaps short textbook problems, that can be completed within the classroom, usually within one or two class periods. For example, the *Handbook*'s exercises in the sections on purpose [1b] or tone [1d] can be performed collaboratively and result in a brief written summary of findings.

➣ **Short essays or brief research papers** of relatively short duration but which require that groups meet outside class.

➣ As preliminary exercises for extended research papers, collaborative groups can be sent to the library to do exploratory research on their topic. After consulting all information resource systems, students can collaboratively write a report that discusses their topic's major issues.

➣ **Major projects,** such as multi-part reports, which are long-term assignments of several weeks' duration requiring extensive nonclassroom work for completion. (See below for examples of major collaborative projects.)

➣ **Term-long projects,** whether quarter or semester, which are the focus of a course. Ideally, term-long projects should be undertaken in the second of a two-term sequence after students have had several opportunities to write with others.

We find that teaching collaboration works best if it is introduced gradually and sequentially over the course of the term. In the beginning, we assign short-term projects that minimize logistical difficulties and give us an opportunity to assess individual and group dynamics. In addition, several short-term assignments, undertaken early in the semester or quarter when the class is focusing on group roles and peer response techniques, gives students a chance to adapt their customary approaches and behavior patterns to the requirements of collaborative group work before embarking on longer assignments. These brief, out-of-class assignments can also serve as group invention exercises, providing students with an occasion to gather and organize information even as they refine their paper topics. At last, after several brief in-class assignments and at least one short out-of-class exercise, students should be sufficiently comfortable with their group members' working styles and the unique requirements of collaborative writing to embark on a major project. In our classrooms, major projects take about three weeks to complete, which allows time for two or three drafts and for at least two in-class peer response sessions. While we think it is important to ease students into collaborative writing, we also think that students should work on several assignments simultaneously. Life is rarely one discrete task after another, and being required to turn in drafts of major projects even as they begin short writing tasks relevant to their next major project teaches them to manage their time and intellectual activity.

Breaking the Ice

It is important for the instructor in the collaborative writing classroom to recognize the essential nature of writing teams. Therefore, it is good practice to allow a little time at the beginning of each class meeting for groups to chat. (At first, you might have to explicitly tell students that they have about five minutes to catch up on group gossip before class gets rolling.) Before groups are assigned—and certainly right after they have been—it will be necessary to orchestrate some ice-breaking exercises that will give individual students a chance to meet one another and to find out that collaborative writing can actually be fun. Here are some ideas for getting the ball rolling:

Warming Up: In-class Collaborative Assignments

➣ Students compile the group's schedule and phone list.

➣ Students interview each other and report back to the group what they have discovered. This can also lead to the enumeration of expertises, equipment, or capabilities that each member brings to the group.

➣ While students understand the concept of audience in a general way, they also find writing for others intimidating. The following collaborative exercise can help students overcome this anxiety and simultaneously explore the concrete characteristics of an audience.

➣ Divide the class into groups of three to five.

➣ Ask your class to envision a group of refugees rescued from the primitive conditions of nomadic life and brought to a modern American city. Even after being shown how to operate the lights and faucets in their apartments, the refugees remained so innocent of the technologies that we take for granted that they washed their clothes by soaking them in the sink and then pounded them with heavy objects—just as they had done by river banks for generations.

➣ Ask each group to craft a set of instructions that would tell the refugees how to wash and dry their clothes using a modern washer and dryer. Students will have to bear in mind that they cannot

123

take what they would consider "common knowledge" for granted. Even simple commands like "open the lid" or "check the lint filter" will require careful explanation—perhaps even illustration.

In this exercise, the social nature of the interaction forces students to *articulate and practice* what they know about audience needs. By visiting each of the groups as they work, you can gather a few representative comments demonstrating what your students already know about their audience to share with the entire class when it comes time to synthesize what was learned during the activity.

Create an Ongoing Discussion about Writing Projects

Another way that the collaborative writing instructor can point student groups toward success is to require numerous individual writing assignments that ask students to reflect consciously on what they are learning as a result of writing with others. We usually require three kinds of analytical writing from our students in addition to the brief, short, and major assignments described above:

1: THE WORK PLAN—a descriptive essay that specifies the group's paper topic and outlines the way they anticipate addressing it. The work plan takes the form of a collaboratively produced memo addressed to the instructor which spells out how the work will be organized and the labor divided. Work plans should specify which paragraphs and/or sections each group member will write, who will type the drafts, who will make copies (if required for peer response work), who will proofread, and who will be responsible for the paper getting in on time. In addition, the work plan can be used to encourage students to think about group roles—who will act as facilitator, or questioner, or idea person. There are several advantages to this assignment:

> ➤ by introducing "first-timers" to collaborative writing through a comparatively short, concrete project, you give them a chance to adapt to each others' working and writing styles with minimal grade pressure;

> ➤ by asking group members to assign themselves specific tasks during the drafting process, you encourage them to think in detail about how they will organize their writing in advance; and

> ➤ by getting students to commit to a plan of action, you can evaluate and respond to the "do-ability" of their projects before too much time and energy has been expended on ideas that will not work. While a work plan constrains students to plan their writ-

ing in advance, it need not suggest—as traditional outlines some-times do—an inviolably rigid structure into which all ideas discovered during writing must fit. In fact, for another short, graded writing task that encourages a critical awareness of the writing process, you can ask students to write a follow-up report that analyzes the ways in which producing the final draft differs from the work plan.

2: THE COLLABORATIVE LOG—an ongoing diary of what the group is doing even as they do it. The collaborative log should articulate the group's agenda for each meeting and should report on who came to the meetings, what each person contributed, and evaluate the degree to which the group's agenda was met. To insure that students keep their collaborative logs up, the instructor can collect them for review about halfway through a major project. As an alternative effort to keep abreast of developments within the group, we have occasionally asked that students write progress reports based on their collaborative logs.

3: THE POST-PAPER ANALYSIS—a synthesis and analysis of how and to what degree the group's project changed from the time of the work plan until the day the final draft was handed in for evaluation. The post-paper analysis (one of our students renamed this paper the "postmortem") should also summarize how the student felt about the work his or her group did. Does the writer consider the group's effort to be good collaboration? What grade does the student think the paper deserves and why? Should everyone receive the same grade?

These writing assignments tend to represent all of James Moffet's "modes of discourse" from the basic *recording* and *reporting* of experiences in collaborative writing groups (as formalized by the collaborative logs) to *generalizing* and *theorizing* (as made available in the postpaper analyses and work plans, respectively). The collaborative writing classroom as we have envisioned it requires many different written products, and the assignments have been created to teach the "content" obtaining to the writing classroom while at the same time encouraging students to make *how* they write an object of reflection and analysis. Thus, we can, through one series of short writing assignments, reinforce classroom discussions of readers' needs and Moffet's modes of discourse, gather "insider" information into the workings of collaborative groups, and give students plenty of practice in writing.

Leave Room for Innovation and the Imagination

Recent research on small group dynamics suggests that the quality and number of ideas generated by invention is enhanced by having group members first engage individually in such prewriting activities as mapping, clustering, and focused free-writing before coming together for group brainstorming. During group brainstorming, collaborative groups should select a "scribe" to record all reactions and ideas that surface as the group works on an assignment. Before the group pursues its topic any farther, have its members repeat the individual-first, group-second prewriting process on the new, narrower idea.

If you are lucky enough to be in a classroom equipped with tables and moveable chairs, you can supply each group with large sheets of butcher paper so its members can map out invention topics while seated around a table. Group mapping also works if your room has multiple chalkboards. Just be sure your groups are supplied with enough chalk to map their ideas at one of the boards. When students map together they can pool their resources for generative topic ideas and organizational strategies.

■ DESIGNING COLLABORATIVE WRITING ASSIGNMENTS THAT WORK

Selecting a Topic

In general, we think that students rather than instructors should select paper topics. Student motivation is stimulated when they are allowed work on subjects that pique their interest. Of course, the teacher can point students in productive directions. We find that supplying students with a general purpose or genre provides them with a lens through which to focus their interests. Thus, instead of handing students a menu of paper topics, we assign papers dealing with specific themes (see below). For example, the paper on public policy asks student groups to gather as much information as possible on any issue that is an object of law. Within the large purpose of reporting all sides of a public policy debate—or the history of a public policy that directly affects them—students have the freedom to select any of a hundred topics ranging from legislation concerning drinking and voting ages to proposals for solving the nation's growing health-care crisis to the debate surrounding gays in the military. The principle of using topic selection to encourage student motivation can also apply within the groups themselves. Thus, you will want to emphasize to your students the importance of choosing a topic that everyone in the group agrees to. Consensus rather than majority rule is the key to successful collaboration. A student left out of the initial decision may feel no subsequent commitment to the group effort.

Once groups have selected a topic, we ask each group to write a well-developed audience profile. Have the groups articulate exactly whom they would expect to read their work. For example, if the group decides to write a paper on the parking problem on campus, group members should be clear about whom they see as their primary audience. Do they perceive a secondary audience for their writing as well? What can they assume their primary and secondary audiences know and do not know about the parking problem? How much background will they need to include in their paper to be sure that their readers fully understand the issues they raise? What kind of tone is appropriate for the audiences they have identified? Writing a statement of purpose for their writing can be a useful preliminary to tackling a major project: for example, "This paper will persuade the administration to schedule classes in a way that minimizes parking lot overcrowding at eight in the morning." Alternately, the individual members of the group could write separate statements of purpose, comparing and combining them afterwards.

The Teacher's Role in Drafting

As described above, the teacher in the collaborative learning and writing environment moves to the periphery of the learning activity in order to allow students to step up and take responsibility for their educations. This in no way minimizes the importance of the teacher. The instructor must create an environment hospitable to collaborative learning by creating a variety of in-class and out-of-class exercises that will give students hands-on experience with the vast array of principles and skills that conduce to good writing. Though working around the edges of classroom activity, the teacher must be alert to the sometimes subtle signals that a group is struggling, and must then decide when and if to intervene. The teacher must also be able to move from group to group, and be ready to suggest alternatives, answer questions, point students toward useful resources, or simply to share a joke. If much of the collaboration takes place online, the teacher may need the ability to "lurk" in some group conversations and activities.

Thus, even punctuation lessons can be an opportunity for student interaction. Instead of defining such abstract notions as what commas are and why participle, infinitive, and absolute phrases need them [24c], the teacher can set a task that will require students in groups to read, review, analyze, and use the comma rule information in their *Handbooks*. Or students can identify such sentence-level units as restrictive and nonrestrictive elements [24f], coordinate adjectives [24e], and transitional and parenthetical expressions [24g] in their own writing. To encourage them to synthesize and apply the abstract information in the *Handbook* to their own, very concrete writing, students also could be asked to create short documents that report how many of which kind of unit they discovered and whether or not a comma should be used in such a case. Thus even learning punctuation rules can be fun when students learn, analyze, and apply their new-found knowledge together. Ask each member of a group to be the "expert" on a particular mark of punctuation: commas, periods, semicolons, colons, quotation marks, and so forth. In proofreading, let each "expert" find the errors and explain to the writer how to correct them. On successive papers, have the students rotate the punctuation assignments, so that each gains expertise in all areas of punctuation. For underprepared students, starting with just commas, say, or periods, is less intimidating than learning and applying all punctuation rules at once. Peer discussion and reinforcement of the rules provides a more effective learning experience than asking individual students to correct teacher-marked errors.

Modify Assessment and Grading

Some instructors assign a single grade to the entire group; others assign grades individually, and others use some combination of the two methods, each student receiving both a group grade and an individual grade. While it is typical practice to assign grades based on the technical quality and discursive maturity of the final text, the success of a collaborative assignment should derive from other bases as well:

> the completion of the project
> the finding of an appropriate solution or resolution to the problem or case
> the group's equitable allocation of work or tasks
> nonwritten aspects of the completed project (such as oral presentation, visuals, and the evaluation and presentation of numerical data)
> the students' sense of successful completion
> the students' having learned something about group processes

Whether an instructor measures these factors in formal assessment or informally for course development, we believe that each represents an important part of what is taught through the collaborative project. We have heard it jokingly suggested that teaching collaborative writing will diminish an instructor's workload by having students work collaboratively. Would that it were true! We have found that even though the collaborative method causes the exchange of twenty-five individual papers and drafts for eight or so collaboratively produced papers and drafts, the time it takes to evaluate collaboratively produced papers evens the scale. And, of course, instructors must also judge the information they gain from all those smallish writing assignments that help students analyze and synthesize the writing process.

Creating Prompts That Encourage Analysis, Synthesis, and Self-reflection

For the collaborative writing instructor, the most demanding expenditure of creative energy is planning writing assignments that can accomplish many goals simultaneously. As discussed above, the writing instructor must deploy a wide range of writing assignments—and at the right time—in order to teach students how to collaborate effectively and how, when collaborating, to write with precision and power. Despite the difficulty of creating workable prompts, we usually follow a few general principles:

➤ Prompts should lay out an activity that encourages conversation, information exchange, and speculation, and that results in a written product.

➤ Prompts should ask students either to analyze a content-oriented issue in a sample text or synthesize the group's discussion of the prompt.

➤ Prompts should make it the students' responsibility to discover what principles apply to a given problem. It defeats the purpose of collaborative learning if you tell them what they will find if they look closely enough at the situation you have drawn to their attention. Likewise, prompts should ask students to engage in an activity that gives them practice using a particular concept (e.g., the audience analysis and discovering purpose exercise described above).

➤ Prompts should solicit self-reflection. Individuals should be urged to respond personally to the situations and issues that your prompts bring into focus.

In addition to this general advice about creating prompts, we further suggest that you avoid leading groups into discussing and writing about volatile, irresolvable subjects. Collaboration works when students can share and develop concepts and ideas. Positions set in stone are rarely amenable to any kind of modification, and an inability to negotiate a position on an issue will likely make negotiation of writing processes impossible as well. Topics like abortion, gun control, religious beliefs, or family values do not work very well as discussion or paper topics because—despite our students' natural attraction to them—they are not conducive to the development of congenial relations among group members nor to the development of balanced papers.

■ DIAGNOSING PROBLEMS IN THE COLLABORATIVE GROUP

Collaborative learning, collaborative writing, and collaborative projects are extraordinarily useful, but not unproblematic, tools for the teacher of writing. As teachers new to collaborative writing soon learn, despite their best efforts, sometimes collaborative projects simply do not work. While the benefits of collaboration in the writing classroom are manifold, it is important to be aware of what we call "collaborative breakdown." Because the dynamics of each class can vary widely, **monitor each group's progress.**

Among the clues to incipient breakdown are:

➤ Individual student anxiety as interim or final deadlines approach;

➤ A group's inability to decide what to do or how to do it;

➤ Students asking to change groups or have an assignment modified; and

➤ A work load that seems inequitably distributed.

To increase the likelihood that the instructor will learn of any problems in time to intervene, part of every collaborative project should include individual assessments by the students. These can take the form of conferences, journals, or the memos and/or progress reports we referred to above. Equally important, the instructor should schedule group work on regular class days so that he or she can sit in on each group to evaluate how well they are functioning.

Watching for the Five Fields of Dissonance

In our studies of student collaborative work, we have identified five major causes of trouble: 1) logistical difficulties; 2) personality conflict; 3) differing cognitive abilities; 4) differences in epistemological development; and 5) differences in social background. While these vexing spirits can rarely be cast out by the instructor, being able to identify them may permit a teacher to modify an assignment or better evaluate its success.

THE LOGISTICS OF COLLABORATION. Perhaps there are a fortunate few instructors who have no students who are working at least one job to make ends meet and gain work experience while they are in school. But many of us expect that at least half our students will have one or two part-time jobs in addition to their full-time class load. In some cases, students have family responsibilities, too. In one of our early collaborative writing classes, Chuck reported, "Tom, Michelle, and I all work different hours, and getting together to write out drafts of our paper was impossible." Competing demands on our students' time may make it impossible or extremely difficult for them to work outside the classroom as a group and, as we have already mentioned, the instructor should make every effort to minimize scheduling conflicts. Providing interactive Web-based tools can help students work around differing schedules and time constraints.

DIFFERENCES IN COGNITIVE ABILITY. Another area of difficulty that can work against successful collaboration is differing cognitive maturity. Cognitive development specialists tell us that the composing process comprises a tremendous variety of mental operations, ranging from understanding the assignment, to remembering relevant facts, to imagining and seeking to meet the needs of an audience, to organizing data in such a way that it may be presented in a clear and logical manner (e.g., Flower and Hayes, 1984), but it also includes the basics of literacy—reading and writing. Thus, when we speak of the cognitive maturity of a writer or a group of writers we are referring to the facility with which that writer or that group can usefully conceptualize and execute the requirements of a writing task. And of course, not all students are created with equal abilities. Some students will be able to conceptualize problems and propose solutions posed by and directed toward a writing task more adequately than their facility with the language will allow them to demonstrate on paper. Conversely, there are writers who are extremely facile with the language, but whose thinking is nevertheless superficial.

In the context of collaborative work, a form of cognitive dissonance occurs when students with varying levels of cognitive maturity tackle a problem together—a situation which holds both pedagogical promise and peril. The promise is that students, regardless of maturity, can learn problem-solving techniques and efficient strategies for reading, writing, and organizing more effectively from one another than from a textbook or a teacher (Daiute, 1986). The peril lies in the fact that cognitive dissonance frequently leads to frustration and impatience, and even to the formation of factions or the dissolution of the group itself. The more cognitively mature student may become impatient with her less advanced group members and usurp control of the project.

EPISTEMOLOGICAL DEVELOPMENT IN CONFLICT. In his study of Harvard students, William G. Perry (1970) proposed a nine-stage scale of epistemological development along which the individual moved from **dualism**—an authoritarian, black-or-white view of the world, to **multiplicity**—the recognition of other points of view; and finally a commitment in **relativism**—taking a personal stand while also accepting other points of view. Epistemological dissonance occurs when different members of a group are at different stages along Perry's continuum. The problem for classroom collaboration is not only that students may be operating at different epistemic levels, but also that students cannot comprehend the "ways of knowing" of their co-members. The dualist, regardless of the sophistication of his or her writing abilities, cannot understand how the group can develop alternative solutions to a problem. A student at the multiplistic stage may be able to recognize views other than his or her own, but be unable to evaluate their relative strengths. Achieving consensus can be difficult when a member of a group does not know how to compare and choose among alternative solutions that may appear to have equal merit. Such a student may bow to the loudest voice or, unsure of his or her own position, say simply "do what you guys want to do." Even a student who may have attained the upper reaches of Perry's scale (and we do not believe that "a commitment in relativism" is the likely endpoint for most individuals) may not tolerate the dogmatism or apparent "wishy-washyness" of the less epistemologically advanced student and may react either by withdrawing from the group or by attempting to dominate it.

PERSONAL DISSONANCE. Most instructors know when they have a personality problem in class. A student's aberrant behavior or argumentative stance manifests itself early in the term. In a work setting, such an individual would be weeded out—or at least pruned—early in his or her employment history, but rarely is a student so disruptive that he or she is ejected from class. Yet even a small disruptive element is antithetical to group process, and a perverse streak may totally sabotage a group's work. Other personality problems are the aggressive student whose personality force dominates the other students and the shy or quiet student who is unable to present his or her views or is unable to take on the parts of the assignment that he or she is best suited for. Related to this phenomenon is the dissonance that can arise from students who have differing levels of motivation. Students who need high GPAs in order to qualify for scholarships in their majors will not appreciate being grouped with students who are taking your class credit/no-credit. Some students want to put forth the least amount of work possible while others take great pride in each task. Even without considering grades, students do not always come to class with the same priorities and degree of commitment. The instructor cannot change a student's personality or supply motivation, but she can teach students about the ways in which personality and motivation factors can affect group interaction. The teacher can also consider these factors when assigning groups—when logical considerations do not completely dictate groupings.

SOCIAL DISSONANCE. This little-discussed area of interpersonal friction can be defined as the clashing work behaviors that derive from differing socioeconomic backgrounds and which influence task representation, work ethic, and degree of imagination or risk-taking. Rather than viewing the matter in stereotypical terms—"working class attitudes," "women's ways of knowing," etc.—we see this area of dissonance as deriving from differing "dialects of behavior." Although what we have called the "dialect of behavior" shares much conceptually with a "discourse community," we believe that the behavioral dialect encompasses more than shared discourse. It was only after teaching at three very different institutions that we became aware of the considerable differences in response that could be engendered by the same assignments. For example, in responding to an ethics case regarding a corrupt politician, students in Arcata, California, and Columbus, Ohio, saw it as only the behavior problem of one individual. Students in Youngstown, Ohio, on the other hand, assumed mob connections and a general corruption in politics. In Arcata, environmental concern among students is taken for granted; in Columbus, it is much less widespread. As another example, in the Youngstown area, positions of authority and responsibility are accorded considerable deference. Thus, on second reference in a newspaper, a lawyer is identified as "Attorney Smith." Professors with doctorates are always "Dr." In both Columbus and Arcata, "Dr." is usually reserved for physicians and dentists, and attorneys are not accorded special status.

Behavioral dialect may also account for the degree of comfort a student experiences with hierarchical or nonhierarchical structures; the degree to which a student resists responsibility for her or his education; and the expectation the student has for the location of authority—all of which have implications for the decentered, nonhierarchical, shared-authority collaborative classroom. Such social factors can cause collaborative breakdown when members of a group do not share the same behavioral dialect or when a shared behavioral dialect does not permit satisfactory completion of an assignment. Interestingly, factors attributable to behavioral dialect often supersede attitudes or behaviors predicted from class, ethnic, or gender theory.

Mediating Conflict

While there are many potential sources of collaborative breakdown in the writing classroom, those considering teaching collaborative writing for the first time should know that complete breakdown is the exception and not the rule. Most groups instinctively compensate for tensions and imbalances—if for no other reason than they want to pass the class. But most frequently, collaborative groups demonstrate that human beings are thoroughly social animals with considerable reserves of tolerance, understanding, and humor to smooth their ways to successful completion of a shared task—whatever the perceived reward. This table distills responses that experience has shown can help teachers of collaborative writing nurture students' innate social strengths:

FIELD OF DISSONANCE	INSTRUCTOR RESPONSE
LOGISTICAL	• Acknowledge students' scheduling difficulties by showing flexibility on due dates and course expectations. • Allow in-class group work time. • Set up online conferencing sites • Arrange groups with consideration for schedules.
PERSONAL	• Solicit students' self-appraisals and preferences. • Provide alternative models for behavior in groups (suggest such roles as "idea person," "elaborator," and "group scribe") to minimize reliance on traditional leader-follower paradigm. • Be willing to give a disruptive personality an individual assignment rather than insisting on group participation.
COGNITIVE	• Recognize that all students are not created with equal abilities nor does their cognitive development proceed at the same pace. • Graduate the complexity of assignments over the course of the term to permit what development can take place to take place. • Group students at different cognitive levels only when motivation appears equal. • Accept that students' intellectual contributions may not be equal.
EPISTEMIC	• Recognize that students at the lower end of the development scale cannot perceive the views of those in positions above them. • Because students at the lower end of the epistemic scale may be incapable of responding to open-ended assignments or assignments in which a group is expected to develop its own approach, be prepared to provide explicit directions.
SOCIAL	• Develop awareness of and adjust to local knowledge. • Provide in-class opportunities for encountering and discussing other perspectives, other norms.

■ ASSIGNMENTS THAT WORK

Some Field-tested Prompts To Get You Started

Ultimately, the only way to learn how to teach writing in a collaborative classroom is to devise the best syllabus you can and give it a whirl. All of the advice presented in these pages derives from years of trial and error, and while we have had some spectacular failures along the way, we do not think that those classes where failures occurred learned less about writing that those we conducted according to the more traditional model. Collaborative writing, like democracy, may be the worst way to teach writing—except for all other ways of teaching it. What follows are several assignments that have proven winners in many collaborative writing classes. We hope that, like us, you will be amazed at how creative students can be when they are fully engaged in the learning and writing process.

Research Paper 1: Thinking Green

Everyone is talking about our deteriorating environment—deforestation, strip mining, acid rain, overfishing, overfertilization, the difficulties of disposing of toxic and nuclear wastes. But what are the facts? What do you really know about any environmental issue? Where does your information come from? How reliable is it? This assignment lets you gain some expertise in at least one area of environmental concern and draw your own conclusions.

What information you will need: Once you have decided on a topic, you will need to dig up information on at least three issues: 1) the physics of the problem—how the environmental impact occurs; 2) the biology of the problem—what happens to the plants and animals affected by the problem, and 3) the socioeconomics of the problem—the human activities and needs that occasion the environmental impact. (Some papers will also have to consider the "chemistry of the problem"—what chemical compounds are released as a result of the environmental impact and what chemical reactions result from this release.)

How you actually organize the paper will, as always, be dependent on the logic that best explains your chosen topic. However, generally speaking, the reader can understand the biology of a problem better than he or she already understands why the affected organisms are in harm's way in the first place. It may be, though, that you find it more sensible to explain the socioeconomics of the problem you are studying even as you relate how that problem occurs. In any case, you will need to work out a provisional strategy and present it in your work plan.

Editorial

As stated in the syllabus, you will work collaboratively with several other students to develop and write a persuasive essay on a subject upon which you all agree. To get to this point, you will need to do some legwork.

STEP 1: Write brief papers (approximately 350–500 words) in which each of you explains the significance of the issue you have chosen.

STEP 2: Each member of the group will write a paper explaining the facts of the issue.

STEP 3: Divide the group. One half will write a pro paper and the other half, a con paper.

STEP 4: Finally your group will reach consensus on the issue and write a persuasive essay advocating the position you have agreed on. You will use secondary sources to build your case. (If students struggle to come to consensus on a position, they may try to develop a Rogerian argument instead.)

GRADING: Significance: 3 points, Facts: 5 points, Pro/Con: 7 points, Final Essay: 10 points—for a total of 25 points.

As you have learned from the editorials that you have read and those shared in class, educated opinions are the basis of strong persuasion, and facts are the basis for educated opinions. Persuading others to follow the course of action you advocate—whether voting for a candidate, contributing to the United Way, or wearing seat belts—requires that you not only provide sound reasoning but that you consider the audience you are trying to persuade and the purpose you have in persuading them.

While it may be said that "everyone is entitled to his or her opinion," everyone is not entitled to have that opinion listened to. There are good opinions and bad ones; part of your job in this assignment is to determine which opinions are valid and which are not.

In general, opinions whose credibility relies on higher authority (the government, the Constitution, the Bible, etc.) are not arguable and only rarely can they be used to bring about change in the hands of the editorial writer. Thus, any argument you wish to advance that uses the Bible or other religious work as authority will probably be inappropriate in this class. Rather, your job is to seek out the facts that explain and issue—taking great care in the source of those facts—sort through those facts, write opinions that support each side of an issue (for example, on using or not using motorcycle helmets) and then write an editorial, or public policy statement, on that issue—a fact-based persuasive essay.

Pick a subject all of you are content with. Obviously, any topic on which you cannot be objective is out: no gun control, abortion, prayer in the schools, or anything else which causes members of the group to raise their voices. Instead, select a subject which is interesting, which is under contention, and for which information is readily available.

A good editorial runs about 500 to 750 words, almost never more. However, an explanation of the facts and a discussion of opinion may, in fact, run a lot longer. One of the jobs of the editorial is to distill those facts to educate the reader.

While your facts and opinion essay must be documented, the final editorial should not be.

Research Paper 2: How Public Policy Is Created

It is easy to criticize government officials: to say they are crooks, they don't keep promises, they aren't principled, or they just do not use common sense. But these easy criticisms fail to consider the difficulty of creating laws that are simultaneously intelligent, fair, and politically possible. The question remains: What influences shape public policy? What information is considered? What pressures do special-interest groups exert? How do such abstract and occasionally relative moral values like right and wrong figure in the making of public policy? The ultimate goal of this assignment, then, is to pick a public policy issue, to figure out what is being said about it and by whom, and to explain to your readers how power, fact, opinion, and belief have influenced (or are influencing) law and behavior.

What information you will need: Choose an area of public policy that interests you, read all you can about it, and write a report that explains what you found out. The possibilities are almost endless—health care, gay marriage, America's role in Iraq (or anywhere else), standardized testing in public schools, campaign finance reform, "sin taxes" on items, such as alcohol or cigarettes, stem cell research, drug testing of athletes—*you* name it! But watch it! This is *not* a persuasive paper; you will not be arguing one point of view or another. Instead, you will be presenting *all* the points of view on a given issue in a way that fairly represents them.

Stuck for ideas? Read through the front sections of the *Washington Post* or the *New York Times* or *Los Angeles Times* for the last couple of weeks and see what public policy issues they are discussing. Your group should find something you think is crucial.

Organizing your research: You will probably find it most logical to begin by discussing the problem that the public policy you are investigating has been proposed to solve. What is its history? What is its social impact? Who is affected? What would the proposed policy do to change the status quo? What is the hoped-for result? It would be all right to give more weight to the legislative history of your issue than its social effects, but you must discuss some of both.

■ MORE ABOUT COLLABORATION

While collaborative writing has become an important focus of composition studies in the past ten years, the idea of an individual's copyright to "intellectual property" is relatively new. The history of writing extends back five thousand years, but the notion that a solitary individual can create "original" written work and then possess that work as property has only existed for a little over two hundred years (cf. Ede and Lunsford, 1–6). Prior to the seventeenth century, books frequently compiled the written work of others and only infrequently cited the original writers. Prior to the seventeenth century, written ideas, like talk, belonged to everyone in a linguistic community. Indeed, before mass literacy and the widespread availability of inexpensive printed materials, written ideas were only available to most through oral transmission. These communal notions about intellectual property gradually changed as it became increasingly possible for individual writers to achieve fame and fortune through their pens. Yet, even as novelists, poets, and playwrights became increasingly more concerned with the ownership of their words, the industrial revolution created its own species of corporately owned language (Ede and Lunsford, 5). Throughout the nineteenth century and into our own time, written discourse in science, business, and industry has become a corporate product. Most scientific reports rely on the work and ideas of teams of researchers. Corporations frequently distribute information to shareholders and the public that acknowledges no one but the company.

Today our students are bewildered by the range of views on intellectual property. While software companies and the music and movie industries wage international war on copyright "pirates," those same companies ask their employees to imagine their individual efforts as contributions to a large team. One might well create a new software program for Microsoft, but one should not expect authorship credit. Preparing for their careers, students pass through an academic establishment that is deeply concerned that students *do their own work*. Plagiarism and cheating are represented as moral bankruptcy while the sharing of information is discouraged. Graduate students in the sciences might well find themselves conducting experiments and writing reports for senior scientists for which they receive no name credit in institutions where they could be expelled for passing off the words of others as their own. English majors could easily find themselves taught to value the individual genius and unique creative power of Virginia Woolf in classes entitled "Woolf and the Bloomsbury Circle."

It is in this conflicted context that recent research on collaborative writing has been conducted. Beginning as early as 1963, Derek J. de Solla Price noted the increase in the number of scientific articles written by large teams. From the mid-sixties until the early seventies, Price (1963), Hagstrum (1964), Clarke (1964), Price and Beaver (1966), Zuckerman (1967), Weinberg (1970), and Crane (1972) identified the research and reporting practices of those working in the sciences and social sciences. In 1973, Kenneth Bruffee introduced the fledgling discipline of composition studies to "practical models of collaborative learning." Response to Bruffee's early work was slow in emerging, however. In the 1970s, composition studies were largely preoccupied with the claims of "expressivist" and "writing-as-process" schools of thought—both of which emphasized the importance of the *individual's* voice, ideas, and composing processes. It was not until the early 1980s, when Richard Gebhardt (1980) and John Clifford (1981) each published essays discussing the ways in which collaboration affects writing pedagogy, that a large number of researchers began to examine collaborative learning and writing from the compositionist's point of view.

Since the early 1980s, research on collaborative writing has divided itself into three main strands: 1) studies and analysis of collaboration in "nonacademic settings"; 2) defining and describing models of collaboration; and 3) the interpersonal dynamics of collaborative groups. Beginning with Faigley and Miller's "What We Learn Writing on the Job" (1982), it is clear that research into the collaborative activities of those working outside the academy has become the most important research site. Odell and Goswami's *Writing in Nonacademic Settings* (1985) is perhaps the most logical starting place for those interested in off-campus collaborative activity. Introduced in Odell and Goswami's collection are several oft-cited essays on collaborative writing research, including Paul Anderson's "What Survey Research Tells Us about Writing at Work" and Paradis, Dobrin, and Miller's "Writing at EXXON ITD: Notes on the Writing Environment of an R&D Organization." Yet, despite the historical importance of Odell and Goswami's collection, the "seminal" text on collaborative writing is Ede and Lunsford's superbly researched *Single Texts/Plural Authors* (1990), which presents a history of notions of authorship, statistical information on what kinds of writing really are done in the world outside the academy, and a rationale for a collaborative pedagogy. Other important texts on nonacademic collaboration are Lay and Karis's *Collaborative Writing in Industry: Investigations in Theory and Practice* (1990) and Burnett and Duin's *Collaboration in Technical and Professional Communication: A Research Perspective* (1995).

The second important area in collaborative research is composed of those studies which consider the various kinds of collaboration. While many of those investigating what collaboration is and how it works do their work in nonacademic settings, the emphasis on models of collaboration can derive from any research base. Killingsworth and Jones's and Couture and Rhymer's 1989 studies, for example, pay particular attention to defining what workplace collaboration is and when it occurs, while Beard, Rhymer, and Williams focus their 1989 essay on how properly to assess collaborative writing groups. Several essays describing nonacademic models for collaboration, including those by Debs and Selzer, can be found in Fearing and Sparrow's collection *Technical Writing: Theory and Practice* (1989). One can also find important essays discussing conceptual frameworks for understanding collaboration in Forman's *New Visions of Collaborative Writing* (1992). Other useful texts discussing models of small groups are Hare's somewhat dated *Handbook of Small Group Research* (1976), Swap's *Group Decision Making* (1984), and Hirokawa and Poole's *Communication and Group Decision Making* (1986). Those particularly interested in how collaborative models drawn from industry have been translated into collaborative writing pedagogy should consult Phillips's *Teaching How to Work in Groups* (1990).

The last major area in collaborative writing research investigates the "sociology" of small groups. In addition to the aforementioned collection by Forman, one will find a good overview of relevant small-group dynamics in Blyler and Thralls's *Professional Communication: The Social Perspective* (1993). Included in this volume is Burnett's "Conflict in Collaborative Decision Making," which those new to teaching collaborative writing should find valuable as a summary of research into how conflict can either mediate or enhance the quality of collaborative efforts. Our own "Fields of Dissonance in the Collaborative Writing Classroom" builds on Burnett's work by presenting an even more complex picture of the small-group working dynamic. In addition to small group "conflict," gender studies perspectives have also been brought to bear on research into collaboration. Lunsford and Ede's "Rhetoric in a New Key" (1990), for example, distinguishes between a predominantly male "hierarchical mode of discourse" and the predominantly female "dialogic mode." Lay's "The Androgynous Collaborator: The Impact of Gender Studies on Collaboration" (1992) also asserts the importance of gender in determining interpersonal dynamics in groups, suggesting that attention must be paid to gender stereotyping when students evaluate their collaborative groups. Raign and Sims's 1993 "Gender, Persuasion Techniques, and Collaboration" amplifies the issues raised in Lunsford and Ede and also in Lay. In addition to these important articles, Nadler, Nadler, and Todd-Mancillas's *Advances in Gender and Communication Research* (1987) provides a good starting point for those interested in exploring communications theory, gender, and language.

Still other researchers have urged the importance of incorporating self-monitoring strategies into collaborative work—most notably, Forman and Katsky's article discussing the importance of groups remaining aware of both writing and group processes (1986). To build a solid general background in how small groups work we suggest reading around in Morse and Phelps's *Interpersonal Communication: A Relational Perspective* (1980), Klauss and Bass's *Interpersonal Communication in Organizations* (1982), Rolloff and Miller's *Interpersonal Processes: New Directions in Communication Research* (1989), Ross's *Small Groups in Organizational Settings* (1989), Napier and Gershenfeld's *Groups: Theory and Experience* (fifth edition, 1993), and Frey's *Group Communication in Context* (1994).

WEB RESOURCES FOR PART II (TEACHING COLLABORATIVE WRITING)

Web Resources can be found at **www.prenhall.com/troyka** under Instructor's Resources.

WORKS CITED

Beard, John D., Jone Rymer, and David L. Williams. "An Assessment System for Collaborative-Writing Groups: Theory and Empirical Evaluation." *Journal of Business and Technical Communication* 3 (1989): 29–51.

Bruffee, Kenneth. "Collaborative Learning: Some Practical Models." *College English* 35 (1973): 634–42.

——. "Collaborative Learning and the 'Conversation of Mankind.'" *College English* 46 (1984): 635–52.

Burnett, Rebecca E. "Conflict in Collaborative Decision Making." *Professional Communication: The Social Perspective.* Eds., Nancy R. Blyler and Charlotte Thralls. Newbury Park, CA: SAGE, 1993. 144–62.

Burnett, Rebecca E. and Ann Hill Duin. *Collaboration in Technical and Professional Communication: A Research Perspective.* Hillsdale, NJ: Erlbaum, 1995.

Clarke, Beverly. "Multiple Authorship Trends in Scientific Papers." *Science* 143 (1964): 822–24.

Clifford, John. "Composing in Stages: The Effects of a Collaborative Pedagogy." *Research in the Teaching of Writing* 14 (1981): 37–53.

Couture, Barbara and Jone Rymer. "Interactive Writing on the Job: Definitions and Implications of 'Collaboration.'" *Writing in the Business Professions.* Ed. Mura Kogan. Urbana, IL: National Council of the Teachers of English, 1989.

Crane, Diane. *Invisible Colleges: Diffusion of Knowledge in Scientific Communities.* Chicago: University of Chicago Press, 1972.

Daiute, Collette. "Do 1 and 1 Make 2?: Patterns of Influence by Collaborative Authors." *Written Communication* 3 (1986): 382–408.

De Solla Price, Derek J. *Little Science, Big Science.* New York: Columbia University Press, 1963.

De Solla Price, Derek J. and Donald Beaver. "Collaboration in an Invisible College." *American Psychologist* 21 (1964): 241–63.

Ede, Lisa and Andrea A. Lunsford. *Single Texts/Plural Authors: Perspectives on Collaborative Writing.* Carbondale, IL: Southern Illinois University Press, 1990.

Faigley, Lester and Thomas Miller. "What We Learn from Writing on the Job." *College English* 44 (1982): 557–69.

Fearing, Bertie E. and W. Keats Sparrow. *Technical Writing: Theory and Practice.* New York: Modern Language Association, 1989.

Flower, Linda and John R. Hayes. "Images, Plans, and Prose: The Representation of Meaning in Writing." *Written Communication* 1 (1986): 120–60.

Forman, Janis. *New Visions of Collaborative Writing.* Portsmouth, NH: Boynton/Cook, 1992.

Forman, Janis and Patricia Katsky. "The Group Report: A Problem in Small Group or Writing Processes?" *The Journal of Business Communication* 23 (1986): 23–35.

Frey, Lawrence R. *Group Communication in Context: Studies of Natural Groups.* Hillsdale, NJ: Erlbaum, 1994.

Gebhardt, Richard. "Teamwork and Feedback: Broadening the Base of Collaborative Writing." *College English* 42 (1980): 69–74.

Hagstrum, Warren O. "Traditional and Modern Forms of Scientific Teamwork." *Administrative Science* Quarterly 9 (1964): 241–63.

Hare, A. Paul. *Handbook of Small Group Research.* New York: Free Press, 1976.

Hirokawa, Randy Y. and Marshall S. Poole. *Communication and Group Decision Making.* Beverly Hills: SAGE, 1986.

Killingsworth, M. Jimmie and Betsy G. Jones. "Division of Labor or Integrated Teams: A Crux in the Management of Technical Communication?" *Technical Communication* 36 (1989): 210–21.

Klauss, R. and B.M. Bass. *Interpersonal Communication in Organizations.* New York: Academic, 1987.

Lay, Mary M. "The Androgynous Collaborator: The Impact of Gender Studies on Collaboration." *New Visions of Collaborative Writing.* Ed. Janis Foreman. Portsmouth, NH: Boynton/Cook, 1992. 82–104.

Lay, Mary M. and William M. Karis. *Collaborative Writing in Industry: Investigations in Theory and Practice.* New York: Baywood, 1990.

Lunsford, Andrea A. and Lisa Ede. "Rhetoric in a New Key: Women and Collaboration." *Rhetoric Review* 8 (1990): 234–41.

Moffett, James. *Teaching the Universe of Discourse.* Boston: Houghton Mifflin, 1983.

Morse, B.W. and L.A. Phelps. *Interpersonal Communication: A Relational Perspective.* Minneapolis: Burgess, 1980.

Nadler, Lawrence B., Marjorie K. Nadler, and William R. Todd-Mancillas. *Advances in Gender and Communication Research.* Lanham: University Press of America, 1987.

Napier, Rodney W. and Matti K. Gershenfeld. *Groups: Theory and Experience.* Boston: Houghton Mifflin, 1993.

Odell, Lee and Dixie Goswami. *Writing in Nonacademic Settings.* New York: Guilford, 1985.

Perry, William G. *Forms of Intellectual and Ethical Development in the College Years.* New York: Holt, 1970.

Phillips, Gerald M. *Teaching How to Work in Groups.* Norwood: Ablex, 1990.

Putnam, Linda L. "Conflict in Group Decision Making." *Communication and Group Decision Making.* Eds., Randy Y. Hirokawa and Marshall S. Poole. Beverly Hills: SAGE, 1986. 175–96.

Raign, Kathryn Rosser. "Gender, Persuasion Techniques, and Collaboration." *Technical Communication Quarterly* 2 (1993): 89–104.

Rolloff, M.E. and G.R. Miller. *Interpersonal Processes: New Directions in Communication Research.* Beverly Hills: SAGE, 1989.

Ross, Raymond S. *Small Groups in Organizational Settings.* Englewood Cliffs, NJ: Prentice Hall, 1989.

Swap, George and Associates. *Group Decision Making.* Beverly Hills: SAGE, 1984.

Thralls, Charlotte and Nancy Roundy Blyler. *Professional Communication: The Social Perspective.* Newbury Park: SAGE, 1993.

Trimbur, John. "Consensus and Difference in Collaborative Writing." *College English* 51 (1989): 602–16.

Weinberg, Alvin M. "Scientific Teams and Scientific Laboratories." *Dædelus* 99 (1970): 1056–75.

Zuckerman, Harriet. "Nobel Laureates in Science: Patterns of Productivity, Collaboration, and Authorship." *American Sociological Review* 32 (1967): 391–403.

PART THREE

Using Portfolios for Learning and Assessment
by Laurel Black, *St. John Fisher College*

■ INTRODUCTION

I began using portfolios the first semester I ever taught. As a graduate student enrolled in a summer course to train teaching assistants, I was overwhelmed by all that I had to learn in such a short time. We spent part of one class talking about portfolios as an option for grading. The professor was experienced at using portfolios, and I'm sure what he told us was much more complex than what I got out of his presentation. However, all I heard in my anxiety about grading papers was that I could let students revise as often as they wanted and not grade them until the final portfolio. They could pick some papers to put into a folder, I'd average the grades of the pieces, and the whole scary grading process would be over in one fell swoop at the end of the semester when I was more secure in my ability to evaluate writing. It wasn't much, but it was a plan.

I went into that semester without any real theoretical understanding of portfolios, nor any sense of structuring my class around any goals other than to avoid embarrassment and confrontation. I didn't think of portfolios as part of a larger context of assessment issues. My first-year students were also new to portfolios and saw the revision and selection process—and the deferral of grades—as a wonderful improvement over high school English. They responded enthusiastically and evaluated the course highly. I decided I would keep using portfolios—they had done the job for me. However, as colleagues asked me questions about how I constructed my class, I realized how little I had thought about the relationship between the shape of my course and my pedagogical beliefs, that I had never thought seriously about the connections between assessment and goals, and that I couldn't explain and didn't understand the theory undergirding the practice of portfolios.

I am still using portfolios in almost every class I teach. My students still respond enthusiastically to them; we are both still learning about writing and assessment through their use. Recently, one student told me, "It's hard work to put one of these together, but you know, it's kinda cool, too, to work like this." What does "like this" mean? What are portfolios, and how are students and teachers prepared to work with portfolios? What follows helps define portfolios but is not "definitive": one of the hallmarks of portfolios is their ability to be shaped to meet the demands of local contexts. It is important to remember that writing portfolios are constructed in a context, usually a classroom. This context helps shape portfolios. In fact, Sandra Murphy ("Portfolios and Curriculum Reform," 1994) asks us to consider the way in which a "portfolio culture" is developed in a classroom. Each institution, each class presents its own challenges. Thus my suggestions for preparing students to work with portfolios and my advice to help instructors avoid problems aren't all-encompassing. If you choose to use portfolios as part of your classroom, however, they should help you understand better the opportunities and difficulties they present. A major component of using portfolios in teaching today is helping students incorporate computer skills into writing, evaluating, and designing their portfolios. Troyka & Hesse's *Simon & Schuster Handbook for Writers*, 8th ed., offers many kinds of help integrating computers into the writing process, especially Chapters 1–2, 31–33, and 40–43, which discuss how computers shape the writing process, planning, shaping, drafting, and revising, research (including online research) and documentation, business and public writing, oral presentations incorporating multimedia, document and Web design. If a teacher wants to emphasize a particular subject area in the portfolio, Troyka & Hesse' offers chapters on writing in various disciplines (Chapter 37), writing about literature (Chapter 38), and writing in the social and natural sciences (Chapter 39).

■ WHAT IS A PORTFOLIO?

As an object, a portfolio is simply a collection of items. In fact, Peter Elbow writes that a portfolio is "nothing but a folder, a pouch—an emptiness: a collection device and not a form of assessment" (in *New Directions in Portfolio Assessment*, 40). In fact, a teacher may use portfolios in her classroom and not change much in her practice at all—students simply collect their writing at the end of the semester, allowing the teacher to see the body of work all at once.

But portfolios are most often defined by the activities involved in constructing them; they are most often seen as part of a process that eventually results in a product. What are often called the defining features of portfolios (Yancey, "Portfolios for the Writing Instructor," 84) are actually the defining features of the *work* of constructing portfolios, work done by both teacher and student. The features usually considered in defining a portfolio include *collection, selection, revision, reflection, presentation*, and *evaluation*. Yancey also includes communication among her list of features; this is certainly part of portfolios, just as it is part of any text. While these features are easily listed separately as products—that is, a student could say, "Here is a selection of my writing"—they are inseparable in practice. When a student presents a portfolio that is a selection of work completed over the course of a semester or unit, all of the processes listed above have gone into its construction. The portfolio provides teachers with a holistic view of the student's abilities and strengths.

Collection

Students *collect* materials for a portfolio. Often, everything a student has written is collected in what is called a "working portfolio": first notes for a paper, journal entries connected to essays, drafts, revisions, responses and evaluations from teachers and peers, and all other related materials. I've had students save notes passed in class, letters to a girlfriend, and hard copy of electronic mail correspondence—all writing that they felt was important or representative of the kinds of writing they do by assignment or choice.

Selection

From the messiness of this writer's portfolio the student is usually asked to select materials for a "showcase" or "presentation" portfolio. When portfolios are used for assessment purposes (they need not be, as Edward White and Peter Elbow [*New Directions in Portfolio Assessment*] point out), it is usually the presentation portfolio that is evaluated. When students select particular pieces for a presentation portfolio, they may follow guidelines set for them by the teacher (who may be following guidelines set for her by a department or university), or they may select pieces based on principles they themselves have determined. It may be that a teacher and student have negotiated the selection principles, or perhaps the class as a group has worked with the teacher to determine how pieces will be selected.

Revision

While the pieces that have been culled from the working portfolio may be presented "as is," it is often the case that students will *revise* at least some of the chosen pieces before they are presented. They may revise to meet specific criteria, or they may revise in response to earlier suggestions offered by peers or their teacher. In many classrooms, work on the remaining pieces in the working portfolio is excluded from the presentation portfolio, and students focus on the selected pieces instead. The portfolio grading system and use of computers in the writing process encourage students to spend more time revising. (See Part Seven of this teacher's manual for detailed help with computers and revision, and see Troyka & Hesse's Chapter 2, "Planning, Shaping, Drafting, and Revising.")

Students also may revise because the purpose of the portfolio has changed or the audience for the piece has changed. For example, a student may rework a piece drawn from a child psychology course to present it as part of a portfolio for an English class.

Reflection

Reflection appears to be a crucial defining feature of a writing portfolio and of the learning that we hope will take place as students construct a portfolio. Whether the portfolio is specifically for assessment, learning, or both, a piece of writing that could be considered reflective distinguishes a writing portfolio from a simple collection in a folder. In some cases, students write an introduction to their portfolio that goes beyond simple description of the portfolio's components, while in other cases, students assess themselves and their writing. The form of the reflection may be a single piece or may involve "memos" attached to each piece in the portfolio. For many teachers and students, writing reflectively is a new experience and an exciting part of a portfolio-based course. (See Appendix B and C for samples of reflective assignments.)

Presentation

Students *present* their portfolios to someone. That someone may be a teacher, a peer, or even themselves, especially if the portfolio is being used as a learning portfolio and not for formal assessment. In presenting a portfolio, students acknowledge that they have written in a social context, that readers—or the writer's concept of potential readers—of the portfolio have shared in some way in its construction. Even when a portfolio is a learning portfolio, the student is attempting to understand what the portfolio "re-presents" about herself or himself as a writer. This feature, too, separates a portfolio from a simple collection in a folder. Students usually take great pride in designing their portfolio, an act that underscores for both the student and teacher that this collection is special (see Troyka & Hesse's *Simon & Schuster Handbook for Writers*, Chapter 42, on designing documents and Chapter 1 on audience and purpose). The more students are able to use the computer's design features, the more excited and proud they usually will be. A word of caution: students may at times spend more time and effort in designing attractive final products than in revising those products into final drafts. Reinforcing the importance of demonstrating their strengths as writers may remind students to balance the time spent in developing and revising the portfolio's content with the time spent preparing it for presentation.

Evaluation

Not all portfolios are *evaluated* formally. However, in most writing classrooms, a final portfolio will be evaluated by a teacher and possibly also by peers. Grant Wiggins (see the Works Cited section of this chapter's bibliography) argues that criteria for evaluation of any performance be clear and available to the student before he or she attempts that performance. As students select and revise pieces for a portfolio, they are probably taking those criteria into account, practicing evaluation on their own.

These processes are interconnected. In selecting pieces to showcase or present, a student evaluates and reflects; in revising, a student also evaluates and reflects; and in both selection and revision, the knowledge that this portfolio will be presented to someone will be a part of the process. A student may return to the original "working portfolio" collection after working for some time on a piece and ultimately rejecting it; the process begins again as he or she reflects on this decision and selects another piece from the working portfolio to revise and present to a reader for response and/or evaluation.

■ WHY USE PORTFOLIOS?

Increasingly, portfolios are used as a means of showcasing our work, providing a rich picture of our strengths and weaknesses. Beyond the classroom, portfolios are useful tools for placement and program evaluation. Portfolios can be used to assess ourselves as instructors or even to assess departments or institutions.

When I chose to use portfolios, the rationale I offered my students was that a final grade based on how well they wrote at the end of the semester—instead of an average of grades over the course of a semester—was a more valid grade. I still feel that's right, although as I confessed earlier, that's not why I came to use portfolios. Many teachers (particularly at the high school level) are required by administrators to use portfolios; this is also sometimes the case with new teaching assistants who must, at least initially, follow departmental guidelines. I have continued to use portfolios because they are a central part of a classroom that is student-centered, process-oriented, and focused on active and collaborative learning, and they lend themselves to learning and assessment. I like, too, that portfolios create a space for diverse voices to be heard, that they change the way time is used in the classroom and in learning, and the ways they support a sense of the social nature of writing and learning.

Diverse Voices

Because portfolios are shaped by the local context, particularly the classrooms in which they are constructed, they permit teachers to adapt assessment to the students. Teachers of developmental, nontraditional, and ESL students often come to portfolios because they feel portfolios change the whole nature of the classroom, making it less frightening for their students. Portfolios allow students to develop their abilities before being graded on them, and they enable teachers to avoid giving "discouraging" grades earlier in the term to students whom they are trying to encourage. Pat Belanoff (in *New Directions for Portfolio Assessment*) points out that in many classrooms, nontraditional students—students of diverse backgrounds, cultures, and language—outnumber "traditional" college students. We cannot assume any longer that our students are homogeneous and that traditional ways of teaching and assessing are a match for every classroom. Portfolios are a way of allowing diverse voices to be heard. Sandra Murphy (in *New Directions for Portfolio Assessment*) suggests that particularly for students whose native language is not English, portfolios reduce some of the stress associated with the structure of traditional ways of teaching and assessing writing where one essay follows another in quick succession and the demand for each is perfection.

Portfolios are used to demonstrate progress, to showcase writing, to evaluate students' writing and thinking, and to encourage collaborative learning and reflection. Colleagues have asked me why the same things can't be achieved without using portfolios; my response is that they can, but it is often more difficult for both teacher and student. There are a number of reasons why this is so.

Time

Portfolios change our sense of time in significant ways. Because portfolios are at the very least collections of work, they must be constructed over an extended period of time. This is very different from an essay that must be written by Monday (and too often is composed on Sunday night!), followed by another two weeks later, followed by another one. . . . Because portfolios are usually selections of work, they require that students examine their work as it appears over time; this consideration helps them understand what it is they have learned and how what they've learned has manifested itself in writing. They are constantly looking both backward at what they have collected and forward toward the portfolio they will create.

When students have little time to think about each essay, when they feel pressed to create, they often fall back on what they are most familiar with, continuing to use the time-honored strategies that have gotten them decent grades in the past, ignoring what we are trying to teach them about writing in this new collegiate setting. Because students begin a portfolio course knowing that not all they write will "count" in the usual way (but all of it can be acknowledged), they often feel free to explore and experiment. Thus some pieces will count for a grade, but all pieces can count for learning. They have the freedom to decide how much time they will spend on these different pieces and processes.

"Why can't I achieve the same thing by allowing students to revise all semester?" teachers ask. Certainly, knowing they have that option relieves some of the pressure on students. However, receiving grades on their essays often reduces the motivation for students to continue learning and revising. Those satisfied with the grade generally do not revise even if the piece would benefit from revision, and those dissatisfied with their grade often revise with the expectation that any change will result in a higher grade. In addition, many writers, particularly those least familiar with the demands of college-level writing, have difficulty writing each essay, let alone juggling revisions of multiple essays. Generally portfolios provide opportunities for learning reflection and student choice that other assessment methods do not allow.

Most teachers will admit that student writing often improves if the students have time to think over what they've written and how their audiences responded to it. Portfolios are one way of creating that time for students. It also changes the way we teach and respond. When the decision about what and how to revise rests more firmly with the student, our responses to writing as teachers may be less geared toward a grade. We can develop comments that help students learn and improve rather than ones that justify the grade we gave. In other words, our assessment becomes more formative and less summative. We are not simply "putting off" grading; we are grading when the "time is right."

Collaboration

Because students must make decisions about what to include in a portfolio, they must pay attention to what their peers and teacher say about their writing. In this way, collaboration is fostered. In cases where the choice of portfolio contents is left largely to the student, portfolios may vary greatly in their shape. If students share their portfolios with one another in peer response groups which are part of most process classrooms, then writers must explain the kinds of writing they've included and help focus discussion in order to receive the level of response that will help them revise. In essence, they must teach their peers about their writing. This kind of interaction encourages active learning on the part of students; they must make critical decisions about their writing, educate peers and teacher about those decisions, and accept responsibility for the quality of the writing.

If we see writing as performance—like art, theatre, or dance—then portfolios offer one of the best ways to judge that performance (Black, et al., "Connecting Current Research," 1994). Portfolios are complex documents which reflect the complexity of the act of writing. Furthermore, they can be firmly a part of the classroom context, rejecting local standards and concerns. They speak to teachers' and students' needs to learn and assess in ways that standardized tests and externally generated assessments and criteria do not.

■ PREPARING TO USE PORTFOLIOS

New teachers often inherit or are given syllabi that reflect someone else's sets of beliefs or purposes. When they try to integrate portfolios that reflect their own beliefs into the preexisting curriculum, or when they try to tack on to a course a portfolio designed for a different purpose or even simply a different section of the same course, they are likely to find a mismatch. Sometimes, teachers have not thought through clearly what is implied by their practice.

But for portfolios—or any kind of assessment—to support learning, it is important to be able to answer some questions for yourself before your students ask them of you.

When students enter the classroom and read for the first time through a syllabus which states they will be working all semester toward a final portfolio, many of them will be confused and not a little anxious, particularly if they are new to college anyway. It is helpful to provide them with some guidelines, even if those have not been fully worked out yet. They want to know something about what a portfolio is and why they are constructing one; they want to know what it might or should include, how they will organize it, and how it will be assessed. They want to know who will read it.

In order to answer the seemingly simple questions students might pose, an instructor must deal with some thorny issues beforehand. What are the goals for my course? How do these reflect institutional goals? What purpose does my course serve? What purpose does the portfolio serve? What do I believe about learning and writing? How does the portfolio I want my students to construct reflect my beliefs?

Pedagogical Beliefs

As mentioned earlier, it's entirely possible for a teacher to use portfolios and change very little that he or she does in the classroom. Students could still be assigned topics to write on and modes to write in; could still work individually without discussing writing with peers; and could place all their work in a folder with their name on it and submit it to their teacher, who would average all the grades together and give the student a final grade. The instructor controls all learning from the beginning. However, what I've tried to point out above is that the features of portfolio use—and their benefits in terms of learning—come about when students are permitted to share in their learning. What would the portfolio described above communicate about the beliefs of the teacher and the structure of the classroom?

Clearly, portfolios can be designed to serve a number of purposes, and when we consider how we will shape the portfolios that are parts of the courses we teach, we must consider not only what our goals are for the course, but what we believe about learning; we must examine our pedagogical theory. As Sandra Murphy points out, portfolios not only allow students to demonstrate skills or explore issues in depth, they also reflect our theoretical perspectives on teaching and learning ("Portfolios and Curriculum Reform," 1994). She describes several kinds of portfolios and how they reflect differing beliefs. A behaviorist portfolio, for example, would manifest the belief that learning is both observable and measurable as a set of discrete skills; such a portfolio might be a collection of skills in the form of worksheets. In a classroom where the focus is cognitivist, that is, focused on the processes by which we think and learn, portfolios would be constructed to demonstrate the student's ability to collaborate, reflect, self-assess, revise, etc. They would be evaluated not just for evidence of these processes but the level at which they are performed. So, for example, in an institution where there is concern about first-year students' abilities to punctuate properly, two teachers may use portfolios to address those concerns, but in one case the portfolio may show little evidence of "skills and drills," instead seeing skills as inseparably part of various learning processes, while another portfolio may focus more on worksheets and exercises.

One Course Among Many

In designing a course that uses portfolios, we need to think, too, about possible connections among courses. First-year English classes are often considered "service" courses, or may be part of a sequence of writing/English courses. In institutions with strong writing across the curriculum and writing in the disciplines programs, the first-year writing course may be interdisciplinary in nature, filling more than just a niche in the basic skills or "core curriculum" of the institution (see Troyka & Hesse's Chapters 37–39 on writing in the disciplines). Just as any individual assignment within a course is part of a larger context of assignments and learning, each course is part of a larger context of learning. In such cases, teachers must ask themselves questions beyond their own, personal pedagogical goals. These are institutional questions. Does my course prepare students for another course? A series of specific courses? How will my use of portfolios affect student learning and colleagues' expectations for my students when they enter those courses? These are questions that are best discussed in a large forum with all involved faculty. In reality, however, that rarely takes place. Teachers must consider all stakeholders in the assessment. Peter Elbow points out that portfolios

> help us demand the high quality that we want or some other constituency wants: the hard texts themselves, "the real thing," the bottom line. We don't have to accept ineffective writing and justify it to ourselves or to colleagues with defensive talk about the lovely process that lies behind it. On the other hand . . . portfolios reward students for using a good writerly process: to explore a topic in discussion and exploratory writing; to complicate their thinking; to allow for perplexity and getting lost; to get feedback; to revise; and to collaborate. (New Direction in Portfolio Assessment)

Yet I have heard complaints from colleagues that portfolios "distort" what a student is capable of doing. These colleagues are concerned that the time allowed for revision, the collaborative nature of the writing process, and the selection of texts for evaluation produces grade inflation—what I am grading in each portfolio is the work of all my students, and not all the work at that. This complaint may seem at first wrong-headed, but for someone in a field that does not focus on the processes by which they learned to write, in a field where collaboration is less visible and where it is not the writing that is extensively revised but the activities that lead up to the writing, the complaint is very real and must be discussed seriously. This is a case where discussions among faculty as well as discussion in the classroom about contexts for writing and disciplinary expectations is important.

■ Using Portfolios

Sandra Murphy lists a number of purposes for portfolios, ranging from

> tracking student development over time, showcasing student response to a range of assignments, evaluating student work across the curriculum, motivating students, promoting learning through reflection and self-assessment, and evaluating students' thinking and writing processes, to program implementation, program assessment, evaluating curriculum, or establishing exit requirements. The possibilities are multiple. ("Portfolios and Curriculum Reform . . . ," 1994, 179–80)

Clearly, the portfolios designed to meet the purposes listed above will each be different. A portfolio used to place students into the proper course level will likely contain writing that is similar to the kinds of writing taught in the courses under consideration. A portfolio to demonstrate development over time would include writing from a student's earliest courses as well as from later courses, and perhaps from courses in a variety of disciplines. A number of models exist, but portfolios need to grow out of the local context. Regardless of how portfolios are to be used, instructors need to make decisions about content, the kinds of choices available for students as they construct their portfolios, how portfolios will be organized, and how they will be evaluated.

Contents

The contents of a portfolio reflect its purpose and the classroom it grows out of. For example, in a writing course offered for developmental writers, the emphasis of the portfolio might be progress. Rather than constructing a portfolio that showcases only her best work, a student might include her first paper and papers written midway and at the end of the semester. She might also include journal entries that reflect development, drafts of papers showing increasing sensitivity to the needs of readers, and written critiques of others' papers that show how she has learned to constructively respond. If she is required to self-assess, she may not focus on how her final papers deserve an "A" by some outside standards, but on how much she has learned over the semester and how a reader might see that demonstrated in the artifacts in front of him. She might discuss what has been difficult for her to learn and what she wants to get out of the next course she will take.

Such a portfolio will be very different from one constructed by students near the end of their college work who are showcasing their writing for potential employment or graduate school. Such a portfolio would be much more product-oriented than process-oriented, focusing on achievement rather than development. It might include a reflective essay which explores career and life goals, examples of different types of writing—technical, business and professional, "academic," reports, creative writing, journalism or scientific writing—that are important to the field which the student wishes to enter, and even a resume or cv.

A sample of portfolio contents for a course in creative writing follows.

English 372
Poetry

Your portfolio must include at a minimum:

> ➤ Five poems

> ➤ Two critiques of classmates' poetry

> ➤ A revised, two-page section of your critical essay

> ➤ A reflective essay

Other items you could include:

> ➤ additional poems

> ➤ materials generated from your class presentation

> ➤ additional critiques

> ➤ entries from your writer's log

The portfolio contents shown here reflect both my attempt to create in the class a culture of poetry, and the students' desires to keep the focus squarely on the writing of poetry and their development as poets. Responding to poems, speaking about and teaching poetry, and writing critically—extensive reviews, an examination of a particular aspect of poetry, or exploring an issue in poetry—seemed to me to be part of the life of a professional poet in this country. My purpose in the portfolio was for students to present their abilities to write in the range of genres and purposes typically visited by a poet. My students, however, wanted to emphasize in their portfolios their creative writing and their ability to reflect upon their work. Many included several more poems, much draft material, and extensive reflective pieces.

Reflection

In the portfolio guidelines above, I ask students to include a reflective essay. Many find this both the most difficult and most interesting piece they write for the portfolio. Writing reflectively is often a new experience for students. Some students may have kept diaries, but a diary isn't necessarily reflective; it may simply list the day's activities without comment. Reflection can take a variety of forms. In some cases, the reflective essay acts as an introduction to the portfolio. In such an instance, the student's reflection usually touches on most of the items that will follow. The student may discuss the organizing principles she used to construct the portfolio, the relationship between pieces, the purpose she sees her portfolio serving, or may answer direct questions from the teacher. The reflective piece may be entirely separate from the introduction. A student might then focus more on one aspect of her writing or development rather than touch on all the pieces we've read. If the reflective essay is placed last, she can assume certain kinds of knowledge on the reader's part, gained from their experience of the rest of the portfolio. Reflection doesn't necessarily involve evaluation; it may be more descriptive, comparative, or ruminative. However, many teachers ask students to engage in some self-assessment in their reflective piece.

It is important to consider the kind of "reflection" you want students to engage in, to consider the purpose of the essay as part of the portfolio and as part of the whole learning process. Students may need extensive practice in writing reflectively for different purposes; such practice can be built into the curriculum through journal entries, writer's memos, self-evaluations, among other methods.

Choice

One crucial issue in portfolios is choice. Who will decide what constitutes a portfolio and who will decide the criteria by which it will be evaluated? For students to feel they have ownership over their learning, they must be actively involved in making those choices. A portfolio driven by a constructivist pedagogy, Murphy notes, provides "a means for engaging students in self-reflection and for acknowledging their role as collaborators in the learning process" ("Portfolios and Curriculum Reform . . . ," 1994, 190). In most courses, the teacher sets the goals before the students even settle into their seats, before they even register for the class. When that happens, it's difficult for students to consider themselves "collaborators" in their learning. Yet it is possible to accommodate students' goals, as well as allow students choices in how they meet the goals you have set for them. If one course goal is for students to understand the political and ethical dimensions of their writing and the writing of others, for example, not every student needs to demonstrate that in the same way. Making choices is part of active learning. Students benefit most when they solve problems connected with constructing their portfolios, when they make critical decisions about the shape and quantity of the contents, when they articulate and explore the beliefs and goals that shape their individual portfolios. If all the important decisions have been made and room for choices has been narrowed to almost nothing before students even begin to understand what a portfolio is, then many of the perceived benefits of portfolio learning and assessment that convinced a teacher to use portfolios have been lost. When developing the syllabus for a portfolio course, then, it is important to consider how student voices will be heard as each set of choices must be made.

Organization

The organization of the portfolio may also be a matter of the student's choice. The order in which items are to be read can be significant. Perhaps the student wants to emphasize his understanding of his writing process; he might ask us to read first the notes, then the drafts, then the final version for each essay. Perhaps another wants to emphasize that each essay selected has an important connection to a particular issue or concern of the student. She might then organize the portfolio in a circular way, one that emphasizes the recursive nature of her thinking and the items that provoked it. Students often use a table of contents, which may be annotated; they may also use an introduction which not only tells readers what they will be reading but explains the organizing principle and develops a context for reading.

Evaluating Portfolios

How will you evaluate a portfolio? What will the criteria be? Will the criteria assume that development or progress will take place? Or will development be given credit in some way, as many students request? What would development look like on paper? Are the criteria understood by everyone? For example, if "understanding the writing process" is part of the criteria, does that mean a theoretical writing process—collecting and generating ideas and information, developing that information alone and with peers, focusing the topic more tightly, ordering material to meet the needs of the audience as well as the writer, continuing to develop and revise the writing and still meeting an external deadline—or the writer's own process, which may be very different? How would a student demonstrate such an understanding? Through self-assessment? Through responses to peers?

Often as teachers we are so imbedded in the language and assumptions of our fields that we forget that once we, too, didn't know what these words meant. And sometimes, we have never articulated these understandings to ourselves, let alone students. Such articulation is, however, more than just a valuable exercise. It is an important part of demystifying evaluation and opening up the process to those being evaluated. Students may even be involved in establishing criteria for evaluation, particularly if their goals for the course have been built into the portfolio. Some teachers who use port-folios ask their students to participate in the final assessment process, as they have been involved throughout the semester in many ways in their peers' effort to construct a portfolio.

Typically, portfolios are evaluated holistically. That is, each piece is not graded separately, but all of them together present a picture of the writer. A journal entry, which may have errors in punctuation and spelling, miss-ing words, sentence fragments, and other differences from conventional written English, may be an important part of a writer's strategy of demon-strating the ability to generate, develop, and support ideas. Seen in a later form, perhaps an essay, the ideas have been shaped to fit an audience and presented following the conventions of standard written English. Which piece is more important? How do you separate out the journal entry—the generative material—from the product in the portfolio? Such variety in form, purpose, and audience among pieces in a portfolio demands a holis-tic reading.

Some teachers who use portfolios create a rubric that they share with students. In such a rubric, defining features of an "A" portfolio are described, as are the features of portfolios that fall into other grade ranges. (See Appendix D for one such rubric.) Students and teacher can refer to the rubric as they are constructing the portfolio and afterwards, as grades are being anticipated and assigned. Some teachers use the reflective essay as an integral part of evaluation. If a student makes a claim in such a piece that she has improved her ability to organize a long essay, then the teacher may look for evidence in the rest of the portfolio to support such a claim.

At some institutions, portfolios are read by an instructor other than the student's or a group of instructors. In such cases, the student's instructor can act as a coach rather than a grader; it radically changes the teacher/student relationship. Others use a process called "team-grading" or group grading. Instructors exchange portfolios according to a set pattern. Each portfolio may receive multiple grades. Discrepancies between grades are usually resolved through discussion or an additional reader. This method reflects the complexity of reading and grading any written texts, but espe-cially a document as varied in its parts as a portfolio.

■ PREPARING STUDENTS FOR PORTFOLIOS

When the use of portfolios has radically changed the ways in which students participate in learning and writing, even the most familiar practices may be altered, may seem strange or unfamiliar. For example, because I want students to pay attention to one another and to emphasize the social nature of the classroom, I ask students to arrange their desks in a circle. While this doesn't automatically keep students from only addressing me, it works much better than when students are arranged "theatre style" and see only the backs of the students in front of them. But this simple change is problematic for many students, and often it takes weeks to teach them that when they come into class, they should automatically place their desks in a circle. If this small change is so difficult, imagine how difficult it is for students to understand the changes in writing, learning, and assessment that can take place in a portfolio culture!

While the use of portfolios is becoming more widespread, it is still a new concept for many students. We must remember as teachers that if we want students to perform in certain ways and at a particular level at the end of the semester, we must give them practice throughout the course. We cannot reasonably expect students to understand and apply criteria for evaluation without exposure and practice, nor can we expect them to write a reflective essay to include in a portfolio without any exposure to the various forms such writing can take. Also we need to ensure we are giving feedback on their performance throughout the term so that they are not surprised or dismayed when they receive their final portfolio grade.

Introductory Portfolios

One way to begin is with introductory portfolios.* These portfolios include items that introduce the student to his or her classmates. Students select a small number of items that represent various aspects of their lives or selves and write a brief introduction to the items. Often, these items include a photo of the student and family and friends; awards; an example of something the student collects; something to represent the student's career goals. One of my students brought in a large wall map to represent her interest in geography; another brought in a can of children's band-aids to represent her goal of becoming a pediatrician. Another brought in his hockey skates, and yet another brought in a corn-husk doll made for her by her grandmother. As students share these portfolios, they ask each other questions about the items and what they represent; the student whose portfolio is being

---

*I borrowed this wonderful assignment from John Gaughan several years ago.

discussed begins to articulate more clearly her criteria for selection. After sharing is through, students can reconsider items—based on their peers' responses, would they choose something different if they could do it again? They consider what they included in their written introductions. Now that they have heard the responses evoked by the items in their portfolios, would they introduce them differently? As a class and individually, they begin to learn about collection, selection, revision, presentation, and evaluation. This is an example of portfolios for learning, not assessment.

Writer's Memo

Most students are used to handing in essays without generative or draft materials, as if the piece had written itself or sprung from their pens or computers fully developed. Usually, too, students hand in essays without any accompanying explanation of their intent, their process, their successes and failures in the piece as it stands. And typically there's no reason why they should; after all, the teacher assigned it, gave them the topic, and knows more about their writing and why they would write such an essay than they themselves do. But in a portfolio culture, where decision making and problem solving are part of the learning environment, drafts and discussions of essays are important. Jeffrey Sommers (1989) champions the use of "writers' memos" which explain what the student was intending to accomplish by writing this portfolio, what process she used in constructing it, where she encountered difficulty and where it was easiest, what her concerns are, and what she would like the reader to focus on. In writing such a memo, the student looks back through the drafts that preceded the essay the teacher sees. In reflecting on her process and articulating her choices, she begins to understand the power the writer has over her work. In expressing her concerns about the piece, she is working with criteria for "good" or "bad" writing and is learning to evaluate her own work. Such writers' memos function to prepare students to write reflectively at the end of the semester as they provide a context for reading their portfolios. (See Appendix B for a sample writer's memo assignment.)

Mini-Portfolios

Some courses lend themselves to mid-semester portfolios and unit portfolios. These are ways of practicing the process of putting together a portfolio in miniature and with less anxiety. Mid-semester portfolios ask students to go through the same processes that they will engage in at the end of the semester. Although students have less to select from and those pieces are unlikely to have been extensively revised, a mid-semester portfolio provides a momentary point where learning and assessment clearly come together. It helps to high-light the structure and process of their learning, something particularly impor-tant for new students. Unit portfolios help students reflect on learning at points throughout the semester when material changes. They are particularly effective in content courses. I have used them myself in first-year literature courses, asking students to construct portfolios organized around a single text or perhaps two texts. Such portfolios have contained journal responses, class notes, one or more formal essays, notes on the reading, responses to study questions, and other materials. One student included as part of her discussion on her learning process a copy of the cover of the *Cliffs Notes* for the text we were reading—she had purchased it in hopes of "sounding more intelligent," but found it disappointing after our class discussion. Another included a copy of the playbill for a play she was performing in as part of her discussion of why she chose to work with a dramatic text rather than a poetic one.

Rubrics, Scoring Guides, and Team-Grading

Students need practice in evaluating writing if they are going to be asked to make decisions on selecting "best" works or in revising their own or responding to others' work. They can participate in describing in a rubric what "good" writing includes and then modifying that description depend-ing upon the assignment. They can also read and respond to writing in "team grading" sessions. Typically, writing that has already received a grade from teachers is distributed to students for discussion and grading follow-ing the guidelines of a rubric. The teacher explains what grade the paper received and why after students have offered their grades. As the discussion continues, students and teacher can begin to articulate what "organized" or "focused" or "creative" mean both in the context of the classroom and in terms of external standards.

Students can respond, assess, and evaluate each other's portfolios and essays. Although most students are reluctant to give a grade, at least initially, they will place writing into categories such as "young," "teenaged" or "mature" (see Appendix D). They can assess with the assistance of rubrics which they have helped to design. And with a variety of sample portfolios and papers that they have discussed during team grading, they can offer suggestions for improvement. "Well, this one got a B from the teachers and we gave it a B+ and the writer does this," they might say. "You might try that in here." Having practice in writing memos, the author whose work is under discussion can help focus the responses, can explain with more clarity his intent and difficulties.

Students can also participate in creating the final guidelines and crite-ria for evaluation. Even if the teacher had initially established criteria, it may well be that the course has shifted in focus, or that the goals that students articulated have shifted the course to some extent. It has been my experience that when I ask students what an "excellent" portfolio should include, should look like, and should communicate, they demand far more of it than I would. If they have had practice all semester, they will likely have internalized many of the criteria that the teacher has offered them. They will have some of their own as well, and as a teacher, I have always learned important things from listening to what my students value in writing. (Appendix A includes evaluation questions.)

In such a course, the defining features of the process of creating a portfolio are foregrounded again and again. The structure of the course itself and the theory that drives the practice are often on display and under question. Using portfolios often means giving up some of the control traditionally exercised by the teacher. But it is usually an even deal. When control is shared, so is learning.

■ PITFALLS AND PROBLEMS IN PORTFOLIO USE

Borrowing Portfolios: Make Your Own Recipe

When teachers share stories of "what worked in my class" with each other, it's always tempting to simply take a strategy that was successful in one class and apply it to another. But as I've pointed out above, a portfolio—even one designed for another section of the same course—reflects a whole set of beliefs about teaching and learning. Without a serious consideration of what you believe and what goals you have set for the course, it is unlikely that you can simply tack on a portfolio designed by another teacher and find success. The most successful portfolios grow out of the local context: the beliefs, goals, and abilities of the teacher and students who will construct them.

Supporting Portfolios with Course Design

Another difficulty is designing a course to support portfolios. Portfolios flourish in courses with a lot of writing and interaction. In a literature course that involves a great deal of lecture, a limited amount of group work, and a midterm and final, the foundation for portfolios is shaky. In order to make choices in selecting pieces for a portfolio, students must have a sufficient body of work to select from. If students write only three papers over the semester, there are few tough decisions to make when they are asked to select two of them for a portfolio. For a portfolio to include writing other than formal essays, for example, journal entries, drafts, responses to study questions, critiques of peers' work, writing from other courses, or even texts that aren't written—videotaped peer group work, perhaps—students must have the opportunity to produce such texts. They also need to produce them in a quantity sufficient to give them practice in such writing—and presumably then, the opportunity for improvement over time—and to give them a large enough collection to be able to select examples to include in a final portfolio. Thus, if students are asked to write critiques of each other's work only once during the semester and the rest of the time they respond orally, yet in the final portfolio they are asked to demonstrate that they can respond constructively to a peer's text, they will either have to submit their first written critique (quite probably not their best work) or make arrangements to submit an audio- or videotape of their performance.

What is important to remember here is that portfolios cannot simply be "added" to a course. Assessment and curriculum dance with one another in tight steps. They drive one another. If in a traditional literature course the lectures all "teach to the test," which is a single-sitting, timed, final exam, then in a course where students will construct a final portfolio, we must teach to that form of assessment, too. Opportunities for practicing the kinds of writing that will be required in the final portfolio must be built into a syllabus. If a portfolio is to be sensitive to student goals and writing desires, then the syllabus must be flexible enough to support that as well. If you are going to offer students the chance to place a text of their choice in the portfolio, it's important to remember that the chosen text might be a poem or short story they wrote. Will there be time built into the syllabus for such personal or experimental writing? Will there be time built in for the revision and reconsideration of texts at points throughout the semester?

Lost Drafts and Papers, Erased Disks

Most instructors hear at least once a semester: "I left my paper in the library and someone took it" or "I had the whole thing done and then my disk went bad." This problem is magnified when a student loses a whole portfolio or the working portfolio from which she will select material for presentation. Encouraging students to back up their work and to print up-do-date hard copies of their revised pieces is a good first step. Another solution is to ask students to submit copies of drafts and papers to you as they work on them or turn them in. This produces its own logistical problems, even when using disks. Similarly, students can team up in a "buddy system" and submit copies of all their materials to at least one other student. Some campuses may have the resources for students to develop and store electronic portfolios.

Muddy Waters: Grading Portfolios

Reading a portfolio is not entirely unlike reading a single essay, but it does present some additional challenges. When we read a single essay or paper, we may find we have formed an opinion about the writer's skills very early in our reading, perhaps in the opening paragraphs. This opinion may well be correct, particularly if the paper is short; after all, in a five paragraph theme we will have read one-fifth of the paper after one paragraph! But a portfolio often contains many pieces, and those pieces may vary widely in their quality.

It is tempting to read an introductory portfolio essay and feel confident in your evaluation of the writer's abilities. But it is likely that within the next few pieces your evaluation will shift back and forth. An insightful journal entry may prompt us to expect the next piece to be a wonderful paper; we may discover, however, that the student had difficulty making a transition from informal to formal writing. We also know as readers of many papers at one sitting that if we read a merely competent essay right after a very poorly written essay, the competent essay may receive a higher grade than it otherwise would. It is important to practice reading portfolios to get a feel for the ways in which these "glow" and "roller coaster" effects within portfolios influence our grading (Sommers et al., 1993). The ability to withhold judgment is crucial when reading portfolios. In some ways they are like collages; they do not always have the same kinds of coherence that single essays do.

Holistic grading is unfamiliar not only to most students and many faculty, but also to some administrators. This may present a problem. Will you as the instructor be able to explain holistic grading well enough to satisfy a student unhappy about a grade? A student's parents if necessary? If a grade is challenged, will the departmental administrators—the department chair or the Writing Program Administrator—support a holistic portfolio grade, that is, a "C" for an entire body of work? If you are in the position of "pioneering" portfolio use, you may find it necessary to acquaint some of your colleagues or administrators with your grading practices. Developing clear grade descriptions or rubrics can help you clarify for yourself and others what a "C" means on a portfolio. Even though you are grading holistically, you need to have criteria upon which you are making your judgments. Just as we expect students to support assertions with evidence, it is wise for teachers to note evidence the student provided for meeting or not meeting the grading criteria.

Reading the Writer, Not the Writing

There is another aspect of reading portfolios that is also important to remember. Most of us have found ourselves at one point or another really offended by what one of our students has written. We may have found ourselves judging and grading the student more than the writing. When we draw back a bit and think about it, we realize that we are reading just one paper, probably not a very long one at that, and the student's views are probably much more complex than what appears in the essay. Portfolios, however, provide us with not just a more complete picture of the writer's abilities, but of the writer him- or herself. The more complete and complex the picture, the more likely it is that we will respond to some aspect of the portfolio that is not part of the agreed-upon criteria. It becomes easier to "like" or "dislike" the author of a portfolio, and more difficult to maintain the kind of professional stance—that tightwire act we juggle all the time when we respond honestly to our students and their work—that we need to draw on when grading.

Reflective essays are especially sites where the personal aspects of the writer/student/teacher/evaluator relationship may become even more complicated than usual. As Glenda Conway (1994) and Nedra Reynolds (1994) point out, it is in a reflective essay (often used to both self-assess and introduce the portfolio) that students try most apparently to negotiate that relationship. They are aware keenly of their audience, but the multiple purposes of the essay often become entangled. Depending upon the assignment for the essay, students may be compelled to discuss their weaknesses as a writer, even though the portfolio is supposedly their best work. They may feel compelled to compliment the teacher (I really liked the way you responded to my work, I think you could relate to me), evaluate the course (I'm weak because I didn't get any practice in this area), or even adopt a stance that sets them apart from their classmates and teacher (while you want this portfolio to showcase work, I want to emphasize effort and progress). Given that reflective essays are often introductory essays and likely to be the first substantive materials in a portfolio, they are often given more weight and importance than other pieces. They set the tone and establish the relationship between reader and writer. This is very problematic when the reader must also actually grade the portfolio. Practice in writing reflectively, attention to issues of audience, and attention to the final portfolio's shape are important. One solution is to place annotated tables of contents or clearly introductory essays first and reflective essays last. Another is to examine the ways in which description becomes evaluation. Finally, Conway suggests that each teacher examine the ethics of asking students to draw attention to weaknesses in such an essay.

Grading Logistics: Dealing with the Paper Load

I have heard colleagues say they don't use portfolios because there is too much to evaluate during the last week of a semester—the grading load is overwhelming. Often, these same colleagues have never used portfolios, but they see as unwelcome the prospect of reading three essays and many other pieces from each student when their own desire to assess fairly and completely combines with the fast-approaching deadline for a final grade. It has not been my experience, however, that grading portfolios takes much more time than grading final essays and then averaging together the grades for various essays, quizzes, etc., completed over the course of the semester. In fact, I've often found that I have more difficulty assigning a final grade I feel comfortable with when I am considering one piece of writing as the major source of that grade: final exams often count for 40 percent or more of the final course grade. I am reading responses to the same questions over and over, trying to distinguish one from another by the time I've reached the end.

Even a well-designed final exam seems inadequate to me after the experience of reading the multitextual, complex body of work that is a portfolio. My sense is that most teachers would prefer to be able to sit down with a student and talk together over a large quantity of her writing, identifying strengths and weaknesses, areas of great development, and directions for further writing. When I read a portfolio, I feel as if I could and wanted to do that; I also feel as if my students could participate in such a conversation without the usual apologies for test performance: "Well, it was timed, I could've done better with more time;" "I read the book and I thought it was neat that X did this or that but I couldn't remember the name of the guy who . . . . so I missed that question. . . ."

Portfolios are usually read holistically, which means that I can sit back with my coffee cup and read straight through without a pen in my hand. Most of the writing is familiar to me; I have seen it in draft several times, and I have a sense of the history of each piece as I read. The most recent piece, a reflective essay, is the least familiar to me and often the piece my students play with the most. It is a joy to read essays so full of voice and hope and learning. Each is different from the next.

My students and I have created and discussed the grading rubric; we understand the terms we are using, the criteria which are flexible and those that are not. Each portfolio has a copy of the rubric in it. I usually write a quick narrative response, highlighting the strengths of the portfolio and using some of the key words from the rubric. There is little else to consider for the final grade—perhaps a whole semester journal, a classroom presentation, or participation or attendance. Even these aspects of a grade have been discussed and negotiated in my courses.

There is certainly no less work involved in using portfolios instead of a more traditional approach. Like other teachers, I think long and hard about my syllabus as I am constructing the outline of the course; I put time into creating materials to support the various kinds of writing my students are asked to do or may choose to do on their own; I spend a great deal of time helping my students learn to do much of the work themselves as the course progresses. In the end, they give me for a grade a multilayered artifact that we both can say presents their best work—not their best work under the circumstances. Because I am not grading each piece individually, because I have responded to most of this work in earlier drafts, because my response is global and holistic, I can respond swiftly and comfortably to each portfolio.

■ CONNECTING PORTFOLIOS TO THE *SIMON & SCHUSTER HANDBOOK FOR WRITERS*

Much of the material in the handbook can also be applied to the construction of a portfolio. The handbook concentrates on writing to inform and persuade, as these are two of the most common purposes of writing in an academic setting. However, a course designed around writing for these purposes can offer opportunities for both personal and public writing, writing that is expressive and transactional. An instructor might encourage writing that is poetic *and* persuasive—are listeners persuaded by the lyrics of a song? By the imagery of a poem? Such a course may in addition be organized topically, with students selecting one topic to explore over the course of the semester. A final portfolio for such a course might include journal entries about the topic selected, for example, the effect of television violence on viewers. The journal entry is private writing: the audience is the writer and the purpose may be exploratory, an attempt to discover. But in response to assignments that vary audience and purpose, a writer may: produce a mini research paper in which she summarizes the positions generally taken on the topic and the support offered for each; attempt to persuade a local cable company not to offer a particular channel, arguing the violence is damaging to children; write a short children's story which teaches them about television violence; or write up limited original research after surveying peers about their viewing preferences. A final course portfolio could be used to provide information and persuade readers of the writer's position at the end of the semester. The reflective essay for such a portfolio might include a TV-viewing autobiography and a consideration of the connections between the writer's TV viewing and the position, arguments, even the imagery used in the rest of the portfolio.

In an alternative, nontopical final portfolio, rather than focusing on one topic the writer might include essays on various topics and for various audiences, selected and organized to show the writer's increasing sensitivity to the demands of each rhetorical situation.

As students begin working on a portfolio, they might be reminded of what they have learned about the various processes that are part of writing, including newly learned skills in writing on the computer and using the Internet for research. For example, students often want their portfolios to showcase their best work, to demonstrate the breadth of their writing skills, and to provide evidence of progress and effort. But too many purposes will make it difficult to select pieces and revise them. As they construct their final portfolio, students will need to apply what they've learned about narrowing a topic when writing individual essays.

Similarly, the instructor must think carefully about the purpose of the reflective essay and the ways in which the audience for such an essay will effect "reflection." In honest reflection in a private journal, I might admit that I really didn't read the whole book I wrote about for one essay; I just read a few chapters and listened to what was discussed in class. I might wonder how much more I might have learned if I'd read the whole thing, and I might consider how that would change my essay. Personally, I think that's worthwhile reflecting on. But if I knew that my reader was also going to grade me on my portfolio and that essay is part of it, I would be tempted instead to write about why I was interested in the topic of the portfolio— something safe and relatively easy. Students and instructor need to talk about purpose and audience for the reflective essay, as well as topic. Are there some things that the student *must* discuss? Or is the topic wide open, as long as there is some connection to the portfolio?

Students might look back at Chapter 4 in the *Handbook* and consider how they will "think beyond the obvious" as they write an introduction to their portfolio. The reader will make obvious connections, but what are the connections he might not see, and what are the implications of connecting these pieces together in such a way? Instructors might, too, point out the ways that introductions and reflections may appear to be informational in purpose, but are very important in persuading a reader to adopt a certain position as she reads and finally evaluates.

■ CONCLUSION

I hear about portfolios everywhere I turn now. They are being required by administrators who have not read one themselves, explored and even mandated by state legislative bodies, and are following students from grade to grade at all levels of learning. They are being used to place students in courses, to evaluate programs, and to demonstrate competency in major fields. They are being used by teachers themselves in rank and tenure applications. They are being tacked onto courses at all levels of learning and at institutions nationwide.

Portfolios present unique opportunities for both learning and assessment because they focus our attention at various times on both the processes of writing and the products that we construct. They are often complex and challenging both to create and evaluate. But they are one assessment instrument among many, and are certainly not the only way to help students learn. By themselves they are not a panacea for the problems presented by standardized testing, essay tests, and the passivity that can result from lectures and a lack of student involvement in everyday classwork. When they are part of a carefully considered and designed curriculum, however, they can support and help create active learning, collaboration, and the development of critical learning skills such as problem-solving, small-group communication, generating, developing and supporting ideas, and critical thinking and questioning. They do not make teaching easier, but they do change its shape. Faculty who use portfolios as an integral part of their teaching may rediscover themselves as learners. Teachers who have constructed a portfolio themselves, either as a participant in their own class or as part of their professional responsibilities—a teaching portfolio for rank and tenure considerations—find that the processes of learning and writing are foregrounded in ways they have not been for years as we have written professionally, working on individual pieces in the kind of academic writing we are comfortable with. Instructors using portfolios in their classrooms may rediscover or discover for the first time how much their students really know. Too often we see students as their essays, as three pages here, four there. Portfolios show us our students as more than the sum of their parts.

FURTHER READING AND RESOURCES

There are a number of newsletters and journals that are devoted to assessment, some exclusively to portfolio use. In addition, there are several recently published collections of essays about portfolio use that may prove helpful. The articles cited in this introduction provide a good starting place for specific questions you might have about portfolios. And professional conferences in English studies usually offer a number of sessions on portfolio assessment.

The following journals and newsletters are available at many academic libraries. Publishers of these journals may also offer additional instructional aids and resources for study.

AAHE Assessment Forum. American Association for Higher Education. One Dupont Circle, Suite 600, Washington, DC 20036-1110.

Assessing Writing. Ablex Publishing Corporation, 355 Chestnut St., Norwood, NJ, 07648.

CWA Newsletter. Missouri Colloquium on Writing Assessment. Missouri Western State College, St. Joseph, MO 65407.

Notes from the National Testing Network in Writing. National Testing Network in Writing. cuny, 535 East 80th St., New York, NY 10021.

Portfolio Assessment Newsletter. Northwest Evaluation Association. 5 Centerpoint Drive, Suite 100, Lake Oswego, OR 97035.

Portfolio News. c/o San Dieguito Union High School District, 710 Encinitas Boulevard, Encinitas, CA 92024.

Portfolio—The Newsletter of Arts PROPEL. Harvard Project Zero, 323 Longfellow Hall, Harvard Graduate School of Education, 13 Appian Way, Cambridge, MA 02138.

Quarterly of the National Writing Project and Center for the Study of Writing and Literacy. Graduate School of Education, University of California, Berkeley, CA 94720.

* * *

The following recent collections offer essays dealing with the theory and practice of portfolios at levels from elementary through professional.

Black, Laurel, Donald A. Daiker, Jeffrey Sommers, and Gail Stygall, (eds.). *New Directions in Portfolio Assessment.* Reflective Practice, Critical Theory, and Large-Scale Scoring. Portsmouth, NH: Heinemann, Boynton/Cook, 1995.

Belanoff, Pat, and Marcia Dickson, (eds.). *Portfolios: Process and Product.* Portsmouth, NH: Heinemann, Boynton/Cook, 1991.

Farr, Roger C., and Bruce Tone. *Portfolio and Performance Assessment: Helping Students Evaluate Their Progress as Readers and Writers.* 2nd ed. Fort Worth, Tex.: Harcourt Brace, 1998.

Gearhart, Maryl, and Joan L. Herman. "Portfolio Assessment: Whose Work Is It? Issues in the Use of Classroom Assignments for Accountability." *Educational Assessment* 5.1 (1998): 41–55.

Howard, Rebecca Moore. "Memoranda to Myself: Maxims for the Online Portfolio." *Computers and Composition* 13.2 (1996): 155–67.

Huit, Brian A. "Computers and Assessment: Understanding Two Technologies." *Computers and Composition* 13.2 (1996): 231–43.

Mondock, Sheryl L. "Portfolios—The Story Behind the Story." *English Journal* 86 (Jan. 1997): 59–64.

Nelson, Alexis. "Views from the Underside: Proficiency Portfolios in First-Year Composition." *Teaching English in the Two-Year College* 26.3 (Mar. 1999): 243–53.

Purves, Alan C. "Electronic Portfolios." *Computers and Composition* 13.2 (1996): 135–46.

Sommers, Jeffrey. "Portfolios in Literature Courses: A Case Study." *Teaching English in the Two Year College* 24 (Oct. 1997): 220–34.

Wilcox, Bonita L. "Writing Portfolios: Active vs. Passive." *English Journal* 86 (Oct. 1997): 34–37.

Yancey, Kathleen Blake (ed.). *Portfolios in the Writing Classroom.* Urbana, IL: NCTE, 1992.

———. *Situating Portfolios: Four Perspectives.* Logan, Utah: Utah State UP, 1997.

WEB RESOURCES

Web Resources can be found at **www.prenhall.com/troyka** under Instructor's Resources.

WORKS CITED

Black, Laurel, Edwina Helton, and Jeffrey Sommers. "Connecting Current Research on Authentic and Performance Assessment Through Portfolios." *Assessing Writing* 1.2 (1994): 247–266.

Black, Laurel, Donald A. Daiker, Jeffrey Sommers, and Gail Stygall, (eds.). *New Directions in Portfolio Assessment.* Reflective Practice, Critical Theory, and Large-Scale Scoring. Portsmouth, NH: Heinemann, Boynton/Cook, 1995.

Belanoff, Pat. "Portfolios and Literacy: Why?" *New Directions in Portfolio Assessment.* Eds. Laurel Black, Donald A. Daiker, Jeffrey Sommers, and Gail Stygall. Portsmouth, NH: Heinemann, Boynton/Cook, 1994.13–24.

Conway, Glenda. "Portfolio Cover Letters, Students' Self-Presentation, and Teachers' Ethics." *New Directions in Portfolio Assessment.* Eds. Laurel Black, Donald A. Daiker, Jeffrey Sommers, and Gail Stygall. Portsmouth, NH: Heinemann, Boynton/Cook, 1994: 83–92.

Elbow, Peter. "Will the Virtues of Portfolios Blind Us to Their Potential Dangers?" *New Directions in Portfolio Assessment.* Eds. Laurel Black,

Donald A. Daiker, Jeffrey Sommers, and Gail Stygall. Portsmouth, NH: Heinemann, Boynton/Cook, 1994. 40–55.

Murphy, Sandra. "Writing Portfolios in K–12 Schools: Implications for Linguistically Diverse Students." *New Directions in Portfolio Assessment*. Eds. Laurel Black, Donald A. Daiker, Jeffrey Sommers, and Gail Stygall. Portsmouth, NH: Heinemann, Boynton/Cook, 1994. 140–156.

——. "Portfolios and Curriculum Reform: Patterns in Practice." *Assessing Writing* 1.2 (1994). 175–206.

Reynolds, Nedra. "Graduate Writers and Portfolios: Issues of Professionalism, Authority, and Resistance." *New Directions in Portfolio Assessment*. Eds. Laurel Black, Donald A. Daiker, Jeffrey Sommers, and Gail Stygall. Portsmouth, NH: Heinemann, Boynton/Cook, 1994. 201–209.

Sommers, Jeffrey, Laurel Black, Donald A. Daiker, and Gail Stygall. "The Challenges of Rating Portfolios: What WPAs Can Expect." *WIPA: Writing Program Administration* 17.1–2 (1993): 7–30.

——. "The Writer's Memo: Collaboration, Response, and Development." *Writing and Response*.

Theory Practice and Research. Ed. Chris Anson. Urbana, IL: NCTE, 19899. 174–86.

White, Edward M. "Portfolios as an Assessment Concept." *New Directions in Portfolio Assessment*. Eds. Laurel Black, Donald A. Daiker, Jeffrey Sommers, and Gail Stygall. Portsmouth, NH: Heinemann, Boynton/Cook, 1994. 25–39.

Wiggins, Grant. "Assessment: Authenticity, Context, and Validity." *Phi Delta Kappan* (1993): 200–214.

——. "The Truth May Make You Free But the Test May Keep You Imprisoned: Toward Assessment Worthy of the Liberal Arts." Paper presented at the fifth American Association for Higher Education (AAHE) Conference on Assessment, Washington, D.C., 1990.

Yancey, Kathleen Blake. "Portfolios for the Writing Instructor: Some Definitions, Some Guidelines, Some Recommendations." *Resource Guide*. 12th ed. Prentice Hall Handbook for Writers. Eds. Melinda G. Kramer, Glenn Legget, C. David Mead. Englewood Cliffs, N.J.: Prentice Hall, 1995. 82–104.

Advanced Composition: English 251

■ COURSE WRITING ASSIGNMENTS

1. Minimum two entries weekly in a journal
2. Introductory profile
3. Five essays: four open and one reflective essay
4. Grammar presentation and workshop
5. Written responses to a peer's paper

■ FINAL PORTFOLIO REQUIREMENTS

1. Table of contents
2. Reflective essay
3. Two essays, revised from earlier drafts
4. Five journal entries

OPTIONAL: Additional journal entries, worksheets, critiques, in-class writing exercises, ?—What else have you been working on that you'd like to include?

■ FINAL COURSE GRADE

The class has decided that final course grades will be computed using the following formula:

Portfolio:	60%
Journal:	15%
Presentation:	5%
Participation:	20%

■ EVALUATING PORTFOLIOS FOR ENGLISH 251

As I read through your portfolio, I will be asking myself the following questions. These questions are based on our discussion over the course of the semester, and particularly on our discussion on "excellence" last week. As you construct your portfolios, you can ask yourself the same questions.

➤ Does the writer demonstrate the ability to develop and support a thesis where necessary?

➤ Does the writer demonstrate the ability to ask questions of her material that allow her to fully explore her topic?

➤ Does the writer demonstrate the ability to think critically about the material with which he is working?

➤ Does the writer demonstrate the ability to make what he or she writes interesting to a reader

➤ Does the writer engage the reader?

➤ Does the writer demonstrate the ability to use language appropriate to the rhetorical situation?

➤ Does the writer demonstrate the ability to write following the conventions of standard written English?

➤ Does the writer demonstrate the ability to write for a variety of purposes?

I don't ask these questions about each single piece in the portfolio, but I ask them when they appear appropriate. I won't ask that a journal entry be free from error, but I do expect that your essays be free from error. I may feel that you have suggested some abilities and demonstrated others as I read through the whole portfolio. The more you are able to demonstrate, rather than suggest, the higher your portfolio grade will be. You and I will have met in a conference as you are making portfolio decisions, and we will read and respond to each other's rough portfolios in class before they are due.

Writer's Memo Assignment

A **writer's memo** is a way of letting readers in on the purpose you had in composing your essay. It also helps readers understand the process you used in constructing your writing. Readers will be better able to understand why you put this particular piece of support here, an anecdote there, why you chose your title, why you concluded what you did. A writer's memo is a way of following your essay around, explaining the things you might if you were sitting with you readers, talking about your writing.

When this memo is intended for a teacher who will give you response and a grade, it provides other kinds of information as well. For example, the teacher may come to understand that you have definite ideas and plans for your writing but have difficulty turning plans into writing in certain situations. She may then be able to offer you some advice or guidance. The teacher may also be better able to understand how you evaluate your writing and share with you her evaluation.

Another way the memos help you is the practice they give you in writing reflectively and writing about writing. Over the course of multiple drafts and a whole semester, you will have written a number of these memos. If you look back at them at the end of the semester, you may be able to see how you have developed successful techniques for approaching assignments, that you have learned how to write about writing, or that you have continued to struggle with one aspect of your writing but been successful with others.

As you write your memo consider giving the reader answers to the following questions:

➤ When did you start thinking about this paper? What ideas did you consider? Why did you reject the others and select this one to work with?

➤ When did you actually start writing the paper? What prompted you to write or what kept you from writing? Did you use a different process when writing this paper from one that you used in the past?

➤ What were the major decisions you made while writing the first draft? When you revised? Why did you decide what you did?

➤ What did you learn—if anything—from writing this paper? Should we as readers be able to tell what you learned as we read the paper?

➤ What are the strengths of this paper? Why?

➤ What parts of the paper aren't quite as strong? Why?

➤ What grade would you give this paper right now and why?

➤ What would you like your readers to get from this paper?

➤ What would you like your readers to focus on as they prepare to respond to the paper or prepare suggestions for revision?

As you write your memo, imagine you are having a dialogue with an interested reader, someone who wants to know how you did what you did and why, someone whom you trust to respond honestly and constructively.

Reflective Essay Assignment

Your reflective essay introduces readers to your portfolio. It allows you to share with readers the choices you made while constructing this portfolio. It helps readers understand your writing process and your learning throughout the term. Readers will be better able to understand why you selected the pieces you did and what achievements they should expect to see in your portfolio.

Through the term, you have produced writer's memos for each essay assignment you've submitted. Referring to these writer's memos can provide you with ideas to use in your reflective essay. Look for ways your writing has changed over time, areas you have been struggling with throughout the term, approaches or strategies that have been effective for you, what you have learned, what your strengths are, and so forth. As you develop your essay, ask yourself how and why these changes have occurred.

In addition to looking back on your writer's memos, responding to some of the following questions may help you write your reflective essay:

> Which pieces did you choose to include and why? What do these pieces show us about you as a writer or learner?

> What did you learn about writing, about yourself as a writer, or about yourself as a learner through the course of the semester?

> What strategies for finding, developing, or revising ideas did you find most helpful and why? Least helpful? (Consider discussing your process in the context of one of your portfolio pieces.)

> How have you improved, and how could someone reading this portfolio see that improvement?

> What do you consider to be your strengths and weaknesses as a writer? Why?

> Which piece do you feel best shows your achievements as a writer? Why?

> What goals did you have when beginning this course? Did you achieve them? If so, show how. If not, discuss why. What are your future goals for writing?

> What would you like your readers to get from this portfolio?

> What did you get from compiling this portfolio?

Like any essay, your reflective essay should be well crafted and well developed. When you make assertions about your learning or your writing, you will need to support them with evidence from your work. Although the reflective essay helps gives readers a framework for understanding your portfolio, even more importantly, the reflective essay is for you. During a busy semester, students are often so busy reading and writing that they forget to consider what they have learned through the process. Use your reflective essay as a place to think about what you have accomplished.

APPENDIX D
Portfolio Response Rubric*

Young Portfolio—A portfolio that is full of possibilities not yet realized. The reader has a sense that the portfolio as a whole is undeveloped. It is often short and lacks substance. The writing may be free from errors, but it does not possess a strong voice. There may be no clear sense of audience or purpose. There may also be recurring problems in content and style. The reflective essay may substitute surface narrative and summary for reflection. The writing may rely on formulas and cliches. On the other hand, there may be moments of effective writing, places where the writer hints at strengths that are yet to be developed.

Teenaged Portfolio—In this portfolio we see pretty clearly the shape of things to come. The writing is competent in both content and style. There may be an unevenness of quality or underdevelopment in places—perhaps the reflective essay doesn't offer a full picture of the writer's work, or several pieces seem to need attention to bring them up to the level of development seen in another piece. The reader may want "more" to be fully convinced of the writer's ability to use language effectively. But the writer takes more risks with her work. Her voice is stronger, more original. She has a clearer sense of where she stands with her writing and her audience.

Mature Portfolio—This portfolio is substantial in development and accomplishment. It engages its readers, invites them into a mature dialogue. It uses language effectively and creatively. The reflective essay moves well beyond summary to help provide a context for understanding the writer and the writing. At the upper range of this group, mature portfolios take risks that work and challenge their readers by trying something new.

Remember: No portfolio is perfect, and each of these groups represent a range and a variety (a thirteen-year-old is different from a nineteen-year-old, yes?). So as you respond to your peers, keep in mind that you might make even finer, more accurate analogies for them.

---

*These descriptions draw on Miami University's scoring guide for placement portfolios. Edwina Helton suggests the terms "starting," "working," and "polished" for these three levels. I have found students enjoy the category descriptors used above, even adding a few of their own in close-knit peer groups: "infant" and "old man."

PART FOUR:

Multilingual Writers in the Composition Class
by Cynthia Myers, *Iowa State University*

■ INTRODUCTION

When I was in my second semester of teaching freshman composition as a graduate student, I had an articulate and motivated Colombian student in my class. I enjoyed having Julio in class and optimistically hoped that my course could help him mature as a writer. One day after class, he approached me with a paper I had corrected and kindly asked me to explain a few of the mistakes he had made: He wanted to thoroughly understand which situations required the present perfect and which required the past perfect. I launched into an explanation, but as I talked, I suddenly realized that I had only a vague notion of the answer. I knew it had something to do with time frame, but why exactly couldn't Julio say "I have lived in Kansas since six months ago"? It was not something I had ever really considered, nor was it a grammar question that had come up in my teaching of high school English to native speakers.

I began to notice how many grammar errors I had corrected on Julio's paper: the page was covered with green ink. I also began to suspect that my corrections were probably not going to help him avoid making the mistakes another time. I noticed how few substantive comments I had made to help him with revising his material and reorganizing his ideas. I began to feel embarrassed, and then apologetic, and finally inadequate. How could I help him improve his writing without becoming mired in long and confusing grammar explanations? How could I help him improve his grammar when I had such an incomplete understanding of the language myself?

I tell the story because I believe my feelings of incompetence at that time have probably been felt by many teachers suddenly faced with nonnative students whose questions and whose presence in a class with native speakers are disquieting. As teachers of writing, we want to help all students, but without specialized training we may be uncertain how to proceed. Will we embarrass a quiet Japanese student if we ask him to share an especially poetic description with the rest of the class? Is it useful to mark the many errors that appear on an Indonesian student's first draft? Should we tell a Puerto Rican student that her lateness to class is disruptive since we know that her Latin American sense of time is different from our own? Should we avoid calling on a Chinese student whose spoken English is difficult to understand? And, in addition to the many questions we may have about individual nonnative speakers, how do we handle classroom dynamics to encourage the native-speaking students to include nonnative speakers when they choose collaborative or peer review groups? How can we foster an atmosphere in which all students feel empowered?

My role as coordinator of a program of cross-cultural freshman English classes at a large state university has given me some insights into the challenges faced by composition teachers who work with classes made up of native and nonnative English speakers, particularly when the teachers have little experience in teaching ESL (English as a second language). It has also given me a new appreciation for the stimulating diversity of a composition class with students from varied backgrounds and also for the benefits to the U.S. students in a class with international classmates.

Of course, not all nonnative English speakers are international students. Some are migrants or recent immigrants who have been educated in U.S. schools (also called "generation 1.5"). Often times these students demonstrate fluency with spoken English, but ESL errors manifest themselves in their writing. Generation 1.5 English language learners bring varying levels of fluency in their native language and varying levels of education to the college classroom (Harklau, Losey, & Siegal, 1999).

Whether English language learners comprise half a class or are scattered more sparsely throughout sections of freshman English, the insights and experiences of international students can enrich any class. Students learn to collaborate with students from different backgrounds, gaining skills that will make them more cosmopolitan citizens of the world. Goals of a writing course may include encouraging students to draw material from multiple perspectives, growing beyond a narrow view of the world, and thinking critically, goals which can be facilitated when differing views are represented. Regardless of their cultural background, students can learn to accept accents, tolerate ambiguity, and avoid automatic judgments, and having a culturally mixed class can broaden the perspectives of both U.S. and international students. Students can also learn that culture is much more than an assemblage of curious customs, that it is at the very root of our personalities, ideas, and beliefs.

Though English language learners may be initially apprehensive about taking a composition course, they have much to gain from the experience. In many universities, freshmen enroll primarily in large lecture classes; a composition class may be one of the few in which professors know their names, or in which they have a chance to get acquainted with their classmates. Some international students spend much of their time associating with a support group of other students from their own cultures; though they may wish to make American friends, international students often do not find opportunities to get well acquainted with U.S. students. The intimate setting of a composition class can be an ideal opportunity for an international student to make U.S. friends. Additionally, the more chances an international student has to practice listening, speaking and writing the more likely she will be to improve her abilities to communicate in English. This practice occurs with more intensity and frequency in the writing classroom than in many content area classes.

The first section of this chapter examines cultural issues that make studying in U.S. colleges a challenging situation for many multilingual students, particularly internationl students, and suggests ways in which a composition teacher can integrate multilingual students into the classroom. It also discusses some of the general concerns in cross-cultural education and provides insights into the differing perspectives of multilingual students. The second section describes some of the difficulties new international students may have in speaking and listening. It discusses classroom activities that have proved useful in helping English language learners improve their listening comprehension and speaking abilities. The third section looks more specifically at writing pedagogy for the multilingual student, covering such issues as understanding differences in rhetorical expectations of native and nonnative students, handling errors in ESL students' writing, and adapting pedagogical techniques like peer review and collaborative writing to a class including multilingual writers, both international students and generation 1.5 students.

■ CULTURAL ISSUES

New international students face big adjustments when coming to the U.S. to study. Not only is the language a challenge, but even well-meaning Americans can cause distress for newly arrived students. Mui, from Malaysia, wrote this in her journal:

> When I first came, I was very frightened because I did not understand the American way of doing things. I can clearly remember my first time on the campus. It was a afternoon, but the campus was as quiet as midnight because the university was closed for winter break. I was walking alone with a campus map in my right hand and worrying that I would not be able to find all my classes. An American guy approached me as I walked along the sidewalk.

As he got closer, he said "Hi." I looked around and there was nobody else except the two of us. "He must be saying hi to me," I thought. I was so scared! I whispered in my heart, "My goodness, I hope he won't attack a helpless girl like me. He must be a crazy person." I walked faster with my head down and ignored him. My heart was beating and I could hardly breath. I just couldn't believe it when he passed me by without any assault! Later, as I was here a longer time, I realized that saying "hi" or smiling to strangers was to be friendly to them. I hoped that the guy wouldn't misinterpret that foreigners were cold and unfriendly.

Reading her journal, we cannot help but sympathize with Mui's terror. If this situation caused her to panic, one might imagine that other, more complex situations could be very confusing. New international students sometimes have great difficulty knowing what is appropriate or expected in a given situation. For example, a new student in one of my ESL classes confided to me that he had been unable to sleep for a week because his American roommate would enter their dorm room at two or three in the morning talking loudly to friends, would turn on the light and the stereo, and would often not go to bed until dawn. To the international student, his roommate's behavior was incomprehensibly rude, yet my student was uncertain whether or not this unkindness was inappropriate for an American. He had no idea whether or not he should complain, either to the roommate or to someone else. And in the meantime, he was attempting to attend class and study through a blur of exhaustion.

These two situations were resolved favorably: Mui noticed the differences in greeting customs and began to feel comfortable with them; my tired student spoke to his RA and eventually arranged to move into another room. But other situations may continue to provoke uneasiness, discomfort, or confusion. The anthropologist Edward Hall (1959) explains that ". . . culture is more than mere custom that can be shed or changed like a suit of clothes" (p. 46), and ". . . culture controls behavior in deep and persisting ways, many of which are outside of awareness and therefore beyond conscious control of the individual" (p. 48).

Some students may never feel entirely comfortable with the relaxed, "anything goes" atmosphere in an American classroom: It violates all they have been taught about the teacher's proper authority and the respect owed by a student. Though they may manage to understand and function in a U.S. classroom, they may never feel completely "at home" in a class where students interrupt the teacher or pack up their books to leave while the teacher is still talking. Another student may grow to understand that American friends are not intending to be rude when they say "Let's get together sometime?" but never call, yet it may continue to seem impolite.

International students are not the only ones who face cultural differences at college; generation 1.5 students, although often quite assimilated in U.S. culture, may feel isolated from their native language and culture and even their families as they move into the academy. These students sometimes feel like they don't belong in either culture. Immigrant students are likely to have experienced ethnic labels and stereotypes or imposed identities. Increasingly, families who immigrate to the United States do so in search of better economic opportunity, often bringing with them very few resources and taking on very low-wage jobs. Some students feel pressured to attend college to pull themselves and their families out of poverty, but may feel alienated once they get there. Frequently, generation 1.5 students were placed in low-ability classes while attending U.S. high schools, so they may inexperienced with the culture and conventions of the academy (Roberge, 2005).

We need to recognize rather than trivialize the differences in deeply rooted cultural values. As Hall (1959) points out, the most useful aspect of learning about cultural differences is gaining a deeper understanding of one's own culture. "The best reason for exposing oneself to foreign ways is to generate a sense of vitality and awareness—an interest in life which can come only when one lives through the shock of contrast and difference" (p. 53). If teachers understand the complex challenges facing their multilingual students, they can work to make the composition classroom a place where some cultural issues can be explored. At the very least, they can provide a supportive atmosphere where U.S. and international classmates can learn together.

It is also well worth remembering that multilingual students are an amazingly diverse group of people. They come from backgrounds very different from one another, have widely varying goals and attitudes about living and studying in the United States, and certainly have different skills. My comments are not meant to minimize these differences, nor am I intending to "lump" all international students into one large, easily explainable group. However, certain difficulties reappear among students from many backgrounds, and several issues about cross-cultural communication are worth exploring. The following suggestions may help to clarify areas of confusion, misinterpretation, and difficulty experienced by many international students.

Nonverbal Communication

Anyone who has done reading on cultural diversity is aware that students from other cultures may interpret matters of personal space and body language very differently than the "average American." My consciousness was raised about this issue during my first semester as a teaching assistant. A Nigerian student in my class frequently came for office hours to get extra advice about this writing. I enjoyed talking with him and got to know him well from our frequent conversations. We would begin the conference with me behind my desk and him on the chair to the right of the desk where all my students sat when they came in to talk to me. As we talked about his writing, he would invariably gather up his papers and move his chair so that we were sitting side by side. Though I didn't feel threatened by him, I found myself feeling uncomfortable sitting with our shoulders touching, and I would unconsciously edge my chair farther away. As we talked, my student would scoot his chair closer; I would move farther. I finally realized what was happening when I found that I was leaning into the wall at the left side of my desk: inch by inch, he had pursued me there. He felt comfortable at a closer distance than I did—a phenomenon I had read about but never experienced before.

Hall (1959) provides insights into this phenomenon for his U.S. readers:

> In Latin America the interaction distance is much less than it is in the United States. Indeed, people cannot talk comfortably with one another unless they are very close to the distance that evokes either sexual or hostile feelings in the North American. The result is that when they move close, we withdraw and back away. As a consequence, they think we are distant or cold, withdrawn and unfriendly. We, on the other hand, are constantly accusing them of breathing down our necks, crowding us, and spraying our faces. (p. 209)

Students from other cultural backgrounds may also have differing conventions for who may touch whom and in what circumstances. A Japanese student may feel that her space has been invaded if an American student puts his feet on the back of her chair. Asian students often express surprise at U.S. couples publicly hugging or kissing, yet may find the taboo against same-sex touching odd. One assumes, until one has reason to know otherwise, that all people operate under the same unspoken rules for nonverbal appropriateness, and it may come as a disquieting shock to realize that one's own internalized rules are not held by others. "Since most people don't think about personal distance as something that is culturally patterned, foreign spatial cues are almost inevitably misinterpreted" (Hall & Hall, 1990, p. 12).

Eye gaze varies across cultures, too, with some cultures encouraging direct eye contact and others considering direct eye contact too forward or insulting. Once during a discussion of this topic, a student told me that he would never stare at a woman's eyes. He felt that she would certainly interpret this as him indicating sexual interest in her. When I asked what place was the appropriate spot for his eyes, he responded seriously, "Her chest." It is often pointed out that Vietnamese students show respect by directing their eyes downward, not by making direct eye contact. Conversely, students from the Middle East may feel that Americans do not keep eye contact long enough.

Teachers tend to be focused on the verbal channel of expression, and may not have a conscious awareness of nonverbal communication (Morain, 1978). They should educate themselves about some of the differences in nonverbal communication, especially if international students comprise a good portion of their students. Differences in gesture, eye contact, touch, and movement are interestingly discussed by many writers. Particularly accessible are collections by Valdes (1986), and Byrd (1986) as well as the classics by Hall. Other resources for a teacher interested in cross-cultural differences include Genzel & Cummings (1994), Fox (1994), and Levine, Baxter, & McNulty (1987).

Trying to define one's own cultural expectations for nonverbal communication can be an interesting topic of class discussion if several nationalities are represented. A teacher can have students discuss questions like these:

➤ How do you enter a classroom if you are late and arriving after the class has begun?

➤ How do you greet a friend of the opposite sex after not seeing him/her for several months? Of the same sex? How do you greet a friend when you see him/her for the second time in the same day?

➤ What body language would you use when you meet your parents at the end of the school year?

➤ In what circumstances, if any, would you expect to be able to smell a friend? Would you find it offensive, normal, embarrassing?

➤ In which circumstances would you walk hand in hand or arm in arm with a friend?

➤ What gestures are considered rude in your culture? Why?

Although issues such as these do not go to the root of cultural differences, they can raise students' awareness and make them more sensitive not only of their classmates but also their own cultural assumptions.

Time Codes

Most North Americans have heard of the Spanish term "mañana" and realize that the expression says something about the relative cultural importance of being on time or doing things "right now." U.S. residents assume that this stereotype simply means that Latin Americans "put off for tomorrow what they should do today," yet the underlying cultural values are much more complex. Levine (1985) interviewed Brazilian students to better understand their sense of time, and noted that the Brazilian students felt less regret about being late and were less likely to be bothered that someone else was late than students from North America. As a matter of fact, the Brazilian students believed that a consistently late person was probably more successful than one who was on time.

Hall & Hall (1989) describe the distinction between "monochromatic" and "polychromatic" time. People who are monochromatic focus on one thing at a time, while in polychromatic cultures, people are comfortable with doing many things at once. The U.S. is a monochromatic culture: time is seen as linear, and it is scheduled, compartmentalized, and talked about as if it were tangible. It can be "'spent,' 'saved,' 'wasted,' and 'lost'" (p. 13). In polychromatic cultures, keeping to a schedule is less important than interacting with people, and students with a polychromatic sense of time may have trouble understanding why it is important to their teachers for them to come promptly to class or an appointment. Students would opt to be late for an appointment rather than rudely end a conversation they are having with a friend.

Being aware that a student is not intentionally trying to be rude may help a teacher interpret this behavior correctly. It is also helpful to clarify classroom expectations of behavior with students on the syllabus and in class discussion. Most students who would not worry about the clock in their home countries will make an effort to be on time when they are in the United States once they understand that promptness is expected.

An American student wrote about her growing understanding of a Puerto Rican classmate's different sense of time:

> I talked to Ana one day during class and she mentioned that she was uncomfortable with the way people here said, "Hi, how are you?" without waiting for a response. She said it was rather shallow. It didn't dawn on me that I said those words often until I heard myself saying them to Ana herself two days later. I was in a big hurry to get to one of my classes and I saw Ana on one of the paths. I was practically running when I saw her, and because I was happy to see Ana, I said 'Hi, how are ya?' as I kept on going. As soon as

the words came out of my mouth, I knew I had said something really stupid. I stopped to talk to her for awhile and I left feeling a little happier. Even though I was in a hurry, I still made it on time.

This kind of insight into another person's perspective is exactly what we can hope for in a class where students are working together with others from different cultures.

Sensitive Cultural Issues

One of the instructors in our program recently raised an interesting question: "What if an ESL student writes a paper setting forth cultural values that the teacher simply cannot accept?" (Falck-Yi, personal communication). This teacher was imagining a situation in which a student made a claim that men were superior to women, or that an oldest child was evil if he did not care for aging parents, or that one's government must be obeyed blindly.

It is certainly true that students from other cultures will have, and will express, values that are not shared by many U.S. teachers. However, this also occurs in writing classes for U.S. students: the teacher with a liberal perspective will feel uncomfortable about a student's praise of Rush Limbaugh; many writing teachers have disagreed with student papers containing racist comments. Given that the situation is not uncommon, most teachers will attempt to approach such writing with sensitivity. A teacher can ask the student questions to help him more clearly define his ideas, a teacher can suggest alternative viewpoints or point out inconsistencies in his arguments, but in the end, a teacher must respect the student's right as an individual to hold differing beliefs.

At times, teachers may find they have unexpectedly strayed into "taboo" areas. Several years ago, I thought I would try a creative descriptive assignment in an ESL class. I brought several varieties of apples to class, gave one to each class member, and asked them to describe the apples in detail. I suggested they look carefully at the outside of the apple, but also that they take several bites to describe the taste and texture. The class included two students from Malaysia, one from Indonesia, one from Saudi Arabia, and one from Egypt, and I noticed several minutes into the activity that none of them were eating their apples. Suddenly, it struck me: we were in the month of Ramadan when Muslims fast during daylight hours! I was momentarily afraid that I had offended them, but they graciously took the opportunity to explain their religious beliefs to the rest of the class. My mistake provided an opportunity for learning.

Some culturally sensitive topics are worth exploring in the classroom. Teachers may find that with some international students, they not only need to explain techniques for avoiding sexist language (Ch. 12f in *Simon & Schuster Handbook for Writers*, 8/e), but also may need to explain the rationale behind the concept. In addition, with current concerns about sexual harassment, students from different cultures may need to be sensitized to the fact that their "normal" manner of approaching people of the opposite sex can be misinterpreted. A student from Honduras recently told one of the teachers in our program that when he saw college women sunning themselves on public lawns, he assumed he would be welcome to go up next to them, sit down, and begin a conversation. When his American classmate said that the sunbathing woman might think he was harassing her, the student was puzzled. "Why is it worse to go up and talk to someone," he asked, "than it is to stare at them without speaking the way the U.S. men do?" To the Honduran student, the impersonal staring of the American men was more insulting than the approach he perceived as direct and friendly.

Tyler (1994) describes a situation in which a male tutor from India was working with an American female undergraduate in a volunteer situation. The female student complained that the tutor had made sexual advances during the tutoring session because his leg had brushed against hers several times and he had not apologized. Tyler notes that it was clear that the touch had been unintentional, and that the Indian tutor had not recognized that this casual contact required an apology.

Teachers should be aware that students from some cultures may not feel at all comfortable criticizing their government or their parents, will balk at topics that offend their religious sensibilities, and may have differing attitudes about relations between the sexes. Teachers should also avoid singling out international or immigrant students to speak as experts on their native cultures. Although they often can provide unique insights or alternative perspectives, they are individuals and do not represent the whole of a culture, nor may they want to be called upon to be the voice of the "other." Teachers should attempt to understand their students' viewpoints and appreciate the diversity they bring to the classroom. At the same time, giving all students more complex insights into societies and culture can also be a useful goal.

Another issue that may come up with some nonnative speakers, particularly those who are immigrant or migrant students, is a sense of resistance to language development. Some may see the acquisition of a new language as a threat to their native culture and even to their family relationships. Learning language changes us; it changes our understanding of the world.

For some, that change is undesirable, and they may subvert efforts to become fluent in standard English. Richard Rodriguez and other writers have shared this sense of conflict in their autobiographical pieces. This conflict is not limited to learning a second language, either. Other writers, such as bell hooks and Amy Tan, have described the conflict between using the language of home and the language of the institution and how these changes in their language affected their relationships and even their sense of identity. Reading about and discussing these conflicts can help students pinpoint the source of dissonance they may feel in learning academic English. Students can find space to write about these issues in narrative, descriptive, compare and contrast, or argumentative essays.

■ LISTENING AND SPEAKING SKILLS FOR MULTILINGUAL STUDENTS

Although the focus of a composition course is writing, an international student needs to be able to comprehend and speak in order to participate fully in the class. U.S. students can be sensitized to the difficulties facing the international students, and a teacher can encourage communication between native and nonnative speakers.

Listening

Especially for newly arrived students, coping with the average American's idiomatic, connected speech can be challenging. Many students from East Asian countries have learned a sort of "textbook" English, focusing on translation, memorizing model texts, and rigorously studying formal English grammar. Some have never taken a class in which they had to speak; some have never communicated with a native speaker; many have learned from British English models. Imagine the surprise a Korean student feels when she hears her American partner on the first day of class say something that sounds like "Whaddayawanna do?" She can, without difficulty, read the words "What do you want to do?" but her classmate's pronunciation is unexpectedly confusing.

Of course most native speakers realize that English is not always spoken the way that it is written, that words like *thought, throughout,* and *rough* share common spelling but have different pronunciations. However, many native speakers don't realize that the natural speech patterns for Americans are not easily predictable from written text. Words within phrases are linked, as in the previous example, and vowels in unstressed syllables may be reduced (not pronounced clearly) or omitted entirely. For instance, the phrase *back and forth* will be spoken "back 'n forth" and *wants to go* is said "wants t' go." Native speakers probably write *should of* rather than *should have* because, as it is spoken, the word sounds more like *of* than *have*.

Sound changes also occur—are said to be assimilated—when certain consonants occur together. For example, *could you* becomes *couldja* where the *d* and *y* combine into a sound like *dj*, or "What was your name?" becomes "What *wazshur* name?" Finally, stress patterns in English sentences can affect meaning in a way quite unusual in other languages. "He's leaving on *Friday*," "*He's* leaving on Friday" and "He's *leaving* on Friday" are appropriate in slightly different contexts. Similarly, "I went to the white *house*" is not the same as "I went to the *White* House!" It's no wonder that new international students sometimes appear puzzled! (See pronunciation texts like Gilbert, 1994 for detailed explanations of these phenomena.)

Academic idioms can make understanding classroom spoken English even more difficult for a new student. Academic discourse is rife with idiomatic expressions: "Will you *pass back* the *handout*"; "There's a *pop quiz* today"; "I'll *post the scores* at *midterm*"; "You can take a *make-up test.*" The vocabulary of the writing classroom may be just as opaque for a new international student. *First draft, peer editing, brainstorming,* and *prewriting* may not only be unfamiliar terms, but may not link into an already existing schema in the international student's mind.

Even more troublesome for international students are the many idioms and slang expressions that native speakers use unconsciously in their informal speech. I recall standing in line behind an international student on a trip to a local fast food restaurant one summer. The young woman behind the counter asked the student if his order was "Fer here or t' go." The student looked at her with wide eyes; her speech was uncomprehensible to him. Even when she slowed down and enunciated the phrase—"for here or to go," the expression still did not make any sense to this international student. Consider other common expressions that are not immediately transparent to a nonnative English speaker: "That was over my head," "It's on the tip of my tongue," "It was lost in the shuffle," and "We're in for it now." Sports idioms, like "way out in left field," "extra innings," "slam dunk," "out of bounds," or "coming down the home stretch," are used frequently in everyday language, but are meaningless to a student who is unfamiliar with American sports culture. And slang expressions from "goth" to "bling" to "awesome," "cool," or "hot" also can confuse the second language learner.

Many nonnative students are eager to learn new idioms, but they may not always have an effective strategy for acquiring them. I recall one diligent student who was studying a small paperback book as I walked into class. When I asked Ming what he was reading, he told me he was learning American slang from his book, which provided translations into Chinese. I expressed enthusiasm for his efforts, and asked him to give me an example. He looked down, and read his most recently learned idiom: "Paint the town red." I explained that that particular idiom was rather outdated, and commiserated about the difficulty of keeping up to date on slang. I confided that I frequently had to ask my teenage children to explain popular expressions. Ming decided to ask some of his American friends for current alternatives before he began to say "Paint the town red."

The complexities of comprehending spoken English may seem overwhelming, but encouraging the nonnative speakers to use their native classmates as "slang informants" is useful for both the U.S. and international students. The nonnative students should be encouraged to bring their questions about idiomatic expressions; it is an enlightening experience for the native speakers to attempt to define terms that they use without thinking, and identifying idioms can raise their awareness. For example, international students frequently ask "When I thank people, why do they say 'sure' or 'you bet' instead of 'you're welcome'? or "What exactly should I say when an American says 'What's happening'?" A student recently asked me, "What's the difference between 'Oh boy' and 'Oh man'? Why don't you say 'Oh girl' or 'Oh woman'?" Struggling with questions like these makes a native speaker more sensitive to his or her own language. If the nonnative students seem to feel uncomfortable asking their classmates for help with idioms, students can use their journals for recording expressions and terms they don't understand. This allows a teacher to give feedback privately.

Often, students who are not following class discussion or who do not understand something their teachers have said may not indicate that they are having trouble; the problems only become evident when the teacher collects a homework assignment. Students may be reluctant to show that they do not understand because they consider asking questions insulting, since it would communicate that the teacher had not explained well enough. Other students may simply be too shy or fearful to tell the teacher that they don't understand. Putting instructions in writing can be a helpful way of backing up oral comments. Additionally, encouraging students to come for individual help in an office conference can be a nonthreatening way for them to ask questions.

Native-speaking students may need some guidance to respond to their ESL classmates in a helpful way. Levine, Baxter & McNulty (1987) quote a nonnative speaker who was frustrated talking with an American, "When I say . . . 'Please repeat,' he often repeats everything he said before, only louder, and faster. Why doesn't he speak more slowly when he repeats? Why does he repeat so many sentences? Usually, after he repeats, I still don't understand"

(p. 65). If several nonnative students in a class appear to be having difficulty with listening, the teacher may wish to address the issue directly. One can request that the native speakers speak slowly (not more loudly) and be willing to stop to explain expressions their classmates don't know. Additionally, rather than repeating the exact words that were initially misunderstood, the native speaker can try paraphrasing, using different expressions to communicate the same idea. Paraphrasing what other speakers said is a useful listening activity for native and nonnative English speakers alike. The teacher can model this technique if it seems that students are having trouble communicating. Also, if the teacher occasionally stops to explain an idiom to the nonnative students, the U.S. students in the class may wish to add their perspectives or suggest alternative idioms, and will become sensitized to the difficulties of the nonnative speaker in understanding these expressions.

Speaking

While nonnative students' listening problems may not be obvious, especially if they seem to be paying attention, their speaking abilities are often more apparent. A student may know what she wants to say, but not be able to articulate her ideas; another may speak quickly, but with impenetrable pronunciation.

Speaking fluency will improve with practice, and I encourage my students to take advantage of every opportunity to talk they can find. However, even students who wish to practice interacting may feel inhibited raising their hands in class and may never feel comfortable enough to interrupt a classmate. Some may avoid speaking because they worry that others will not understand their accent. One should recognize that nonnative students may have differing expectations regarding what goes on in a classroom. Students may feel that the best and proper way to learn is to sit silently and diligently take notes on the professor's lecture. Many are unaccustomed to small or large group class disucssions, and they may be surprised to be expected to participate in class discussion. Others may attempt to participate but not find a way to "get a word in edgewise." Research into communication patterns reveals differences even between New Yorkers and Californians in their sense of the length of silent pauses between speakers or their tendency to interrupt one another (Tannen, 1984). If speakers from the U.S. differ, one can assume that speakers from various parts of the world will have very different unconscious expectations about how to get the attention of a classmate or how to take a turn in the conversation.

In a class with mixed nationalities, a teacher may find, at least initially, that the native speakers are dominating class discussions. However, a teacher can provide positive reinforcement when a nonnative student does respond to a question, can call on the nonnative speakers to encourage their participation, and should model supportive behaviors like repeating a difficult to understand comment so that the whole class can understand or providing an appropriate phrase or word if a student is struggling to find one. The teacher may also find it helpful to moderate class discussions to ensure that all who want to get to participate. Other techniques, such as allowing wait time before calling for a response, having students freewrite about a topic before discussing it, beginning discussion in small groups before opening it to the whole class, are useful ways to encourage more talking for native and nonnative English speakers alike.

Even though reticent students may never eagerly participate in a whole-class discussion, such students often open up in the safer context of a small group or pair. For this reason, using small groups for discussion of a reading, for examining sample student writing, or for a revision exercise can encourage the international students to participate. Other small group activities can include collaboratively gathering information, problem solving, and annotating or evaluating readings (Reid, 1993).

Small group work may also be a new experience for international students, but if the groups are structured carefully, they can be an effective way of encouraging discussion from quiet students. Assigning groups allows the instructor to mix international and U.S. students and avoids a situation in which the U.S. students choose their friends, leaving the international students to feel like the last ones picked for the seventh grade soccer game. On the other hand, a native speaker may feel excluded if several students from the same language background carry on a discussion in their language rather than in English, and ground rules about using English in class are sometimes useful. Just as with native speakers, gender balance can also affect group dynamics; for example, a Muslim woman may feel more uncomfortable than a U.S. woman if asked to work with a group of male classmates. Ideally, the teacher of a culturally mixed language class should avoid stereotyping her students (the Muslim woman might be just as outspoken and confident as her American classmate), but should remain sensitive to the cultural and gender makeup of student groups.

Of course native speakers can dominate the discussion of small groups, or they may take over a collaborative project without consulting the international students. It is often useful to specifically discuss some of the benefits and problems in cross-cultural communication before students are placed into groups. Additionally, one can set ground rules for discussions which include the participation of every member to encourage native speakers to solicit the ideas of the nonnative students. Or, if students regularly discuss class readings in small groups, rotating the "chair" or "reporter" who summarizes the group's work will necessitate that all the students have a turn. Structuring the group exercises, too, can guarantee that each student gets a voice: for example, if the assignment requires recording responses and ideas from every group member and incorporating those ideas into a summary, then each student's opinions will, by the nature of the assignment, be solicited.

Group activities certainly allow students to use and develop listening and speaking skills in the writing classroom. (Schlumberger & Clymer, 1989) Additionally, teachers should not hesitate to encourage nonnative students' participation in whole class activities and in group oral presentations. More specific comments on using peer review and collaborative writing will follow in the next section.

■ WRITING SKILLS FOR MULTILINGUAL STUDENTS

New teachers should remember that English language learners vary widely in their writing abilities. A teacher should not automatically assume that the nonnative English speakers will be the ones with the most pressing problems. On the contrary, teachers often say that the international students are among the best writers in their classes, willing to take on serious issues and work hard at improving their writing. Certainly, the nonnative speakers are often highly motivated students, and they may be more focused on their academic goals than some of their native-speaking classmates.

In our multicultural society, a student with a non-English name and appearance may well be as "American" as the blonde Jane Smith sitting beside her. Generation 1.5 and second generation immigrants can have interesting cultural perspectives, but their writing skills will be indistinguishable from other U.S. students. A permanent resident, immigrant student who learned English in a U.S. junior high school may be fluent in spoken English, yet may retain nonnative-like problems in grammar or expression. Leki (1992) describes one such Vietnamese student who did not want to take an ESL class for "foreigners" because she clearly wished to be considered an American; however, the student struggled in the regular composition class because of her English abilities. At some U.S. colleges, the distinction between first language basic writers and ESL writers has become blurred with the effects of bilingual education as well as the fact that students have immigrated at different ages (Santos, 1992). Certainly, too, students' educational backgrounds in their first languages will affect their abilities in the new language.

Given that there is no "typical" nonnative speaker in a composition class, how can a teacher meet the diverse needs of multilingual students in helping them gain greater writing skills? Teachers can be reassured that many of the techniques used to teach writing to native speakers work equally well with multilingual students. However, understanding culturally based writing differences and gaining insights into English language learners' expectations will help teachers evaluate their students needs more accurately.

Assumptions About Writing and Learning to Write

Since composition classes are such an expected feature of U.S. college and university curricula, it may come as a surprise that many students who come from different educational backgrounds have not had instruction in writing in their own language (Leki, 1992). In some cultures, writing instruction may embody very different values. I have already mentioned that students may feel uncomfortable with the casual atmosphere in U.S. classrooms and may be surprised that they are supposed to participate in class discussions. Other aspects of the U.S. composition class may also be unexpected.

If they come from university systems in which students can freely choose whether or not to attend lectures during the semester, students may feel that the frequent, daily homework assignments given in typical freshman-level classes are unnecessary busywork. One South American student commented that these classes were like high school classes, with the teacher always checking up on the student and attendance expected. He was accustomed to more freedom at the university level. On the other hand, some students adapt to these expectations and indicate that they appreciate the frequent practice and feedback. I often mention at the beginning of a course that a writing class is very different from most others: instead of absorbing a body of knowledge, students are developing skills. Many students do not realize that reading, writing, speaking, and listening are interrelated skills, thus regular reading assignments and verbal interaction are typical in a composition class. For these reason homework, frequent reading and writing assignments, as well as regular attendance are essential in giving students practice in the skills they are learning.

Other differences may not be as obvious but may deeply affect a student's ability to write compositions. Although writing as process permeates most U.S. composition classrooms, the concept of writing more than one draft may be surprising to many international students. Some students may have come from traditions in which the appearance of a piece of writing is judged as an important feature, and thus may be very uncomfortable handing in drafts that have cross-overs, arrows, or marginally added phrases. Many are unaccustomed to receiving feedback, especially from peers, and using that feedback for revision. They may not appreciate or know how to incorporate comments and suggestions received from others, nor may they feel confident offering feedback to other students. Additionally, some students may have come from educational systems in which they were expected to do exactly as the teacher says. The respect and honor that they give to their teachers may be flattering, but a composition teacher can find it frustrating to find his own ideas and suggestions incorporated, whole cloth, into a student's papers. Many English language learners are so concerned about making grammar errors or using English properly that they do not spend as much time considering the content they are trying to convey.

Additionally, typical U.S. college writing assignments or topics may be very unfamiliar to or uncomfortable for international students. Although many writing teachers begin their courses with narrative writing, believing that students will write better about topics with which they are familiar, many international students are unaccustomed to writing personal narratives. Some may find particular assigned topics too personal to write about. Some topics or readings may be culturally biased, and students from foreign cultures may not have a basis for understanding or responding to them. Teachers may find that some students resist taking a strong personal stance in an argument or that, having taken a stance, the student does not feel a need to support or defend it. Some students may show reluctance to critique an essay. These differences can make a mismatch between the teacher's and the multilingual students' expectations in a class.

Because generation 1.5 students are often experienced with writing as process and may be familiar with typical writing assignments encountered in U.S. colleges, teachers may not realize that they, too, may require special consideration in the writing classroom. Teachers often assume that since many generation 1.5 students are fluent in spoken English that they will also be fluent in written academic English. However, generally generation 1.5 have missed formal grammar instruction, learning language mostly aurally and orally, and retain "fossilized" forms of nonstandard English. Often their first language education was interrupted to learn English, causing them to attempt to build second language literacy without first language literacy (Roberge, 2003). Valdes (1992) argues that it's essential to differentiate between "incipient bilingual," those who are in the process of learning English, and "functional bilinguals," those who have learned English, but who persistently use nonstandard forms of English in their writing. The latter group likely does not need ESL instruction, but may need more direct grammar instruction than may be typically offered in a freshman composition course.

Finally, many English language learners and teachers alike have unrealistic expectations about time to fluency. Language acquisition is a complex and long-term process; one acquires language in different ways than one learns a body of knowledge. In fact, the efficacy of error correction and explicit grammar instruction for second language learners is a hotly debated topic since some research on these methods has indicated that they have no, or perhaps even a detrimental effect on writing development. Clearly, it is unrealistic to expect that the writing of most ESL students will sound like that of a native English speaker. Most English language learners will speak and write with an accent.

Rhetorical features

A student once mentioned that the Chinese have a saying to describe the way that writing should work: "Open the door and see the mountain." She explained that the Chinese writer would paint a picture for the reader, building detail by detail, until finally, the mountain was revealed. If, on the other hand, one considers "the mountain" to be the main purpose of a piece of English writing, then we might imagine that the appropriate approach when writing in English is to first tell the reader she is gong to see a mountain before she ever opens the door! In other words, the approach a writer takes to a piece of discourse—the choices a writer makes about what a reader needs or wants, what evidence to include, and how to organize—is influenced by the conventions of her culture.

A number of researchers have found interesting differences in writing conventions deemed appropriate in different populations. In a series of studies, Purves (1986) found differences between national groups in aspects such as how personal or impersonal writing was supposed to be, whether writing should be abstract or concrete, and how a writer should provide text coherence. People of the same culture tend to agree on what is appropriate proof for an assertion: English readers expect facts and statistics and are not convinced by extensive use of analogy, metaphor, intuition, and the authority of the ancients. "Yet conventions of argumentation in other cultures may require precisely that recourse to analogy, intuition, beauty, or shared communal wisdom" (Leki, 1992, p. 92). Hinds (1987) makes the distinction between "reader-responsible" and "writer-responsible" writing. The Japanese expect the reader to make inferences and may feel insulted if a writer is too explicit, while English readers may see the Japanese approach as circular and vague. I have had Latin American college students balk at my requests for personal examples: to them, a personal example seemed immature or babyish; they preferred theoretical generalizations.

Reid summarizes Robert Kaplan's (1966) exploratory study of nonnative students' organizational patterns. Though these patterns are certainly simplistic, Reid points out that the field of contrastive rhetoric can offer insights into some of the difficulties that the nonnative writer faces in understanding the best way to organize a piece of writing in a specific context. As a matter of fact, I have occasionally drawn Kaplan's diagrams on the board, and asked ESL students to comment about whether or not these simplified patterns seem to represent patterns with which they are familiar. Showing the straightforward expectations of an English-speaking audience as an arrow often brings nods of understanding.

Matalene (1985), who spent a semester teaching in Taiyuan, China, explains that some of her Western expectations baffled her students. She wanted originality, directness, and self-expression; her students valued indirectness, memorization, and references to Chinese classics. Not only was the definition of good writing different, but so was the very function of rhetoric. She concludes that for teachers who work with students from varied backgrounds, "our responsibility is surely to try to understand and appreciate, to admit the relativity of our own rhetoric, and to realize that logics different from our own are not necessarily illogical" (p. 806).

The current theory about contrastive rhetoric does not hold the "deterministic view that speakers of other languages think differently" (Grabe and Kaplan, 1989, p. 264). Instead, literacy skills are learned, are transmitted through the system of education, and are culturally shaped; differences reflect preferred conventions. One should realize that, "as conventions, those that the United States espouses are not better or worse than those espoused in other cultures" (Purves, 1986, p. 50).

As writing teachers, we can be so influenced by our notions of appropriateness in writing, that we sometimes forget that we, too, are looking at writing through a cultural lens. Thus, rather than asserting that the U.S. approach is the "right" or "best" or "only" way of organizing or arguing, I usually present such material as a series of options. I may say that a native speaker of English will expect that a piece of writing be more, rather than less, direct; will prefer concrete, personal examples to an abstract statement of truth; will want explication rather than implications. When phrased in terms of the reader's expectations, learning these conventions becomes like learning customs. Understanding this, too, helps a teacher evaluate students' papers more fairly.

Plagiarism

Given the very different traditions of international students, one might expect differing conventions for citing or copying source material. There is a clear contrast between our emphasis on individuality and finding an "authentic voice" in writing and an emphasis on the commonality of knowledge and a reverence for the wisdom of the elders, and this difference may account for differences in views of plagiarism (Leki, 1992). Matalene (1985) emphasizes that basic literacy in Chinese requires amazing feats of memorization of the thousands of characters in the language. Combine that with the importance of learning texts from classical Chinese writing, memorization of set phrases and proverbs, and one can see that for a Chinese student, learning to write means memorizing, copying, and following well-proven patterns, something very different than the U.S. writing teacher's expectation of originality, authenticity, and creativity.

To students from many cultures, it is a novel idea that a writer owns his words, as if they were property, so students may be surprised at the anger and shock provoked in a teacher when they copy a source without citing it. Additionally, some students have learned to write by memorizing models on specific topics: they are able to churn out an error-free paper by writing the text they have memorized word for word. Students may feel that since the original author conveyed her message so clearly and beautifully, they would be foolish to put that message in their own clumsy prose.

Writing teachers can be sensitive to the fact that plagiarism is not considered as a serious transgression in all cultures. At the same time, composition instructors need to clearly explain the expectations of a U.S. audience, for students certainly will be writing papers for other courses, may be working on scientific reports in graduate work at U.S. universities, and may write in many contexts in which they cannot copy verbatim. As with rhetorical features, I explain the underlying attitudes about plagiarism in the U.S. to my students, emphasizing the importance of learning to quote and paraphrase accurately as an expected skill in U.S. university classes.

These being skills that are also difficult for native speakers, many composition teachers will choose to spend class time practicing summary, paraphrase, and quotation. (See Ch. 35 and Ch. 7 in handbook.) One should realize that these techniques are especially challenging for nonnative speakers, and a teacher will find the time well spent to help students practice and to explain the importance and usefulness of the skills.

Students' Goals

A more troubling issue is that international students often have very different goals for learning to write than do native speakers. Many international students intend to get an education and return to their own countries. Holding these students to the same writing standards that one would expect from U.S. students seems counterproductive (Land and Whitley, 1989). We can also question the goal of having nonnative students use English for self-discovery, since native-language writing would surely be more appropriate for such a venture, and since some students may not see this as a natural purpose for writing (Leki, 1992; Matalene, 1985). If teachers are not aware of these important, and essentially political, issues, they may make unfair and unrealistic assumptions about their ESL students. Leki (1992) covers this problematic issue effectively.

■ HELPING MULTILINGUAL STUDENTS IN THE COMPOSITION CLASSROOM

The needs of English language learners are, as I have indicated, complex and varied, and teachers may wish to keep some of these issues in mind as they plan a syllabus, select a text, consider assignment topics, and respond to their ESL students' writing. For example, if a number of international students can be typically expected in a class, a teacher may wish to choose a cross-cultural reader that includes selections written form international perspectives. (See, for example, Holeton, 1995, Verberg, 1994, or Hirschberg, 1992). These readers can provide a springboard for stimulating class discussions, and they allow students from varied backgrounds to read about attitudes and perspectives different from their own.

Some other currently available multicultural readers naturally focus on the diversity of the U.S. population, and they can be an excellent choice for a class with immigrant and minority students; however, texts focusing on U.S. minorities may have a very "American" bias. Though they are inclusive of the U.S. population, they may not address issues that international students find compelling. On the other hand, some teachers have chosen not to use a multicultural reader and have found that standard readers can be fascinating for international students who are trying to understand U.S. culture. Regardless of whether teachers choose a multicultural reader or one with standard U.S. readings, they should also consider their multilingual students when choosing which readings to assign. Fiction written in dialect can be impenetrable for nonnative English speakers, and lengthy essays take much more reading time for an ESL student. A teacher may wish to consider providing some background for readings that assume a knowledge of U.S. history and culture and plan to give extra help orienting students to long or difficult readings.

Responding to ESL Writing

Recognizing that multilingual students have varied needs and goals, and that they may well have different notions about what makes a piece of writing effective, teachers can be reassured that strategies for responding to ESL writing are really little different from those for responding to native speakers. Most research discourages teachers from focusing on errors early in the writing process, assuming that an early focus on error will not allow a student to think about more substantiative matters. Providing opportunities for students to get feedback as they work on a piece of writing is also quite important. When one does provide feedback on a draft, focusing on content and organization before looking at errors is likely to be most productive. Research has shown that students tend not to pay attention to the comments written on penultimate drafts of their papers, and that these comments can be confusing, contradictory, and unclear (Zamel, 1985). Thus, rather than seeing oneself as an evaluator, stepping in at the last minute to grade the final copies of students papers, a teacher should become involved early in the process. Encouraging students to come in for conferences and to make use of writing resources, such as the Writing Center, providing short mini-consultations during class with individual students, helping students work through the revision process are all useful methods of providing feedback.

Strategies for Dealing with ESL Errors

In order to help ESL students reduce their mistakes in grammar and mechanics, a teacher new to ESL teaching may wish to learn something about current theories of language learning. Brown (1994) notes that "language was not really acquired through a process of habit formation and overlearning, that errors were not necessarily to be avoided at all costs . . ." (p. 71). New views of language learning have necessitated changes in the old "skill and drill" pedagogy. Now we know that language learning occurs as the patterns of the new language are internalized through meaningful communication in a variety of contexts. And pedagogical approaches have changed to provide these rich communicative contexts. Errors are considered a natural part of language learning, not something to be rigorously avoided: they occur for complex reasons, as a learner generalizes about incompletely learned patterns in the new language or guesses about the existence of forms in the new language which occur in the first (Leki, 1992).

Of course these changes in language teaching also affect the teaching of second language writing. Teachers influenced by ESL writing research now spend less effort in correcting errors or in attempting to keep students form making them. Leki (1992) points to two factors that have influenced this turn away from a focus on errors: some research shows that faculty from other disciplines have greater tolerance for ESL students' errors than do English teachers; and, second, correcting those errors has little effect on students' abilities to avoid making mistakes. If students will not be penalized in other courses for occasional nonnative lapses, then what is the purpose of English teachers demanding native-like fluency? And why invest tremendous time and energy correcting errors if this activity has negligible results? For example, in a controlled research study, Robb, Ross, & Shortreed (1986) examined the effect of four types of feedback on written error. Regardless of whether teachers elaborately corrected all student errors, marked the type of error with a coding system, or simply indicated the location of the error, the groups did not show statistically measurable differences. Since error correction can be incredibly time consuming, most ESL teachers do not attempt to correct all the mistakes a student makes, and may wish to consider a certain number of errors as a kind of foreign accent in writing (Harris & Silva, 1993).

However, students may have different expectations about what kind of teacher feedback will help them improve. Leki (1991) points out that a multilingual student's past success with learning English by memorizing grammar rules and focusing on errors may conflict with a writing teacher's wish to emphasize content. Her survey found that English language learners were very interested in their teachers pointing out errors and they claimed to look carefully at their teachers' corrections. However, she notes other studies which indicate that teachers' corrections have little effect on improving student writing. So, though English language learners may expect their teachers to mark all their errors, the usefulness of doing so is in doubt.

The fact does remain, however, that nonnative English speakers may make more serious errors that are distracting and frequent. In his examination of research studies comparing native and nonnative student writers, Silva (1993) notes that ESL students make a larger number of errors than native speakers in many categories, including vocabulary and semantic choice, control of syntax, and problems with verbs, prepositions, articles, and nouns.

Given that composition teachers want to help students reduce the seriousness and frequency of errors, what strategies can they use? First, teachers should avoid the impulse to make all the corrections for the students, and certainly they need not mark every error. When commenting on grammar issues in a multilingual student's writing, focus first on global errors that interfere with the meaning of the student's text. Generally, it is more effective to work with the frequent and distracting errors and the "teach-able" errors, those that are systematic and rule-governed, as opposed to those that are idiosyncratic or are matters of advanced memorization, such as prepositions or idioms. Leki gives the example of *assignments*, which takes a plural ending, and *homework*, which does not (1992, p. 131) as an idiosyncratic example that can't be learned by applying rules. On the other hand, students can learn the system for verb formation to avoid making mistakes like *He can goes. They simply need to apply a predictable formula: following a modal verb (can, could, shall, should, etc.), the next verb takes the "bare infinitive" form (the infinitive without the word to, the most simple form of the verb).

Focusing on only a few types of errors in a particular draft prevents students from feeling overwhelmed. It is sometimes possible to find a pattern that can be pointed out to a student or to focus on a particular type of error that seems distracting in a particular paper. For example, a control of verb tense shifts will be important in a paper that begins with generalized truths ("The relationship of parent and child is important"), moves to personalized statements indicating duration of time ("I have always loved my parents . . ."), and then shifts to an example from the past ("But when I was thirteen . . ."). Showing a student how the tense helps set the time frame of the sentence or paragraph could be productive if she is writing a paper where verb shifts are required. If I see that a student is having trouble with a particular structure, I may have the student proofread his next draft for that one structure only. The student can feel a sense of accomplishment, then, for spotting nearly all the subject-verb agreement errors, or all the sentence fragments, and this makes editing more manageable.

A comprehensive ESL grammar series like *Grammar Dimensions 2* (Riggenbach, 2000) or a small ESL handbook like *Grammar Troublespots* (Raimes, 2004) can provide more background in ESL grammar for a teacher who needs extra help.

Teaching Suggestions

First of all, whether teaching native or nonnative English speakers, the composition classroom should be language-rich, full of talking, listening, reading, and writing. U.S. and international students both appreciate when teachers provide clear expectations for the course and for particular assign-ments. It is especially important that multilingual students receive *written* instructions on assignments. International students also often benefit from seeing student models of essays they will be writing, as it gives them a sense of the rhetorical structure, topic choices, and language use expected on particular assignments.

Many of the assignments and class activities that work for native speakers are also useful for nonnative students. An ungraded journal, popular in many composition classes, can improve the fluency of nonnative speakers. Providing students with frequent opportunities to revise, or using portfolio grading can be a useful way to help multilingual students improve their writing, taking the focus away from producing error-free early drafts. Avoiding this early focus on error is also important so that students can concentrate on more substantial matters of content and organization.

Other common practices are less effective for international students. For example, graded in-class writings are particularly difficult for international students. Under time pressure, they may not be able to write fluently, and certainly will produce many more grammatical errors than they would if they were allowed time to revise. Though for fluency practice, frequent writing is useful, an emphasis on graded in-class writing can be counterproductive, particularly if international students are held to rigid correctness standards. On the other hand, some composition teachers have had success in helping their students improve the ability to understand an essay exam prompt, and to organize and write answers to the kind of exam questions they might be asked on tests in other courses. If the focus is on interpreting the prompt, on organizing, and on finding a few clear details of support, then timed, in-class work can be useful.

It is also productive to guide students through the prewriting process, helping them find new ways of selecting topics, narrowing them, gathering and developing ideas. (See Ch. 2 in handbook.) If students choose their own topics for their papers, new international students may need guidance. Not having the background in writing the kind of personal or persuasive essays that are expected, they may have little idea of the kind of topic which would be appropriate. Showing them typical student papers or referring them to the handbook samples is a first start in helping them see a range of appropriate topics. Students may choose topics which seem extremely broad or vague for a composition class. Keeping in mind that a student is learning new expectations about appropriate conventions for U.S. compositions, a teacher can guide a student to narrow a broad topic or to find a personal angle in the same way that he gives that advice to U.S. students.

If an instructor assigns some of the writing topics for the course, care should be taken to choose topics which will allow international students to write from their own backgrounds and from their own perspectives. Teachers should be careful to avoid topics that require knowledge of U.S. culture, or at the very least provide background for the nonnative students. One student complained that it was impossible to write on the topics her teacher had assigned: high school dating and drugs in American high schools. She had never dated, since girls in her culture did not go out unchaperoned, and she had no knowledge beyond what she read in the papers about drugs in U.S. high schools. Another teacher suggested that a good topic for her half-international class was the meaning of Columbus's discovery of the Americas, yet none of her Asian students had an understanding of Columbus or the effect of his explorations on the New World. Most general topics work effectively:

If a reading unit focuses on topics like family relationships, growing up, political change, education, language, an international student can write with a personal angle. Teachers in our program have also had success with some more culturally based topics. Students have explored different version of familiar folk tales like *Cinderella*, or examined the values expressed in movies like *The Joy Luck Club*. Additional topics have included childhood games, common superstitions, coming-of-age celebrations, and the cultural implications of the architectural design of homes. If there are a number of international students in a class, focusing an assignment on familiar proverbs can be one way of opening students' minds to cultural differences. Several teachers in our program have had students bring "old sayings" from their culture and translate them into English.

Finally, directly examining the idea of cultural stereotypes can be enlightening for U.S. and international students alike. Students can describe typical stereotypes of people from their own culture, explain where the stereotypes originated, and analyze how accurate or inaccurate they are. Becoming aware of the inaccuracy in stereotyping others is one of the great benefits that freshmen can gain in a composition class where these issues have been explored.

A teacher should also respect the international students' wishes about sharing personal material or writing about cultural issues from the perspective of their nationalities. A Russian student in our program complained that all of his teachers wanted him to write about the effects of the fall of the communist government on Russian society. He said he was tired of the topic and that he did not find it interesting or compelling: he never wanted to be asked about it again! Other students may have lived through traumatic times and not wish to share these deeply personal memories with anyone. And others may wish to be assimilated into U.S. society and do not want to draw attention to their differences.

Using Peer Review and Collaborative Writing

Several researchers provide cautions about using peer editing and collaborative projects with multilingual students. Bosley (1993) notes that the manner in which collaborative projects are structured may "represent a Western cultural bias" (p. 51). She points out cultural assumptions about the importance of individualism, of recognizing individual achievement, and of formulating assignments as problem-solving exercises. Similarly, the typical structure of peer review sessions in the U.S. classroom may not be comfortable for students from collectivist cultures like Japan and China (Carson & Nelson, 1994). In the United States, writing groups often function for the benefit of the individual student: students listen to classmates' comments in order to improve their own piece of writing. But students from collectivist cultures are more accustomed to group activities which function for the benefit of the group. They may be reluctant to criticize classmates and may be "concerned primarily with group harmony at the expense of providing their peers with needed feedback on their compositions" (Carson & Nelson, 1994, p. 17). Other problems may relate to different communication styles leading to conflict among collaborators and differing understanding of what makes writing good (Allaei & Connor, 1990).

Keeping these concerns in mind, however, most teachers who have worked with international students do find a number of benefits in using peer review and collaborative writing. Authentic readers provide a greater motivation for students to revise, students receive feedback from multiple perspectives, they better understand how to meet the needs of their readers, and they may discover that other students are also struggling with putting their ideas into writing (Mittan, 1989). Peer review sessions provide valuable opportunities for student to interact. Students are also exposed to various ideas, organizational forms, and rhetorical strategies as they read one another's work.

Several suggestions can make peer review groups go more smoothly. Especially for the nonnative students, it is important to explain clearly what they are going to be doing and what the expected outcome will be. Both native and nonnative students tend to want to focus on editing issues rather than content issues, so it is worthwhile to clarify for all students the process and goals for peer response. If students have done other group activities—discussing readings, for instance—they will be more comfortable with the small group setting. Useful ideas include having students read and discuss articles on differences in cross-cultural communication, and modeling the peer review behavior with a sample piece of writing in front of the class before the peer review sessions begin (Allaei & Connor, 1990; Mittan, 1989; Reid, 1993). Teachers can also have students discuss student drafts from past semesters, photocopied so that students can use them in groups. (I have found my students quite generous in giving me written permission to use their papers anonymously.) This allows students to practice the skills of small group review before they take the emotional plunge of having their own work examined.

When students do bring in their own work, I always have them respond to specific questions, starting positively by identifying something that works well in the writing. Reid (1993) points out that "the goal of peer response/review is not so much to judge . . . as to cooperate in a communicative process, helping others in the classroom community to balance individual purposes with the expectations of the readers" (p. 209). Thus, I never ask my students "What grade would you give this paper?" or "Is this a good or bad paper?" Instead, I have students focus on their responses as readers, by answering questions like these: "Can you easily sum up the writer's main purpose in writing?"; "Was there any place that you wanted more information from the writer?"; and "Were there places where you had trouble following the argument of the writer?" Allowing plenty of time for peer review is important, and having students read drafts aloud and focus on spoken comments during the class period will avoid a silent classroom where students spend the hour writing their responses. Grimm (1986) suggests having students take their notes home to draft written comments for their classmates, and this idea seems especially useful for international students who will take longer to formulate their responses in writing. When peer review is effective, students gain a greater facility in identifying the aspects of their classmates' writing that give them difficulty as readers, and they will be able to transfer that knowledge to their own writing (Allaei & Connor, 1990).

Collaborative projects, too, can be effective in a class with international students. Assignments in which groups or pairs of students work together can draw on the basic understanding and interests of several students. One teacher in our program had his students work in groups to write final projects in which they did original research. One group went to the local mall and tested their hypothesis that the native speakers would be approached more quickly and more positively by the store clerks. Another group drew from their collective knowledge to write a guidebook for new international students who had just come to study at the university: The native speakers were able to contribute their greater knowledge of standard campus procedures and American customs, while the nonnative speakers could provide insights to the problems faced by new nonnative students.

Again, as with peer review groups, specific instruction will be helpful for collaborators. Burnett (1993a, 1993b) notes that co-authors who are willing to criticize one another's rhetorical choices and voice their disagreement in constructive ways produced higher quality documents than those students who simply nodded agreement to whatever their collaborators suggested. She suggests modeling this "substantive conflict" (1993a, p. 134) by providing students with specific information about successful collaborative behaviors and modeling particular "verbal moves" (1993b, p. 73) that a student can use for purposes such as prompting, challenging, or contributing information. Though Burnett's research focuses on native speaker collaboration, this suggestion is even more important for a class with nonnative students who may lack the verbal repertoire for voicing disagreement. Also, showing students that they can provide feedback to their collaborators in a spirit of friendly disagreement may help students understand that it is possible to disagree without causing "loss of face." Burnett also suggests having the teacher model constructive criticism by working in front of the class with a student or colleague to illustrate how writers can improve their collaborations.

In short, the methods used to teach peer review and collaboration to native speakers can be adapted quite readily for a class with ESL students. Both techniques have the added benefits of getting quiet students more involved in the classroom, providing opportunities for speaking and listening practice for ESL students, and building understanding and group solidarity between the U.S. students and their international classmates. Additionally, of course, the most valuable benefit is that these techniques help students improve their writing skills.

■ CONCLUSION

A teacher of writing can welcome multilingual students, knowing not only that the class can be a tremendous help to the students but also that the students may offer much to the class. The stimulating discussions that can occur in the small group setting of the composition class, the opportunity to share their cultural backgrounds and to learn about others' views, and the chance to more clearly understand U.S. academic expectations all benefit the multilingual student tremendously. Additionally, in contributing their unique perspectives, multilingual students add to the education of the U.S. students in the class. One U.S. student wrote this in his evaluation of a cross-cultural composition class:

> My feelings have definitely changed about people from other cultures since I've joined this class. Before this semester I carried with me many misconceptions. The main reason was because before now I had not had the opportunity to talk to people. This class has shown me that people from other parts of the world

share my same frustrations, concerns, joy, and happiness. I have learned to enjoy working with my classmates and working to become more open-minded.

In discussing the benefits of cross-cultural classes, Patthey-Chavez and Gergen write, "the presence of different voices and visions of the world can be transformed into an instructional resources" (p. 76). Whether a teacher has many English language learners or just a few, this resource can be a source of opportunity and inspiration.

REFERENCES

Allaei, S. K. & Connor, U. M. (1990). Exploring the dynamics of cross-cultural collaboration in writing classrooms. *The Writing Instructor*, Fall, 19–28.

Bosley, D. S. (1993). Cross-cultural collaboration: Whose culture is it, anyway? *Technical Communication Quarterly*, 2, I, 51–62.

Brown, H. D. (1994). *Principles of language learning and teaching* (3rd ed.). Englewood Cliffs, NJ: Prentice Hall.

Burnett, R. E. (1993a). Decision making during the collaborative planning of co-authors. In A. Penrose & B. M. Sitko, Eds. *Hearing Ourselves Think: Cognitive Research in the College Writing Classroom* (pp. 125–146). New York: Oxford University Press.

Burnett, R. E. (1993b). Interactions of engaged supporters. In L. Flower, D. L. Wallace, L. Norris, and R. E. Burnett, Eds. *Making Thinking Visible: Writing, Collaborative Planning, and Classroom Inquiry* (pp. 67–82). Urbana, IL: NCTE.

Byrd, P. (Ed.). (1986). *Teaching across cultures in the university ESL program.* Washington, DC: NAFSA.

Carson, J. & Nelson, G. (1994). Writing groups: Cross-cultural issues. *Journal of Second Language Writing*, 3, I, 17–30.

Fox, H. (1994). *Listening to the world: cultural issues in academic writing.* Urbana: NCTE.

Genzel, R. & Cummings, M. G. (1994). *Culturally speaking: A conversation and culture text.* Second Edition. Boston: Heinle and Heinle.

Gilbert, J. (1994). *Clear Speech* (2nd ed.). Cambridge: Cambridge University Press.

Grabe, B. & Kaplan, R. B. (1989) Writing in a second language: Contrastive rhetoric. In D. Johnson & D. Roen, (Eds.), *Richness in* writing: *Empowering ESL students* (pp. 263–283). White Plains, NY: Longman.

Grimm, N. (1986). Improving students' responses to their peers' essays. *College English.* 27. 91–94.

Hall, E. T. (1959). *The silent language.* Garden City, NY: Doubleday & Co.

Hall, E. T. & Hall, M. (1990). *Understanding cultural differences: Keys to success in West Germany, France, and the United States.* Yarmouth, ME: Intercultural Press.

Harklau, L., Losey, K.M., & Siegal, M. (Eds.) (1999). *Generation 1.5 meets college composition: Issues in the teaching of writing to U.S.-educated learners of ESL.* Mahwah, NJ: Erlbaum.

Harris, M. & Silva, T. (1993). Tutoring ESL students: Issues and options. *College Composition and Communication,* 44, 4, 525–537.

Hinds, J. (1987). Reader vs. writer responsibility: A new typology. In U. Connor & R. Kaplan (Eds.), *Writing across languages: Analysis of L2 text.* Reading, MA: Addison-Wesley.

Hirshberg, S. (1992). *One world, many cultures.* New York: Macmillan.

Holeton, R. (1995). *Encountering cultures* (2nd Edition). Englewood Cliffs, NJ: Prentice-Hall.

Kaplan, R. B. (1966). Cultural thought patterns in inter-cultural education. *Language Learning,* 16, 1–20.

Land, R. E. & Whitley, C. (1989). Evaluating second language essays in regular composition classes: Toward a pluralistic U.S. rhetoric. In D. Johnson & D. Roen (Eds.), *Richness in writing: Empowering ESL students* (pp. 284–294). White Plains, NY: Longman, Inc.

Larsen-Freeman, D. (Ed.). (1994). *Grammar dimensions* (four book series). Boston, MA: Heinle & Heinle.

Leki, I. (1991). The preferences of ESL students for error correction in college-level writing classes. *Foreign Language Annals,* 24, 3, 203–211.

——. (1992). *Understanding ESL writers: A guide for teachers.* Portsmouth, NH: Boynton/Cook.

Levine, R. with E. Wolff. (1985) Social time: The heartbeat of a culture. *Psychology Today,* 19, (March), 28–37.

Levine, D., Baxter, J., & McNulty, P. (1987). *The culture puzzle: Cross-cultural communication for English as a second language.* Englewood Cliffs, NJ: Prentice Hall.

Matalene, C. (1985). Contrastive rhetoric: An American writing teacher in China. *College English, 47,* 8, 789–808.

Mittan, R. (1989). The peer review process: Harnessing students' communicative power. In D. Johnson & D. Roen, (Eds.), *Richness in writing: Empowering ESL students* (pp. 207–219). White Plains, NY: Longman.

Morain, G. (1986). Kinesics and cross-cultural understanding. In J. M. Valdes, (Ed.), *Crossing Cultures* (pp. 64–76). Cambridge: Cambridge University Press.

Patthey-Chavez, G. & Gergen, C. (1992). Culture as an instructional resource in the multi-ethnic composition classroom. *Journal of Basic Writing,* II, I, 75–96.

Purves, A. (1986). Rhetorical communities, the international student, and basic writing. *Journal of Basic Writing,* 5, I, 83–51.

Raimes, A. (1992). *Grammar troublespots: An editing guide for students* (2nd ed.). New York: St. Martin's.

Reid, J. M. (1993). *Teaching ESL writing.* Englewood Cliffs, NJ: Regents/Prentice Hall.

Robb, T., Ross, S., Shortreed, I. (1986). Salience of feedback on error and its effect on ESL writing quality. *TESOL Quarterly,* 20, I, 83–93.

Roberge, M. (2003). Generation 1.5 immigrant students: What special experiences, characteristics and education needs do they bring to our English classes? *Proceedings of the 37th Annual TESOL Convention.* Baltimore, MD. Retrieved September 23, 2004, from **http://www.american.edu/tesol/Roberge_article.pdf**.

Roberge, M. (2005, March 16). *Working with Generation 1.5 in College Composition.* Presentation at the Conference on College Composition and Communication, San Francisco, CA.

Santos, T. (1992). Ideology in Composition. *Journal of Second Language Writing,* I, I, 1–15.

Schlumberger, A. & Clymer, D. (1989). Tailoring composition classes to ESL students' needs. *Teaching English in the Two-Year College,* May, 121–127.

Silva, T. (1993). Toward an understanding of the distinct nature of L2 writing: The ESL research and its implications. *TESOL Quarterly,* 27, 4, 657–676.

Tannen, D. (1984). *Conversational style: Analyzing talk among friends.* Norwood, NJ: Ablex.

Tyler, A. (1994). Sexual harassment and the ITA curriculum. *The Journal of Graduate Teaching Assistant Development*, 2, I, 31–41.

Valdes, G. (1992). Bilingual minorities and language issues in writing. *Written Communication*, 9, 85 – 136.

Valdes, Joyce M. (Ed.). (1986). *Culture bound.* Cambridge: Cabmride University Press.

Verberg, C. J. (1994). *Ourselves among others: Cross-cultural readings for writers* (Third Edition). New York: St. Martin's.

Zamel, V. (1985). Responding to student writing. *TESOL Quarterly*, 19, 195–209.

PART FIVE:

Reading and Writing About Literature: A Primer for Students

by Edgar V. Roberts, *Lehman College of the City University of New York*

Foreword

The following primer, which is modified and adapted from the ninth edition of *Writing About Literature* and the fifth edition of *Literature: An Introduction to Reading and Writing*, is written to students, and is designed for their use. It contains a condensed overview of the nature of literature, the ways of reading and reacting to a primary text (which here is "The Necklace," the famous story by Guy de Maupassant), and the methods of moving from early and unshaped responses to finished drafts of essays.

It would be most desirable to duplicate the entire primer for distribution to classes, but barring that, students should at least receive copies of the story and the sample essays to facilitate study and classroom discussion.

It is my hope that the overview provided here will stimulate students to carry out deeper and more methodical explorations of literary works. Literary understanding and appreciation should be acquired as early as possible, and students should never end their quests for the enjoyment, understanding, and power that literature provides.

—Edgar V. Roberts

Reading and Writing About Literature

■ **WHAT IS LITERATURE, AND WHY DO WE STUDY IT?**

We use the word **literature**, in a broad sense, to mean compositions that tell stories, dramatize situations, express emotions, and analyze and advocate ideas. Before the invention of writing thousands of years ago, literary works were necessarily spoken or sung, and were retained only as long as living people continued to repeat them. In some societies, the oral tradition of literature still exists, with many poems and stories designed exclusively for spoken delivery. Even in our modern age of writing and printing, much literature is still heard aloud rather than read silently. Parents delight their children with stories and poems; poets and story writers read their works directly before live audiences; plays and scripts are interpreted on stages and before moving-picture cameras for the benefit of a vast public.

No matter how we assimilate literature, we gain much from it. In truth, readers often cannot explain why they enjoy reading, for goals and ideals are not easily articulated. There are, however, areas of general agreement about the value of systematic and extensive reading.

Literature helps us grow, both personally and intellectually. It provides an objective base for knowledge and understanding. It links us with the cultural, philosophic, and religious world of which we are a part. It enables us to recognize human dreams and struggles in different places and times that we otherwise would never know existed. It helps us develop mature sensibility and compassion for the condition of all living things—human, animal, and vegetable. It gives us the knowledge and perception to appreciate the beauty of order and arrangement—gifts that are also bestowed by a well-structured song or a beautifully painted canvas. It provides the comparative basis from which to see worthiness in the aims of all people, and it therefore helps us see beauty in the world around us. It exercises our emotions through interest, concern, sympathy, tension, excitement, regret, fear, laughter, and hope. It encourages us to assist creative and talented people who need recognition and support. Through our cumulative experience in reading, literature shapes our goals and values by clarifying our own identities—both positively, through acceptance of the admirable in human beings, and negatively, through rejection of the sinister. It enables us to develop perspectives on events occurring locally and globally, and thereby it gives us understanding and control. It is one of the shaping influences of life. It makes us human.

Types of Literature: The Genres

Literature may be classified into four categories or genres: (1) prose fiction, (2) poetry, (3) drama, and (4) nonfiction prose. Usually the first three are classed as **imaginative literature.**

The genres of imaginative literature have much in common, but they also have distinguishing characteristics. **Prose fiction,** or **narrative fiction,** includes myths, **parables, romances, novels,** and **short stories.** Originally, fiction meant anything made up, crafted, or shaped, but today the word refers to prose stories based in the imaginations of authors. The essence of fiction is **narration,** the relating or recounting of a sequence of events or actions. Fictional works usually focus on one or a few major characters who change and grow (in their ability to make decisions, awareness and insight, attitude toward others, sensitivity, and moral capacity) as a result of how they deal with other characters and how they attempt to solve their problems. Although fiction, like all imaginative literature, may introduce true historical details, it is not real history. Its main purpose is to interest, stimulate, instruct, and divert, not to create a precise historical record.

Poetry expresses a monologue or a conversation grounded in the most deeply felt experiences of human beings. It exists in many formal and informal shapes, from the brief **haiku** to the extensive **epic.** More economical than prose fiction in its use of words, poetry relies heavily on **imagery, figurative language, and sound.**

Drama is literature designed to be performed by actors for the benefit and delight of an audience. Like fiction, drama may focus on a single character or a small number of characters; and it enacts fictional events as if they were happening in the present. The audience therefore becomes a direct witness to the events as they occur, from start to finish. Although most modern plays use prose dialogue, on the principle that the language of drama should resemble the language of ordinary persons as much as possible, many plays from the past, such as those of ancient Greece and Renaissance England, are in poetic form.

Nonfiction prose consists of news reports, feature articles, essays, editorials, textbooks, historical and biographical works, and the like, all of which describe or interpret facts and present judgments and opinions. In nonfiction prose the goal is to present truths and sound conclusions about the factual world of history, science, and current events. Imaginative literature, although also grounded in facts, is less concerned with the factual record than with the revelation of truths about life and human nature.

For the purpose of exploring techniques for reading, responding, and writing about literature, the following discussion will focus on the genre of fiction.

■ ELEMENTS OF FICTION

Works of fiction share a number of common elements. For reference here, the more significant ones are **character, plot, structure**, and **idea** or **theme.**

Character

Stories, like plays, are about characters—characters who are not real people but who are nevertheless like real people. A **character** may be defined as a reasonable facsimile of a human being, with all the good and bad traits of being human. Most stories are concerned with characters who are facing a major problem which may involve interactions with other characters, with difficult situations, or with an idea or general circumstances that force action. The characters may win, lose, or tie. They may learn and be the better for the experience or may miss the point and be unchanged.

It is a truism that modern fiction has accompanied the development of a psychological interest in human beings. Psychology itself has grown out of the philosophical and religious idea that people are not evil by nature, but rather that they have many inborn capacities—some for good and others for bad. People are not free of problems, and they make many mistakes in their lives, but they nevertheless are important and interesting, and are therefore worth writing about, whether male or female; young or old; white, black, tan, or yellow; rich or poor; worker or industrialist; traveler or resident; aviator, performer, mother, daughter, homemaker, prince, general, bartender, or checkout clerk.

The range of fictional characters is vast: A married couple struggling to repay an enormous debt, a woman meditating about her daughter's growth, a young man learning about sin and forgiveness, a young woman struggling to overcome the bitter memory of early sexual abuse, a man regretting that he cannot admit a lie, a woman surrounded by her insensitive and self-seeking brothers, a man preserving love in the face of overwhelming difficulties, a woman learning to cope with her son's handicap—all these, and more, may be found in fiction just as they may also be found in all levels and conditions of life. Because as human beings all of us share the same capacities for concern, involvement, sympathy, happiness, sorrow, exhilaration, and disappointment, we are able to find endless interest in such characters and their ways of responding to their circumstances.

Plot

Fictional characters, who are drawn from life, go through a series of life-like **actions** or **incidents,** which make up the story. In a well-done story, all the actions or incidents, speeches, thoughts, and observations are linked together to make up an entirety, sometimes called an **organic unity**. The essence of this unity is the development and resolution of a **conflict**—or conflicts—in which the **protagonist,** or central character, is engaged. The interactions of causes and effects as they develop **sequentially** or **chrono-logically** make up the story's **plot**. That is, a story's actions follow one another in time as the protagonist meets and tries to overcome opposing forces. Some-times plot has been compared to a story's map, scheme, or blueprint.

Often the protagonist's struggle is directed against another character—an **antagonist.** Just as often, however, the struggle may occur between the protagonist and opposing groups, forces, ideas, and choices—all of which make up a collective antagonist. The conflict may be carried out wherever human beings spend their lives, such as a kitchen, a bedroom, a restaurant, a town square, a farm, an estate, a workshop, or a battlefield. The conflict may also take place internally, within the mind of the protagonist.

Structure

Structure refers to the way a story is assembled. Chronologically, all stories are similar because they move from beginning to end in accord with the time needed for *causes* to produce *effects*. But authors choose many different ways to put their stories together. Some stories are told in straight-forward sequential order, and a description of the plot of such stories is identical to a description of the structure. Other stories, however, may get pieced together through out-of-sequence and widely separated episodes, speeches, second-hand reports, remembrances, dreams, nightmares, peri-ods of delirium, fragments of letters, overheard conversations, and the like. In such stories, the plot and the structure diverge widely. Therefore, in deal-ing with the structure of stories, we emphasize not chronological order but the actual *arrangement* and *development* of the stories as they unfold, part by part. Usually we study an entire story, but we may also direct our atten-tion toward a smaller aspect of arrangement such as an episode or passage of dialogue.

Idea or Theme

The word **idea** refers to the result or results of general and abstract thinking. In literary study the consideration of ideas relates to meaning, interpretation, explanation, and significance. Fiction necessarily embodies issues and ideas. Even stories written for entertainment alone are based in an idea or position. Thus, writers of comic works are committed to the idea that human difficulties can be treated with humor. More serious works may force characters to make difficult moral choices—the thought being that in a losing situation the only winners are those who maintain honor and self-respect. Mystery and suspense stories rest on the belief that problems have solutions, even if they may not at first seem apparent. Writers may deal with the triumphs and defeats of life, the admirable and the despicable, the humorous and the pathetic, but whatever their goal, they are always expressing ideas about human experience. We may therefore raise questions such as these as we look for ideas in fiction: *What does this mean? Why does the author include it? What idea or ideas does it show? Why is it significant?*

Fictional ideas may also be considered as major **themes** which tie individual works together. Often an author makes the theme obvious, as in the Aesop fable in which a man uses an ax to kill a fly on his son's forehead. The theme of this fable might loosely be expressed in a sentence like "the cure should not be worse than the disease." A major theme in Maupassant's "The Necklace" is that people may be destroyed or saved by unlucky and unforeseeable events. The accidental loss of the borrowed necklace is just such an event, for this misfortune ruins the lives of both Mathilde and her husband.

The process of determining and describing the themes or ideas in stories is never complete; there is always another theme that we may discuss. Thus in "The Necklace," one might note the additional themes that adversity brings out worth, that telling the truth is better than concealing it, that envy often produces ill fortune, and that good fortune is never recognized until it is lost. Indeed, one of the ways in which we may judge stories is to determine the degree to which they embody a number of valid and important ideas.

■ THE FICTION WRITER'S TOOLS

Narration

Writers have a number of modes of presentation, or "tools," which they may use in writing their stories. The principal tool (and the heart of fiction) is **narration**, the reporting of actions in sequential order. The object of narration is to *render* the story, to make it clear and to bring it alive to the reader's imagination through the movement of sentences through time. The writer of narrative may include all the events leading up to and following major actions, for a narration moves in a continuous line, from word to word, scene to scene, action to action, and speech to speech. As a result of this chronological movement, the reader's comprehension must necessarily also be chronological.

Style

The medium of fiction and of all literature is language, and the manipulation of language—the **style**—is a primary skill of the writer. A mark of a good style is active verbs, and nouns that are **specific** and **concrete**. Even with the most active and graphic diction possible, writers can never render their incidents and scenes exactly, but they may be judged on how vividly they tell their stories.

Point of View

One of the most important ways in which writers knit their stories together, and also an important way in which they try to interest and engage readers, is the careful control of **point of view.** Point of view is the **voice** of the story, the speaker who does the narrating. It is the way the reality of a story is made to seem authentic. It may be regarded as the story's *focus*, the *angle of vision* from which things are not only seen and reported but also judged.

Basically, there are two kinds of points of view, but there are many variations, sometimes obvious and sometimes subtle. In the first, the **first-person point of view**, a fictitious observer tells us what he or she saw, heard, concluded, and thought. This viewpoint is characterized by the use of the *I* pronoun as the speaker refers to his or her position as an observer or commentator. The **speaker**, or **narrator**—terms that are interchangeable—may sometimes seem to be the author speaking directly using an **authorial voice**, but more often the speaker is an independent character—a **persona** with characteristics that separate her or him from the author.

In common with all narrators, the first-person narrator establishes a clearly defined relationship to the story's events. Some narrators are deeply engaged in the action; others are only minor participants or observers; still others have had nothing to do with the action but are transmitting the reports of other, more knowledgeable, witnesses. Sometimes the narrator uses the *we* pronoun if he or she is represented as part of a group that has witnessed the action or participated in it. Often, too, the narrator might use *we* when referring to ideas and interpretations shared with the reader or listener—the idea being to draw readers into the story as much as possible. The second major point of view is the **third person** (*she, he, it, they, her, him, them,* etc.). The third-person point of view may be (1) **limited**, with the focus being on one particular character and what he or she does, says, hears, thinks, and otherwise experiences, (2) **omniscient**, with the possibility that the activities and thoughts of all the characters are open and fully known by the speaker, and (3) **dramatic**, or **objective**, in which the story is confined only to the reporting of actions and speeches, with no commentary and no revelation of the thoughts of any of the characters unless the characters themselves reveal their thoughts dramatically.

Understanding point of view usually requires subtlety of perception— indeed, it may be one of the most difficult of all concepts in the study of fiction. In fuller perspective, therefore, we may think of it as the *total position* from which things are viewed, understood, and communicated. The position might be simply physical: *Where was the speaker located when the events occurred?* or *Does the speaker give us a close or distant view of the events?* The position might also be personal or philosophical, as in the commentary by the narrator in Maupassant's "The Necklace."

Point of view is one of the major ways by which authors make fiction vital. By controlling point of view, an author helps us make reasonable inferences about the story's actions. Authors use point of view to raise some of the same questions in their fiction that perplex us in life. We need to evaluate what fictional narrators as well as real people tell us, for what they say is affected by their limitations, attitudes, opinions, and degree of candidness. For readers, the perception of a fictional point of view can be as complex as life itself, and it may be as difficult—in fiction as in life—to evaluate our sources of information.

Description

Together with narration, a vital aspect of fiction is **description**, which is intended to cause readers to imagine or re-create the scenes and actions of the story. Description can be both physical (places and persons) and psychological (an emotion or set of emotions). Excessive description sometimes interrupts or postpones a story's actions, so that many writers include only as much as is necessary to keep the action moving along.

Mood and **atmosphere** are important aspects of descriptive writing, and to the degree that descriptions are evocative, they may reach the level of **metaphor** and **symbolism**. These characteristics of fiction are a property of all literature, and you will also encounter them whenever you read poems and plays.

Dialogue

Another major tool of the writer of fiction is **dialogue**. By definition, dialogue is the conversation of two people, but more than two characters may also participate. It is of course the major medium of the playwright, and it is one of the means by which the fiction writer makes a story vivid and dramatic. Straight narration and description can do no more than make a secondhand assertion ("hearsay") that a character's thoughts and responses exist, but dialogue makes everything firsthand and real.

Dialogue is hence a means of *showing* rather than *reporting*. If characters feel pain or declare love, their own words may be taken as the expression of what is on their minds. Some dialogue may be terse and minimal; other dialogue may be expanded, depending on the situation, the personalities of the characters, and the author's intent. Dialogue may concern any topic, including personal feelings, reactions to the past, future plans, changing ideas, sudden realizations, and political, social, philosophic, or religious ideas.

The language of dialogue indicates the intelligence, articulateness, educational levels, or emotional states of the speakers. Hence the author might use *grammatical mistakes, faulty pronunciation,* or *slang* to show a character of limited or disadvantaged background or a character who is trying to be seen in that light. *Dialect* shows the region from which the speaker comes, just as an accent indicates a place of national origin. *Jargon* and *cliché* suggest self-inflation or intellectual limitations—usually reasons for laughter. The use of *private, intimate expressions* might show people who are close to each other emotionally. Speech that is interrupted by *voiced pauses* (e.g., "er," "ah," "um," "you know"), or speech characterized by *inappropriate words* might show a character who is unsure or not in control. There are many possibilities in dialogue, but no matter what qualities you find, writers include dialogue to enable you to know their characters better.

Tone and Irony

In every story we may consider **tone**, that is, the ways in which authors convey attitudes toward readers and also toward the story material. **Irony**, one of the major components of tone, refers to language and situations that seem to reverse normal expectations. *Word choice* is the characteristic of **verbal irony**, in which what is meant is usually the opposite of what is said, as when we *mean* that people are doing badly even though we *say* that they are doing well. Broader forms of *irony* are *situational* and dramatic: **Situational irony** refers to circumstances in which bad things happen to good people, or in which rewards are not earned because forces beyond human comprehension seem to be in total control. In **dramatic irony** characters have only a nonexistent, partial, incorrect, or misguided understanding of what is happening to them, while both readers and other characters understand the situation more fully. Readers hence become concerned about the characters and hope that they will develop understanding quickly enough to avoid the problems bedeviling them and the pitfalls endangering them.

Symbolism and Allegory

In literature, even apparently ordinary things may acquire **symbolic** value; that is, everyday objects may be understood to have meanings that are beyond themselves, bigger than themselves. In fiction, many functional and essential incidents, objects, speeches, and characters may also be construed as symbols. Some symbols are widely recognized and therefore are considered as cultural or universal. Water, flowers, jewels, the sun, certain stars, the flag, altars, and minarets are examples of cultural symbols. Other symbols are contextual; that is, they take on symbolic meaning only in their individual works, as when in Maupassant's "The Necklace" Mathilde and her husband move into an attic flat to save money that they need to repay their enormous debt. These new quarters may be taken to symbolize the hardship experienced by the poor.

When a complete story, in addition to maintaining its own narrative integrity, can be applied point-by-point to a parallel set of situations, it is an allegory. Many stories are not complete allegories, however, even though they may contain sections having allegorical parallels. Thus, the Loisels' long servitude in Maupassant's "The Necklace" is similar to the lives and activities of many people who perform tasks for mistaken or meaningless reasons. "The Necklace" is therefore allegorical even though it is not an allegory.

Commentary

Writers may also include **commentary, analysis**, or **interpretation**, in the expectation that readers need insight into the characters and actions. When fiction was new, authors often expressed such commentary directly. Henry Fielding (1707–1754) divided his novels into "books," and included a chapter of personal and philosophic commentary at the beginning of each of these. In the next century, George Eliot (1819–1880) included many extensive passages of commentary in her novels.

Later writers have kept commentary at a minimum, preferring instead to concentrate on direct action and dialogue, and allowing readers to draw their own conclusions about meaning. In first-person narrations, however, you may expect the narrators to make their own personal comments. Such observations may be accepted at face value, but you should recognize that anything the speakers say is also a mode of character disclosure and therefore is just as much a part of the story as the narrative incidents.

The Elements Together

These, then, are the major tools of writers of fiction. For analytical purposes, one or another of them may be considered separately so that the artistic achievement of a particular author may be recognized. It is also important to realize that authors may use all the tools simultaneously. The story may be told by a character who is a witness, and thus it has a **first-person point of view**. The major **character**, the **protagonist**, goes through a series of **actions** as a result of a carefully arranged **plot**. Because of this plot, together with the author's chosen method of **narration**, the story will follow a certain kind of arrangement, or **structure**, such as a straightforward **sequence** or a disjointed series of **episodes.** One thing that the action may demonstrate is the **theme** or **central idea**. The writer's **style** may be manifested in ironic expressions. The description of the character's actions may reveal **irony of situation**, while at the same time this situation is made vivid through **dialogue** in which the character is a participant. Because the plight of the character is like the plight of many persons in the world, it is an **allegory**, and the character herself or himself may be considered as a **symbol**.

Throughout each story we read, no matter what characteristics we are considering, it is most important to realize that a work of fiction is an entirety, a unity. Any reading of a story should be undertaken not to break things down into parts, but to understand and assimilate the work *as a whole*. The separate analysis of various topics, to which this book is committed, is thus a *means* to that end, *not* the end itself. The study of fiction, like the study of all literature, is designed to foster our growth and to increase our understanding of the human condition.

■ READING A STORY AND RESPONDING TO IT ACTIVELY

Regrettably, our first readings of works do not provide us with full understanding. After we have finished reading a work, we may find it embarrassingly difficult to answer pointed questions or to say anything intelligent about it at all. But more active and thoughtful readings give us the understanding to develop well-considered answers. Obviously, we need to follow the work and to understand its details, but just as important we need to respond to the words, get at the ideas, and understand the implications of what is happening. We rely on our own fund of knowledge and experience to verify the accuracy and truth of situations and incidents, and we try to articulate our own emotional responses to the characters and their problems.

To illustrate such active responding, the following story, "The Necklace" (1884), by the French writer Guy de Maupassant (1850–1893), is printed with marginal annotations like those that any reader might make during original and follow-up readings. Many observations, particularly at the beginning, are *assimilative*; that is, they do little more than record details about the action. But as the story progresses, the comments begin to reflect conclusions about the story's meaning. Toward the end, the comments are full rather than minimal; they result not only from first responses but also from considered thought. Here, then, is Maupassant's "The Necklace."

GUY DE MAUPASSANT, an apostle of Gustave Flaubert, was one of the major nineteenth-century French naturalists. He was a meticulous writer, devoting great attention to reality and to economy of detail. His stories are focused on the difficulties and ironies of existence not only among the Parisian middle class, as in "The Necklace," but also among both peasants and higher society. Two of his better-known novels are *A Life* (1883) and *A Good Friend* (1885). Among his other famous stories are "The Rendezvous" and "The Umbrella." "The Necklace" is notable for its concluding ironic twist, and for this reason it is perhaps the best known of his stories.

Guy de Maupassant (1850–1893)

The Necklace   *1884*

Translated by Edgar V. Roberts

She was one of those pretty and charming women, born, as if by an error of destiny, into a family of clerks and copyists. She had no dowry, no prospects, no way of getting known, courted, loved, married by a rich and distinguished man. She finally settled for a marriage with a minor clerk in the Ministry of Education.

She was a simple person, without the money to dress well, but she was as unhappy as if she had gone through bankruptcy, for women have neither rank nor race. In place of high birth or important family connections, they can rely only on their beauty, their grace, and their charm. Their inborn finesse, their elegant taste, their engaging personalities, which are their only power, make working-class women the equals of the grandest ladies.

She suffered constantly, feeling herself destined for all delicacies and luxuries. She suffered because of her grim apartment with its drab walls, threadbare furniture, ugly curtains. All such things, which most other women in her situation would not even have noticed, tortured her and filled her with despair. The sight of the young country girl who did her simple housework awakened in her only a sense of desolation and lost hopes. She daydreamed of large, silent anterooms, decorated with oriental tapestries and lighted by high bronze floor lamps, with two elegant valets in short culottes dozing in large armchairs under the effects of forced-air heaters. She imagined large drawing rooms draped in the most expensive silks, with fine end tables on which were placed knickknacks of inestimable value. She dreamed of the perfume of dainty private rooms, which were designed only for intimate tête-à-têtes with the closest friends, who because of their achievements and fame would make her the envy of all other women.

Marginal notes:

"She" is pretty but poor. Apparently there is no other life for her than marriage. Without connections, she has no entry into high society, and marries an insignificant clerk.

She is unhappy.

A view of women that excludes the possibility of a career. In 1884, women had little else than their personalities to get ahead.

She suffers because of her cheap belongings, wanting expensive things. She dreams of wealth and of how other women would envy her if she had all these fine things. But these luxuries are unrealistic and unattainable for her.

When she sat down to dinner at her round little table covered with a cloth that had not been washed for three days, in front of her husband who opened the kettle while declaring ecstatically, "Ah, good old boiled beef! I don't know anything better," she dreamed of expensive banquets with shining placesettings, and wall hangings portraying ancient heroes and exotic birds in an enchanted forest. She imagined a gourmet-prepared main course carried on the most exquisite trays and served on the most beautiful dishes, with whispered gallantries which she would hear with a sphinx-like smile as she dined on the pink meat of a trout or the delicate wing of a quail.

Her husband's taste is for plain things, while she dreams of expensive gourmet food. He has adjusted to his status. She has not.

5   She had no decent dresses, no jewels, nothing. And she loved nothing but these; she believed herself born only for these. She burned with the desire to please, to be envied, to be attractive and sought after.

She lives for her unrealistic dreams, and these increase her frustration.

She had a rich friend, a comrade from convent days, whom she did not want to see anymore because she suffered so much when she returned home. She would weep for the entire day afterward with sorrow, regret, despair, and misery.

She even thinks of giving up a rich friend because she is so depressed after visiting her.

Well, one evening, her husband came home glowing and carrying a large envelope.

A new section in the story.

"Here," he said, "this is something for you."

She quickly tore open the envelope and took out a card engraved with these words:

The **Chancellor of Education** *and*
Mrs. George Ramponneau
request that
Mr. and Mrs. Loisel
*do them the honor of coming to dinner
at the Ministry of Education
on the evening of January 8.*

An invitation to dinner at the Ministry of Education. A big plum.

10   Instead of being delighted, as her husband had hoped, she threw the invitation spitefully on the table, muttering:

"What do you expect me to do with this?"

"But honey, I thought you'd be glad. You never get to go out, and this is a special occasion! I had a lot of trouble getting the invitation. Everyone wants one. The demand is high and not many clerks get invited. Everyone important will be there."

She looked at him angrily and stated impatiently:

"What do you want me to wear to go there?"

15 He had not thought of that. He stammered:

"But your theater dress. That seems nice to me . . ."

He stopped, amazed and bewildered, as his wife began to cry. Large tears fell slowly from the corners of her eyes to her mouth. He said falteringly:

"What's wrong? What's the matter?"

But with a strong effort she had recovered, and she answered calmly as she wiped her damp cheeks:

20 "Nothing, except that I have nothing to wear and therefore can't go to the party. Give your invitation to someone else at the office whose wife will have nicer clothes than mine."

Distressed, he responded:

"Well, all right, Mathilde. How much would a new dress cost, something you could use at other times, but not anything fancy?"

She thought for a few moments, adding things up and thinking also of an amount that she could ask without getting an immediate refusal and a frightened outcry from the frugal clerk.

Finally she responded tentatively:

25 "I don't know exactly, but it seems to me that I could get by on four hundred francs."

He blanched slightly at this, because he had set aside just that amount to buy a shotgun for Sunday lark-hunts the next summer with a few friends in the Plain of Nanterre.

However, he said:

"All right, you've got four hundred francs, but make it a pretty dress."

As the day of the party drew near, Mrs. Loisel seemed sad, uneasy, anxious, even though her gown was all ready. One evening her husband said to her:

Side notes:

It only upsets her.

She declares that she hasn't anything to wear.

He tries to persuade her that her theater dress might do for the occasion.

Her name is Mathilde.

He volunteers to pay for a new dress.

She is manipulating him.

The dress will cost him his next summer's vacation. (He doesn't seem to have included her in his plans.)

A new section, the third in the story. The day of the party is near.

30   "What's the matter? You've been acting funny for several days."

She answered:

"It's awful, but I don't have any jewels to wear, not a single gem, nothing to dress up my outfit. I'll look like a beggar. I'd almost rather not go to the party."

Now she complains that she doesn't have any nice jewelry. She is manipulating him again.

He responded:

"You can wear a corsage of cut flowers. This year it's all the rage. For only ten francs you can get two or three gorgeous roses."

35   She was not convinced.

"No . . . there's nothing more humiliating than looking shabby in the company of rich women."

She has a good point, but there seems to be no way out.

But her husband exclaimed:

"God, but you're silly! Go to your friend Mrs. Forrestier, and ask her to lend you some jewelry. You know her well enough to do that."

He proposes a solution: borrow jewelry from Mrs. Forrestier, who is apparently the rich friend mentioned earlier.

She uttered a cry of joy:

40   "That's right. I hadn't thought of that."

The next day she went to her friend's house and described her problem.

Mrs. Forrestier went to her mirrored wardrobe, took out a large jewel box, opened it, and said to Mrs. Loisel: "Choose, my dear."

Mathilde will have her choice of jewels.

She saw bracelets, then a pearl necklace, then a Venetian cross of finely worked gold and gems. She tried on the jewelry in front of a mirror, and hesitated, unable to make up her mind about each one. She kept asking:

45   "Do you have anything else?"

"Certainly. Look to your heart's content. I don't know what you'd like best."

Suddenly she found a superb diamond necklace in a black satin box, and her heart throbbed with desire for it. Her hands shook as she picked it up. She fastened it around her neck, watched it gleam at her throat, and looked at herself ecstatically.

A "superb" diamond necklace.

Then she asked, haltingly and anxiously:

"Could you lend me this, nothing but this?"

50   "Why yes, certainly."

This is what she wants, just this.

She jumped up, hugged her friend joyfully, then hurried away with her treasure.

She leaves with the "treasure."

The day of the party came. Mrs. Loisel was a success. She was prettier than anyone else, stylish, graceful, smiling and wild with joy. All the men saw her, asked her name, sought to be introduced. All the important administrators stood in line to waltz with her. The Chancellor himself eyed her.

A new section.
The Party. Mathilde is a huge success.

She danced joyfully, passionately, intoxicated with pleasure, thinking of nothing but the moment, in the triumph of her beauty, in the glory of her success, on cloud nine with happiness made up of all the admiration, of all the aroused desire, of this victory so complete and so sweet to the heart of any woman.

Another judgment about women. Does the author mean that only women want to be admired? Don't men want admiration, too?

She did not leave until four o'clock in the morning. Her husband, since midnight, had been sleeping in a little empty room with three other men whose wives had also been enjoying themselves.

Loisel, with other husbands, is bored, while the wives are having a ball.

55   He threw, over her shoulders, the shawl that he had brought for the trip home—a modest everyday wrap, the poverty of which contrasted sharply with the elegance of her evening gown. She felt it and hurried away to avoid being noticed by the other women who luxuriated in rich furs.

Ashamed of her shabby wrap, she rushes away to avoid being seen.

Loisel tried to hold her back:

"Wait a minute. You'll catch cold outdoors. I'll call a cab."

But she paid no attention and hurried down the stairs. When they reached the street they found no carriages. They began to look for one, shouting at cabmen passing by at a distance.

They walked toward the Seine, desperate, shivering. Finally, on a quay, they found one of those old night-going buggies that are seen in Paris only after dark, as if they were ashamed of their wretched appearance in daylight.

A come down after the nice evening. They take a wretched-looking buggy home.

60   It took them to their door, on the Street of Martyrs, and they sadly climbed the stairs to their flat. For her, it was finished. As for him, he could think only that he had to begin work at the Ministry of Education at ten o'clock.

"Street of Martyrs." Is this name significant?

Loisel is down-to-earth.

She took the shawl off her shoulders, in front of the mirror, to see herself once more in her glory. But suddenly she cried out. The necklace was no longer around her neck!

She has lost the necklace!

Her husband, already half undressed, asked:

"What's wrong?"

She turned toward him frantically:

65   "I . . . I . . . I no longer have Mrs. Forrestier's necklace."

He stood up, bewildered:

"What? . . . How? . . . It's not possible!"

And they looked in the folds of the gown, in the folds of the shawl, in the pockets, everywhere. They found nothing.

They can't find it.

He asked:

70   "You're sure you still had it when you left the party?"

"Yes. I checked it in the vestibule of the Ministry."

"But if you'd lost it in the street, we would've heard it fall. It must be in the cab."

"Yes, probably. Did you notice the number?"

"No. Did you see it?"

75   "No."

Overwhelmed, they looked at each other. Finally, Loisel got dressed again:

"I'm going out to retrace all our steps," he said, "to see if I can find the necklace that way."

And he went out. She stayed in her evening dress, without the energy to get ready for bed, stretched out in a chair, drained of strength and thought.

He goes out to search for the necklace.

Her husband came back at about seven o'clock. He had found nothing.

But is unsuccessful.

80   He went to Police Headquarters and to the newspapers to announce a reward. He went to the small cab companies, and finally he followed up even the slightest hopeful lead.

He really tries. He's doing his best.

She waited the entire day, in the same enervated state, in the face of this frightful disaster.

Loisel came back in the evening, his face pale and haggard. He had found nothing.

"You'll have to write to your friend," he said, "that you broke a clasp on her necklace and that you're having it fixed. That'll give us time to look around."

Loisel's plan to explain delaying the return. He takes charge, is resourceful.

She wrote as he dictated.

85 By the end of the week they had lost all hope.
And Loisel, looking five years older, declared:
"We'll have to see about replacing the jewels."

The next day they took the case which had contained
the necklace and went to the jeweler whose name was
inside. He looked at his books:

"I wasn't the one, Madam, who sold the necklace. I
only made the case."

90 Then they went from jeweler to jeweler, searching
for a necklace like the other one, racking their memories, both of them sick with worry and anguish.

In a shop in the Palais-Royal, they found a necklace
of diamonds that seemed to them exactly like the one
they were looking for. It was priced at forty thousand
francs. They could buy it for thirty-six thousand.

They got the jeweler to promise not to sell it for
three days. And they made an agreement that he would
buy it back for thirty-four thousand francs if the original was recovered before the end of February.

Loisel had saved eighteen thousand francs that his
father had left him. He would have to borrow the rest.

He borrowed, asking a thousand francs from one,
five hundred from another, five louis° here, three louis
there. He wrote promissory notes, undertook ruinous
obligations, did business with finance companies and
the whole tribe of loan sharks. He compromised himself
for the remainder of his days, risked his signature without knowing whether he would be able to honor it, and,
terrified by anguish over the future, by the black misery
that was about to descend on him, by the prospect of
all kinds of physical deprivations and moral tortures, he
went to get the new necklace, and put down thirty-six
thousand francs on the jeweler's counter.

95 Mrs. Loisel took the necklace back to Mrs. Forrestier,
who said with an offended tone:

"You should have brought it back sooner; I might
have needed it."

She did not open the case, as her friend feared she
might. If she had noticed the substitution, what would

° *louis*: a gold coin worth twenty francs.

Side notes:
Things are hopeless.

They hunt for a replacement.

A new diamond necklace will cost 36,000 francs, a monumental amount.

They make a deal with the jeweler. (Is Maupassant hinting that things might work out for them?)

It will take all of Loisel's inheritance plus another 18,000 francs that must be borrowed at enormous rates of interest.

Mrs. Forrestier complains about the delay.

Is this enough justification for not telling the truth? It seems to be for the Loisels.

she have thought? What would she have said? Would she not have taken her for a thief?

Mrs. Loisel soon discovered the horrible life of the needy. She did her share, however, completely, heroically. That horrifying debt had to be paid. She would pay. They dismissed the maid; they changed their address; they rented an attic flat.

> A new section, the fifth.

She learned to do the heavy housework, dirty kitchen jobs. She washed the dishes, wearing away her manicured fingernails on greasy pots and encrusted baking dishes. She handwashed dirty linen, shirts, and dish towels that she hung out on the line to dry. Each morning, she took the garbage down to the street, and she carried up water, stopping at each floor to catch her breath. And, dressed in cheap house dresses, she went to the fruit dealer, the grocer, the butchers, with her basket under her arms, haggling, insulting, defending her measly cash penny by penny.

> They suffer to repay their debts. Loisel works late at night. Mathilde accepts a cheap attic flat, and does all the heavy housework herself to save on domestic help.

> She pinches pennies, and haggles with the local tradesmen.

100 They had to make installment payments every month, and, to buy more time, to refinance loans.

> They struggle to meet payments.

The husband worked evenings to make fair copies of tradesmen's accounts, and late into the night he made copies at five cents a page.

> Mr. Loisel moonlights to make extra money.

And this life lasted ten years.

> For ten years they struggle, but they endure.

At the end of ten years, they had paid back everything—everything—including the extra charges imposed by loan sharks and the accumulation of compound interest.

> The last section. They have finally paid back the entire debt.

Mrs. Loisel looked old now. She had become the strong, hard, and rude woman of poor households. Her hair unkempt, with uneven skirts and rough, red hands, she spoke loudly, washed floors with large buckets of water. But sometimes, when her husband was at work, she sat down near the window, and she dreamed of that evening so long ago, of that party, where she had been so beautiful and so admired.

> Mrs. Loisel (how come the narrator does not say "Mathilde"?) is roughened and aged by the work. But she has behaved "heroically" (¶ 98), and has shown her mettle.

105 What would life have been like if she had not lost that necklace? Who knows? Who knows? Life is so peculiar, so uncertain. How little a thing it takes to destroy you or to save you!

> A moral? Our lives are shaped by small, uncertain things; we hang by a thread.

Well, one Sunday, when she had gone for a stroll along the Champs-Elysées to relax from the cares of the week, she suddenly noticed a woman walking with a child. It was Mrs. Forrestier, still youthful, still beautiful, still attractive.

Mrs. Loisel felt moved. Would she speak to her? Yes, certainly. And now that she had paid, she could tell all. Why not?

She walked closer.

"Hello, Jeanne."

110 The other gave no sign of recognition and was astonished to be addressed so familiarly by this working-class woman. She stammered:

"But . . . Madam! . . . I don't know. . . . You must have made a mistake."

"No. I'm Mathilde Loisel."

Her friend cried out:

"Oh! . . . My poor Mathilde, you've changed so much."

115 "Yes. I've had some tough times since I saw you last; in fact hardships . . . and all because of you! . . ."

"Of me . . . how so?"

"You remember the diamond necklace that you lent me to go to the party at the Ministry of Education?"

"Yes. What then?"

"Well, I lost it."

120 "How, since you gave it back to me?"

"I returned another exactly like it. And for ten years we've been paying for it. You understand this wasn't easy for us, who have nothing. . . . Finally it's over, and I'm damned glad."

Mrs. Forrestier stopped her.

"You say that you bought a diamond necklace to replace mine?"

"Yes, you didn't notice it, eh? It was exactly like yours."

125 And she smiled with proud and childish joy.

Mrs. Forrestier, deeply moved, took both her hands.

"Oh, my poor Mathilde! But mine was only costume jewelry. At most, it was worth only five hundred francs! . . ."

Sidebar notes:

A scene on the Champs-Elysées. She sees Jeanne Forrestier, after ten years.

They seem to have lost contact with each other totally during the last ten years. Would this have happened in real life?

Jeanne notes Mathilde's changed appearance.

Mathilde tells Jeanne everything.

SURPRISE! The lost necklace was **not** real diamonds, and the Loisels slaved for no reason at all. But hard work and sacrifice probably brought out better qualities in Mathilde than she otherwise might have shown. Is this the moral of the story?

■ Reading and Responding in a Journal

The comments included alongside the story demonstrate the active reading-responding process you should apply to everything you read. Use the margins in your text to record your comments and questions, but, in addition, plan to keep a *journal* for lengthier responses. Your journal, which may consist of a notebook, note cards, separate sheets of paper, or a computer file, will be immensely useful to you as you move from your initial impressions toward more carefully considered thought.

In keeping your journal, your objective should be to learn assigned works inside and out and then to say perceptive things about them. To achieve this goal, you need to read the work more than once. You will need a good note-taking system so that as you read, you can develop a "memory bank" of your own knowledge about a work. You can draw from this fund of ideas when you begin to write. As an aid in developing your own procedures for reading and "depositing" your ideas, you may wish to begin with the following "Guidelines for Reading." Of course, you will want to modify these suggestions and to add to them, as you become a more experienced, disciplined reader.

Using the Names of Authors When Writing About Literature

For both men and women writers, you should typically include the author's *full name* in the *first sentence* of your essay. Here are few model first sentences:

> Guy de Maupassant's "The Necklace" is a story that concludes with a surprise.

> "The Necklace," by Guy de Maupassant, is a story that concludes with a surprise.

For all later references, use only the author's last name (such as *Maupassant* for this story). However, for the "giants" of literature, you should use the last names exclusively. In referring to writers like Shakespeare and Milton, for example, there is no need to include *William* or *John*.

In spite of today's informal standards, do not use an author's first name, as in "*Guy* skillfully creates suspense and surprise in 'The Necklace.'" Also, do not use a familiar title before the names of dead authors, such as "*Mr.* Maupassant's 'The Necklace' is a suspenseful and pathetic story." Use the last name alone.

As with all conventions, of course, there are exceptions. If you are referring to a childhood work of a writer, the first name is appropriate, but shift to the last name when referring to the writer's mature works. If your writer has a professional or a noble title, such as "*Judge* O'Connor," "*Governor* Cross," "*Lord* Byron" or "*Lady* Winchelsea," it is not improper to use the title. Even then, however, the titles are commonly omitted for males, so that most references to Lord Byron and Lord Tennyson should be simply to "Byron" and "Tennyson."

Referring to living authors is somewhat problematic. Some journals and newspapers, like the *New York Times*, use the respectful titles *Mr.* and *Ms.* in their reviews. However, scholarly journals, which are likely to remain on library shelves for many decades, follow the general principle of beginning with the entire name and then using only the last name for subsequent references.

RESPONDING TO LITERATURE: LIKES AND DISLIKES

People read for many reasons. In the course of daily affairs, they read signs, labels, price tags, recipes, or directions for assembling a piece of furniture or a toy. They read newspapers to learn about national, international, and local events. They might read magazines to learn about important issues, celebrities, political figures, and biographical details about significant persons. Sometimes they might read to pass the time, or to take their minds off pressing problems or situations. Also, people regularly read out of necessity—in school and in their work. They study for examinations in chemistry, biology, psychology, and political science. They go over noun paradigms and verb forms in a foreign language. They read to acquire knowledge in many areas, and they read to learn new skills, new information, and new ways to do their jobs better.

But, aside from incidental, leisurely, and obligatory reading, many people turn to imaginative literature, which they read because they like it and find it interesting. Even if they don't like everything they read equally, they nevertheless enjoy reading and usually pick out authors and types of literature that they like.

It is therefore worth considering those qualities of imaginative literature that at the primary level produce responses of pleasure (and also of displeasure). You either like or dislike a story, poem, or play. If you say no more than this, however, you have not said much. Analyzing and explaining your likes and dislikes requires you to describe the reasons for your responses. The goal should be to form your responses as judgments, which are usually *informed* and *informative*, rather than as simple reactions, which may be *uninformed* and *unexplained.*

Sometimes a reader's first responses are that a story or poem is either "okay" or "boring." These reactions usually mask an incomplete and superficial first reading. They are neither informative nor informed. As you study most works, however, you will be drawn into them and become *interested* and *involved.* To be interested in a poem, play, or story is to be taken into it emotionally; to be involved suggests that your emotions become almost wrapped up in the characters, problems, outcomes, ideas, and expressions of opinion and emotion. Both "interest" and "involvement" describe genuine responses to reading. Once you get interested and involved, your reading ceases to be a task or an assignment and grows into a pleasure.

Use Your Journal to Record Your Responses

No one can tell you what you should or should not like, for liking is your own concern. While your reading is still fresh, therefore, you should use your journal to record your responses to a work in addition to your observations about it. Be frank in your judgment. Write down what you like or dislike, and explain the reasons for your responses, even if these are brief and incomplete. If, after later thought and fuller understanding, you change or modify your impressions, write down these changes too. Here is a journal entry that explains a favorable response to Maupassant's "The Necklace":

> I like "The Necklace" because of the surprise ending. It isn't that I like Mathilde's bad luck, but I like the way Maupassant hides the most important fact in the story until the end. Mathilde does all that work and sacrifice for no reason at all, and the surprise ending makes this point strongly.

This paragraph could be developed as part of an essay. It is a clear statement of liking, followed by references to likable things in the story. This response pattern, which can be simply phrased as "I like [dislike] this work because . . . ," is a useful way to begin journal entries because it always requires an explanation of responses. If at first you cannot explain the causes of your responses, at least make a brief list of the things you like or dislike. If you write nothing, you will probably forget your reactions. Recovering them later, either for discussion or writing, will be difficult.

GUIDELINES FOR READING

1. OBSERVATIONS FOR BASIC UNDERSTANDING

A. EXPLAIN WORDS, SITUATIONS, AND CONCEPTS. Write down words that are new or not immediately clear. If you find a passage that you do not quickly understand, decide whether the problem arises from unknown words. Use your dictionary, and record the relevant meanings in your journal, but be sure that these meanings clarify your understanding. Make note of special difficulties so that you may ask you instructor about them.

B. DETERMINE WHAT IS HAPPENING. For a story or play, where do the actions take place? What do they show? Who is involved? Who is the major figure? Why is he or she major? What relationships do the characters have with one another? What concerns do the characters have? What do they do? Who says what to whom? How do the speeches advance the action and reveal the characters? For a poem, what is the situation? Who is talking, and to whom? What does the speaker say about the situation? Why does the poem end as it does and where it does?

2. NOTES ON FIRST IMPRESSIONS

A. MAKE A RECORD OF YOUR REACTIONS AND RESPONSES, which you may derive from your marginal notations. What did you think was memorable, noteworthy, funny, or otherwise striking? Did you worry, get scared, laugh, smile feel a thrill, learn a great deal, feel proud, find a lot to think about? In your journal, record these responses and explain them more fully.

B. DESCRIBE INTERESTING CHARACTERIZATIONS, EVENTS, TECHNIQUES, AND IDEAS. If you like a character or an idea, explain what you like, and do the same for characters and ideas you don't like. Is there anything else in the work that you especially like or dislike. Are parts easy or difficult to understand? Why? Are there any surprises? What was your reaction to them? Be sure to use your own words when writing your explanations.

3. DEVELOPMENT OF IDEAS AND ENLARGEMENT OF RESPONSES

A. TRACE DEVELOPING PATTERNS. Make an outline or a scheme: What conflicts appear? Do these conflicts exist between people, groups, or ideas? How does the author resolve them? Is one force, idea, or side the winner? Why? How do you respond to the winner or to the loser?

B. WRITE EXPANDED NOTES ABOUT CHARACTERS, SITUATIONS, AND ACTIONS. What explanations need to be made about the characters? What actions, scenes, and situations invite interpretation? What assumptions do the characters and speakers reveal about life and humanity generally; about themselves, the people around them, their families, and their friends; and about work, the economy, religion, politics, philosophy and the state of the world and the universe? What manners or customs do they exhibit? What sort of language do they use? What literary conventions and devices have you noticed, and what do these contribute to the action and ideas of the story?

C. WRITE A PARAGRAPH OR SEVERAL PARAGRAPHS DESCRIBING YOUR REACTIONS AND THOUGHTS. If you have an assignment, your paragraphs may be useful later because you might transfer them directly as early drafts. Even if you are making only a general preparation, however, always write down your thoughts.

D. MEMORIZE INTERESTING, WELL-WRITTEN, AND IMPORTANT PASSAGES. Use note cards to write them out in full, and keep them in your pocket or purse. When walking to class, riding public transportation, or otherwise not occupying your time, learn them by heart.

E. ALWAYS WRITE DOWN QUESTIONS THAT ARISE AS YOU READ. You may raise these in class, and they may also aid your own study.

State Reasons for Your Favorable Responses

Usually you can equate your interest in a work with liking it. You can be more specific about favorable responses by citing one or more of the following:

➤ You like and admire the characters and what they do and stand for. You get involved with them. When they are in danger you are concerned; when they succeed, you are happy; when they speak, you like what they say.

➤ After you have read the last word in a story or play, you are sorry to part with these characters and wish that there were more to read about them and their activities.

➤ Even if you do not particularly like a character or the characters, you are nevertheless interested in the reasons for and outcomes of their actions.

➤ You get so interested and involved in the actions or ideas in the work that you do not want to put the work down until you have finished it.

➤ You like to follow the pattern of action or the development of the author's thoughts, so that you respond with appreciation upon finishing the work.

➤ You find that reading enables you to relax or to take your mind off a problem or a pressing responsibility.

➤ You learn something new—something you had never before known or thought about human beings and their ways of handling their problems.

➤ You learn about customs and ways of life in different places and times.

➤ You gain new insights into aspects of life that you thought you already understood.

➤ You feel happy or thrilled because of reading the work.

➤ You are amused, and you laugh often as you read.

➤ You like the author's ways of describing scenes, actions, ideas, and feelings.

➤ You find that many of the expressions are remarkable and beautiful, and are therefore worth remembering.

State Reasons for Your Unfavorable Responses

Although so far we have dismissed *okay* and *boring* and have stressed *interest*, *involvement*, and *liking*, it is important to know that disliking all or part of a work is normal and acceptable. You do not need to hide this response. Here, for example, are two short journal responses expressing dislike for Maupassant's "The Necklace":

1. I do not like "The Necklace" because Mathilde seems spoiled, and I don't think she is worth reading about.
2. "The Necklace" is not an adventure story, and I like reading only adventure stories.

These are both legitimate responses because they are based on a clear standard of judgment. The first response stems from a distaste for one of the main character's unlikable traits, and the second from a preference for rapidly moving stories that evoke interest in the dangers that main characters face and overcome.

Here is a paragraph-length journal entry that might be developed from the first response. Notice that the reasons for dislike are explained. They would need only slightly more development for use in an essay:

I dislike "The Necklace" because Mathilde seems spoiled, and I don't think she is worth reading about. She is a phony. She nags her husband because he is not rich. She never tells the truth. I dislike her for hurrying away from the party because she is afraid of being seen in her shabby coat. She is foolish and dishonest for not telling Jeanne Forrestier about losing the necklace. It's true that she works hard to pay the debt, but she also puts her husband through ten years of hardship. If Mathilde had faced facts, she might have had a better life. I do not like her and cannot like the story because of her.

As long as you include reasons for your dislike, as in the list and in the paragraph, you can use them again in considering the story more fully, when you will surely also expand thoughts, include new details, pick new topics for development as paragraphs, and otherwise modify your journal entry. You might even change your mind. However, even if you do not, it is better to record your original responses and reasons honestly than to force yourself to say you like a story that you do not like.

Try to Put Dislikes into a Larger Context

Although it is important to be honest about disliking a work, it is more important to broaden your perspective and expand your taste. For example, a dislike based on the preference for only mystery or adventure stories, if generally applied, would cause a person to dislike most works of literature. This attitude seems unnecessarily self-limiting.

If negative responses are put in a larger context, it is possible to expand the capacity to like and appreciate good literature. For instance, some readers might be preoccupied with their own concerns and therefore be uninterested in remote or "irrelevant" literary figures. However, if by reading about literary characters they can gain insight into general problems of life, and therefore their own concerns, they can find something to like in just about any work. Other readers might like sports and therefore not read anything but the daily sports pages. What probably interests them about sports is competition, however, so if they can follow the *competition* or *conflict* in a literary work, they will have discovered something to like in that work.

As an example, let us consider again the dislike based on a preference for adventure stories, and see whether this preference can be widened. Here are some reasons for liking adventures:

1. Adventure has fast action.
2. It has danger and tension, and therefore interest.
3. It has daring, active, and successful characters.
4. It has obstacles that the characters work hard to overcome.

No one could claim that the first three points apply to "The Necklace," but the fourth point is promising. Mathilde, the major character, works hard to overcome an obstacle: She pitches in to help her husband pay the large debt. If you like adventures because the characters try to gain worthy goals, then you can also like "The Necklace" for the same reason. The principle here is clear: If a reason for liking a favorite work or type of work can be found in another work, then there is reason to like that new work.

The following paragraph shows a possible application of this "bridging" process of extending preferences. (The sample essay that begins on page 270 is also developed along these lines.)

> I usually like only adventure stories, and therefore I disliked "The Necklace" at first because it is not adventure. But one of my reasons for liking adventure is that the characters work hard to overcome

difficult obstacles, like finding buried treasure or exploring new places. Mathilde, Maupassant's main character in "The Necklace," also works hard to overcome an obstacle—helping to pay back the money and interest for the borrowed 18,000 francs used as part of the payment for the replacement necklace. I like adventure characters because they stick to things and win out. I see the same toughness in Mathilde. Her problems get more interesting as the story moves on after a slow beginning. I came to like the story.

The principle of "bridging" from like to like is worth restating and emphasizing: *If a reason for liking a favorite work or type of work can be found in another work, then there is reason to like that new work.* A person who adapts to new reading in this open-minded way can redefine dislikes, no matter how slowly, and may consequently expand the ability to like and appreciate many kinds of literature.

An equally open-minded way to develop understanding and widen taste is to put dislikes in the following light: An author's creation of an *unlikable* character, situation, attitude, or expression may be deliberate. Your dislike might then result from the author's *intentions.* A first task of study, therefore, is to understand and explain the intention or plan. As you put the plan into your own words, you may find that you can like a work with unlikable things in it. Here is a paragraph that traces this pattern of thinking, based again on "The Necklace":

> Maupassant apparently wants the reader to dislike Mathilde, and I do. At first, he shows her being unrealistic and spoiled. She lies to everyone and nags her husband. Her rushing away from the party so that no one can see her shabby coat is a form of lying. But I like the story itself because Maupassant makes another kind of point. He does not hide her bad qualities, but makes it clear that she herself is the cause of her trouble. If people like Mathilde never face the truth, they will get into bad situations. This is a good point, and I like the way Maupassant makes it. The entire story is therefore worth liking even though I still do not like Mathilde.

Both of these "bridging" analyses are consistent with the original negative reactions. In the first paragraph, the writer applies one of his principles of liking to include "The Necklace." In the second, the writer considers her initial dislike in the context of the work, and discovers a basis for liking the story as a whole while still disliking the main character. The main concern in both responses is to keep an open mind despite initial dislike and then to see whether the unfavorable response can be more fully and broadly considered.

However, if you decide that your dislike overbalances any reasons you can find for liking, then you should explain your dislike. As long as you relate your response to the work accurately and measure it by a clear standard of judgment, your dislike of even a commonly liked work is not unacceptable. The important issue is not so much that you like or dislike a particular work *but that you develop your own abilities to analyze and express your ideas.*

■ WRITING ESSAYS ON LITERARY TOPICS

Writing is the sharpened, focused expression of thought and study. It begins with the search for something to say—an idea. Not all ideas are equal; some are better than others, and getting good ideas is an ability that you will develop the more you think and write. As you discover ideas and write them down, you will also improve your perceptions and increase your critical faculties.

In addition, because literature itself contains the subject material, though not in a systematic way, of philosophy, religion, psychology, sociology, and politics, learning to analyze literature and to write about it will also improve your capacity to deal with these and other disciplines.

Writing Does Not Come Easily: Don't Worry—Just Do It

At the outset, it is important to realize that writing is a process that begins in uncertainty and hesitation, and that becomes certain and confident only as a result of diligent thought and considerable care. When you read a complete, polished, well-formed piece of writing, you might believe at first that the writer wrote this perfect version in only one draft and never needed to make any changes and improvements in it at all. Nothing could be further from the truth.

If you could see the early drafts of writing you admire, you would be surprised and startled—and also encouraged—to see that good writers are also human and that what they first write is often uncertain, vague, tangential, tentative, incomplete, and messy. Usually, they do not like these first drafts, but nevertheless they work with their efforts and build upon them: They discard some details, add others, chop paragraphs in half, reassemble the parts elsewhere, throw out much (and then maybe recover some of it), revise or completely rewrite sentences, change words, correct misspellings, and add new material to tie all the parts together and make them flow smoothly.

Three Major Stages of Thinking and Writing

For good and not-so-good writers alike, the writing task follows three basic stages. (1) The first stage—*discovering ideas*—shares many of the qualities of ordinary conversation. Usually, conversation is random and disorganized. It shifts from topic to topic, often without any apparent cause, and it is repetitive. In discovering ideas for writing, your process is much the same, for you jump from idea to idea, and do not necessarily identify the connections or bridges between them. (2) By the second step, however—*creating an early, rough draft of a critical paper*—your thought should be less like ordinary conversation and more like classroom discussion. Such discussions generally stick to a point, but they are also free and spontaneous, and digressions often occur. (3) At the third stage—*preparing a finished essay*—your thinking must be sharply focused, and your writing must be organized, definite, concise, and connected.

If you find that trying to write an essay gets you into difficulties like false starts, dead ends, total cessation of thought, digressions, despair, hopelessness, and other such frustrations, remember that *it is important just to start*. Just simply write anything at all—no matter how unacceptable your first efforts may seem—and force yourself to come to grips with the materials. Beginning to write does not commit you to your first ideas. They are not untouchable and holy just because they are on paper or on your computer screen. You may throw them out in favor of new ideas. You may also cross out words or move sections around, as you wish. However, if you keep your first thoughts buried in your mind, you will have nothing to work with. It is essential to accept the uncertainties in the writing process and make them work *for* you rather than *against* you.

DISCOVERING IDEAS

You cannot know your own ideas fully until you write them down. Thus, the first thing to do in the writing process is to dig deeply into your mind and drag out all your responses and ideas about the story. Write anything and everything that occurs to you. Don't be embarrassed if things do not look great at first, but keep working toward improvement. If you have questions you can't answer, write them down and plan to answer them later. In your attempts to discover ideas, use the following prewriting techniques.

Brainstorming or Freewriting Gets Your Mind Going

Brainstorming or **freewriting** is an informal way to describe your own written but private no-holds-barred conversation with yourself. It is your first step in writing. When you begin freewriting, you do not know what is going to happen, so you let your mind play over all the possibilities that you generate as you consider the work, or a particular element of the work, or your own early responses to it. In effect, you are talking to yourself and writing down all your thoughts, whether they fall into patterns or seem disjointed, beside the point, or even foolish. At this time, do not try to organize or criticize your thoughts. Later you can decide which ideas to keep and which to throw out. For now, *the goal is to get all your ideas on paper or on the computer screen.* As you are developing your essay later on, you may, *at any time*, return to the brainstorming or freewriting process to initiate and develop new ideas.

Focus on Specific Topics

1. **DEVELOP SUBJECTS YOU CREATE WHEN TAKING NOTES AND BRAINSTORMING.** Although the goal of brainstorming is to be totally free about the topics, you should recognize that you are trying to think creatively. You will therefore need to start directing your mind into specific channels. Once you start focusing on definite topics, your thinking, as we have noted, is analogous to classroom discussion. Let us assume that in freewriting, you produce a topic that you find especially interesting. You might then start to focus on this topic and to write as much as you can about it. The following examples from early thoughts about Maupassant's "The Necklace" show how a writer may zero in on such a topic—in this case, "honor"—once the word comes up in freewriting:

> Mathilde could have gone to her friend and told her she had lost the necklace. But she didn't. Was she overcome with shame? Would she have felt a loss of honor by confessing the loss of the necklace?

> What is honor? Doing what you think you should even if you don't want to, or if it's hard? Or is it pride? Was Mathilde too proud or too honorable to tell her friend? Does having honor mean going a harder way, when either way would probably be okay? Do you have to suffer to be honorable? Does pride or honor produce a choice for suffering?

Mathilde wants others to envy her, to find her attractive. Later she tells Loisel that she would feel humiliated at the party with rich women unless she wore jewelry. Maybe she is more concerned about being admired than about the necklace. Having a high self-esteem has something to do with honor, but more with pride.

Duty. Is it the same as honor? Is it Mathilde's duty to work so hard? Certainly her pride causes her to do her duty and behave honorably, and therefore pride is a step towards honor.

Honor is a major part of life, I think. It seems bigger than any one life or person. Honor is just an idea or a feeling—can an idea of honor be larger than a life, take over someone's life? Should it?

These paragraphs do not represent finished writing, but they do demonstrate how a writer may attempt to define a term and determine the degree to which it applies to a major character or circumstance. Although the last paragraph departs from the story, this digression is perfectly acceptable because in the freewriting stage, writers treat ideas as they arise. If the ideas amount to something, they may be used in the developing essay; but if they don't, they can be thrown away. The important principle in brainstorming is to record *all* ideas, with no initial concern about how they might seem to a reader. The results of freewriting are for the eyes of the writer only. (A student once began a freewriting exercise by indicating his desire for a large bowl of ice cream. Although the wish had nothing to do with the topic, it did cause the student to begin writing and to express more germane ideas. Needless to say, the original wish did not get into the final essay.)

2. BUILD ON YOUR ORIGINAL NOTES. An essential way to focus your mind is to mine your journal notes for relevant topics. For example, let us assume that you have made an original note on "The Necklace" about the importance of the attic flat where Mathilde and her husband live after they paid for the replacement necklace. With this note as a start, you can develop a number of ideas, as in the following:

The attic flat is important. Before, in her apartment, Mathilde was dreamy and impractical. She was delicate, but after losing the necklace, no way. She becomes a worker when in the flat. She can do a lot more now.

M. gives up her servant, climbs stairs carrying buckets of water, washes greasy pots, throws water around to clean floors, does all the wash by hand.

While she gets stronger, she also gets loud and frumpy—argues with shopkeepers to get the lowest prices. She stops caring for herself. A reversal here, from incapable and well groomed to coarse but capable. All this change happens in the attic flat.

Notice that no more than a brief original note can help you discover thoughts that you did not originally have. This act of stretching your mind leads you to put elements of the story together in ways that create support for ideas that you may use to build good essays. Even in an assertion as basic as "The attic flat is important," the process itself, which is a form of concentrated thought, leads you creatively forward.

3. RAISE AND ANSWER YOUR OWN QUESTIONS. A major way to discover ideas about a work is to raise and answer questions as you read. The "Guidelines for Reading" will help you formulate questions, but you may also raise specific questions like these (assuming that you are considering a story):

➤ What explanations are needed for the characters? Which actions, scenes, and situations invite interpretation? Why?

➤ What assumptions do the characters and speakers reveal about life and humanity generally; about themselves, the people around them, their families, and their friends; and about work, the economy, religion, politics, and the state of the world?

➤ What are their manners or customs?

➤ What kinds of words do they use: formal or informal words, slang or profanity?

➤ What literary conventions and devices have you discovered, and how do these add to the work? (When an author addresses readers directly, for example, that is a **convention**; when a comparison is used, that is a **device**, which might be either a **metaphor or a** simile.)

Of course you may raise other questions as you reread the piece, or you may be left with one or two major questions that you decide to pursue.

4. USE THE PLUS-MINUS, PRO-CON, OR EITHER-OR METHOD TO PUT IDEAS TOGETHER. A common method of discovering ideas is to develop a set of contrasts: plus-minus, pro-con, either-or. Let us suppose a plus-minus method of considering the character of Mathilde in "The Necklace": Should she be "admired" (plus) or "condemned" (minus)?

PLUS: ADMIRED?	MINUS: CONDEMNED?
After she cries when they get the invitation, she recovers with a "strong effort"—maybe she doesn't want her husband to feel bad.	She only wants to be envied and admired for being attractive (end of first part), not for more important qualities.
She really scores a great victory at the dance. She does have the power to charm and captivate.	She wastes her time daydreaming about things she can't have, and whines because she is unhappy.
Once she loses the necklace, she and her husband become impoverished. But she does "her share . . . completely, heroically" (paragraph 98) to make up for the loss.	She manipulates her husband into giving her a lot of money for a party dress, but they live poorly.
Even when she is poor, she still dreams about that marvelous, shining moment. She gets worse than she deserves.	She assumes that her friend would think she was a thief if she knew she was returning a different necklace. Shouldn't she have had more confidence in the friend?
At the end, she confesses the loss to her friend.	She gets loud and coarse, and haggles about pennies, thus undergoing a total cheapening of her character.

Once you put contrasting ideas side by side, as in this example, you will get new ideas. Filling the columns almost demands that you list as many contrasting positions as you can and that you think about how material in the work supports each position. It is in this way that true, genuine thinking takes place.

Your notes will therefore be useful regardless of how you finally organize your essay. You may develop either column in a full essay, or you might use the notes to support the idea that Mathilde is too complex to be either wholly admired or wholly condemned. You might even introduce an entirely new idea, such as that Mathilde should be pitied rather than condemned or admired. In short, arranging materials in the plus-minus pattern is a powerful way to discover ideas that can lead to ways of development that you might not otherwise find.

5. TRACE DEVELOPING PATTERNS. You can also discover ideas by making a list or scheme for the story or main idea. What conflicts appear? Do these conflicts exist between people, groups, or ideas? How does the author resolve them? Is one force, idea, or side the winner? Why? How do you respond to the winner or to the loser?

Using this method, you might make a list similar to this one:

Beginning: M. is a fish out of water. She dreams of wealth, but her life is drab and her husband is ordinary.

Fantasies—make her even more dissatisfied—punishes herself by thinking of a wealthy life.

Her character relates to the places in the story: the Street of the Martyrs, the dinner party scene, the attic flat. Also the places she dreams of—she fills them with the most expensive things she can imagine.

They get the dinner invitation—she pouts and whines. Her husband feels discomfort, but she doesn't really harm him. She manipulates him into buying her an expensive party dress, though.

Her dream world hurts her real life when her desire for wealth causes her to borrow the necklace. Losing the necklace is just plain bad luck.

The attic flat brings out her potential coarseness. But she also develops a spirit of sacrifice and cooperation. She loses, but she's really a winner.

These observations all focus on Mathilde's character, but you may wish to trace other patterns you find in the story. If you start planning an essay about another pattern, be sure to account for all the actions and scenes that relate to your topic. Otherwise, you may miss a piece of evidence that can lead you to new conclusions.

6. LET YOUR WRITING HELP YOU DEVELOP YOUR THINKING. No matter what method of discovering ideas you use, it is important to realize that *unwritten thought is incomplete thought*. Make a practice of writing notes about your reactions and any questions that occur to you. Very likely they will lead you to the most startling discoveries that you finally make about a work.

DRAFTING YOUR ESSAY

As you use the brainstorming and focusing techniques for discovering ideas, you are also beginning to draft your essay. You will need to revise your ideas as connections among them become more clear, and as you reexamine the work for support for the ideas you are developing, but you already have many of the raw materials you need for developing your topic.

Create a Central Idea

By definition, an essay is *a fully developed and organized set of paragraphs that develop and enlarge a central idea.* All parts of an essay should contribute to the reader's understanding of the idea. To achieve unity and completeness, each paragraph refers to the central idea and demonstrates how selected details from the work relate to it and support it. The central idea will help you control and shape your essay, and it will provide guidance for your reader.

A successful essay about literature is a brief but thorough (not exhaustive) examination of a literary work in light of a particular element, such as **character**, **point of view**, or **symbolism**. Typical central ideas might be (1) that a character is strong and tenacious, or (2) that the point of view makes the action seem "distant and objective," or (3) that a major symbol governs the actions and thoughts of the major characters. In essays on these topics, all points must be tied to such central ideas. Thus, it is a fact that Mathilde Loisel in "The Necklace" endures ten years of slavish work and sacrifice. This fact is not relevant to an essay on her character, however, unless you connect it by showing how it demonstrates one of her major traits—in this case, her growing strength and perseverance.

Look through all of your ideas for one or two that catch your eye for development. If you have used more than one prewriting technique, the chances are that you have already discovered at least a few ideas that are more thought-provoking, or important, than the others.

Once you choose an idea that you think you can work with, write it as a complete sentence. A *complete sentence* is important: A simple phrase, such as "setting and character," does not focus thought the way a sentence does. A sentence moves the topic toward new exploration and discovery because it combines a topic with an outcome, such as "The setting of 'The Necklace' reflects Mathilde's character." You may choose to be even more specific: "Mathilde's strengths and weaknesses are reflected in the real and imaginary places in 'The Necklace.' "

With a single, central idea for your essay, you have a standard for accepting, rejecting, rearranging, and changing the ideas you have been developing. You may now draft a few paragraphs to see whether your idea seems valid, or you may decide that it would be more helpful to make an outline or a list before you attempt to support your ideas in a rough draft. In either case, you should use your notes for evidence to connect to your central idea. If you need more ideas, use any of the brainstorming-prewriting techniques to discover them. If you need to bolster your argument by including more details that are relevant, jot them down as you reread the work.

Using the central idea that *the changes in the story's settings reflect Mathilde's character* might produce a paragraph like the following, which stresses her negative qualities:

> The original apartment in the Street of Martyrs and the dream world of wealthy places both show negative sides of Mathilde's character. The real-life apartment, though livable, is shabby. The furnishings all bring out her discontent. The shabbiness makes her think only of luxuriousness, and her one servant girl causes her to dream of having many servants. The luxury of her dream life heightens her unhappiness with what she actually has.

Even in such a discovery draft, however, where the purpose is to write initial thoughts about the central idea, many details from the story are used in support. In the final draft, this kind of support will be absolutely essential.

Create a Thesis Sentence

With your central idea to guide you, you can now decide which of the earlier observations and ideas can be developed further. Your goal is to establish a number of major topics to support the central idea and to express them in a **thesis sentence**—an organizing sentence that plans or forecasts the major topics you will treat in your essay. Suppose you choose three ideas from your discovery stage of development. If you put the central idea at the left and the list of topics at the right, you have the shape of the thesis sentence. Note that the first two topics have been taken from the discovery paragraph.

CENTRAL IDEA	TOPICS
The setting of "The Necklace" reflects Mathilde's character.	1. Real-life apartment 2. Dream surroundings 3. Attic flat

This arrangement leads to the following thesis statement:

> Mathilde's character growth is related to her first apartment, her dream-life mansion rooms, and her attic flat.

You can revise the thesis statement at any stage of the writing process if you find that you do not have enough evidence from the work to support it. Perhaps a new topic may occur to you, and you can include it, appropriately, as a part of your thesis sentence.

As we have seen, the central idea is the glue of the essay. The thesis sentence *lists the parts to be fastened together*—that is, the topics in which the central idea is to be demonstrated and argued. To alert your readers to your essay's structure, the thesis sentence is often placed at the end of the introductory paragraph, just before the body of the essay begins.

Writing a First Draft

To write a first draft, you support the points of your thesis sentence with your notes and discovery materials. You may alter, reject, and rearrange ideas and details as you wish, as long as you change your thesis sentence to account for the changes (a major reason why most writers write their introductions last). The thesis sentence just shown contains three topics (it could be two, or four, or more), to be used in forming the body of the essay.

Begin each paragraph with a topic sentence. Just as the organization of the entire essay is based on the thesis, the form of each paragraph is based on its **topic sentence**. A topic sentence is an assertion about how a topic from the predicate of the thesis statement supports the central idea. The first topic in our example is the relationship of Mathilde's character to her first apartment, and the resulting paragraph should emphasize this relationship. If you choose the coarsening of her character during the ten-year travail, you can then form a topic sentence by connecting the trait with the location, as follows:

> The attic flat reflects the coarsening of Mathilde's character.

Beginning with this sentence, the paragraph can show how Mathilde's rough, heavy housework has a direct effect on her behavior, appearance, and general outlook.

Use only one topic—no more—in each paragraph. Usually you should treat each separate topic in a single paragraph. However, if a topic seems especially difficult, long, and heavily detailed, you may divide it into two or more subtopics, each receiving a separate paragraph of its own. Should you make this division, your topic then is really a *section*, and each paragraph in the section should have its own topic sentence.

WRITE SO THAT YOUR PARAGRAPHS DEVELOP OUT OF YOUR TOPIC SENTENCES. Once you choose your thesis sentence, you can use it to focus your observations and conclusions. Let us see how our topic about the attic flat may be developed as a paragraph:

> The attic flat reflects the coarsening of Mathilde's character. Maupassant emphasizes the burdens she endures to save money, such as mopping floors, cleaning greasy and encrusted pots and pans, taking out the garbage, and hand-washing clothes and dishes. This work makes her rough and coarse, an effect that is heightened by her giving up care of her hair and hands, wearing the cheapest dresses possible, and becoming loud and penny-pinching in haggling with the local shopkeepers. If at the beginning she is delicate and attractive, at the end she is unpleasant and coarse.

Notice that details from the story are introduced to provide support for the topic sentence. All the subjects—the hard work, the lack of personal care, the wearing of cheap dresses, and the haggling with the shopkeepers—are introduced not to retell the story but rather to exemplify the claim the writer is making about Mathilde's character.

Develop an Outline

So far we have been developing an **outline**—that is, a skeletal plan of organization for your essay. Some writers never use formal outlines at all, preferring to make informal lists of ideas, whereas others rely on them constantly. Still other writers insist that they cannot make an outline until they have finished their essays. Regardless of your preference, *your finished essay should have a tight structure*. Therefore, you should create a guiding outline to develop or to shape your essay.

The outline we have been developing here is the **analytical sentence outline**. This type is easier to create than it sounds. It consists of (1) an *introduction*, including the central idea and the thesis sentence, together with (2) *topic sentences* that are to be used in each paragraph of the body, followed by (3) a *conclusion*.

WRITING BY HAND, TYPEWRITER, OR WORD PROCESSOR

It is important for you to realize that writing is an inseparable part of thinking and that unwritten thought is an incomplete thought.

Because thinking and writing are so interdependent, it is essential to get ideas into a visible form so that you may develop them further. For many students, it is psychologically necessary to carry out this process by writing down ideas by hand or typewriter. If you are one of these students, make your written or typed responses on only one side of your paper or note cards. Doing this will enable you to spread your materials out and get an actual physical overview of them when you begin writing. Everything will be open to you; none of your ideas will be hidden on the back of the paper.

Today, word processing is thoroughly established as an indispensable tool for writers. The word processor can help you develop ideas, for it enables you to eliminate unworkable thoughts and replace them with others. You can move sentences and paragraphs tentatively into new contexts, test out how they look, and move them somewhere else if you choose.

In addition, with the rapid printers available today, you can print drafts even in the initial and tentative stages of writing. Using your printed draft, you can make additional notes, marginal corrections, and suggestions for further development. With the marked-up draft for guidance, you can go back to your work processor and fill in your changes and improvements, repeating this procedure as often as you can. This facility makes the machine an additional incentive for improvement, right up to your final draft.

Word processing also helps you in the final preparation of your essays. Studies have shown that errors and awkward sentences are frequently found at the bottoms of pages prepared by hand or with a conventional typewriter. The reason is that writers hesitate to make improvements when they get near the end of a page because they shun the dreariness of starting the page over. Word processors eliminate this difficulty completely. Changes can be made anywhere in the draft, at any time, without damage to the appearance of the final draft.

Regardless of your writing method, it is important to realize that *unwritten thought is incomplete thought.* Even with the word processor's

box continued on next page➤

> screen, you cannot lay everything out at once. You can see only a small part of what you are writing. Therefore, somewhere in your writing process, prepare a complete draft of what you have written. A clean, readable draft permits you to gather everything together and to make even more improvements through the act of revision.

When applied to the subject we have been developing, such an outline looks like this:

TITLE: How Setting in "The Necklace" Is Related to the Character of Mathilde

1. **INTRODUCTION**
   a. *Central idea*: Maupassant uses his setting to show Mathilde's character.
   b. *Thesis statement*: Her character growth is related to her first apartment, her daydreams about elegant rooms in a mansion, and her attic flat.
2. **BODY**: *Topic sentences* a, b, and c (and d, e, and f, if necessary)
   a. Details about her first apartment explain her dissatisfaction and depression.
   b. Her daydreams about mansion rooms are like the apartment because they too make her unhappy.
   c. The attic flat reflects the coarsening of her character.
3. **CONCLUSION**
   Topic sentence. All details in the story, particularly the setting, are focused on the character of Mathilde.

The *conclusion* may be a summary of the body; it may evaluate the main idea; it may briefly suggest further points of discussion; or it may be a reflection on the details of the body.

Use the Outline in Developing Your Essay

The three sample essays that follow in this section are organized according to the principles of the analytical sentence outline. To emphasize the shaping effect of these outlines, all central ideas, thesis sentences, and topic sentences are underlined. In your own writing, you may underline or italicize these "skeletal" sentences as a check on your organization. Unless your instructor requires such markings, however, remove them in your final drafts.

FIRST SAMPLE ESSAY, FIRST DRAFT

The following sample essay is a first draft of the topic we have been developing. It follows the outline presented here, and includes details from the story in support of the various topics. It is by no means, however, as good a piece of writing as it can be. The draft omits a topic, some additional details, and some new insights that are included in the second draft. It therefore reveals the need to make improvements through additional brainstorming and discovery-prewriting techniques.

How Setting in "The Necklace" Is Related to the Character of Mathilde

[1]   In "The Necklace" Guy de Maupassant does not give much detail about the setting. He does not even describe the necklace itself, which is the central object in his plot, but he says only that it is "superb" (paragraph 47). Rather, he uses the setting to reflect the character of the central figure, Mathilde Loisel.* All Maupassant's details are presented to bring out her traits. Her character development is related to her first apartment, her daydreams about mansion rooms, and her attic flat.†

[2]   Details about her first apartment explain her dissatisfaction and depression. The walls are "drab," the furniture "threadbare," and the curtains "ugly" (paragraph 3). There is only a simple country girl to do the housework. The tablecloth is not changed daily, and the best dinner dish is boiled beef. Mathilde has no evening clothes, only a theater dress that she does not like. These details show her dissatisfaction with life with her low-salaried husband.

[3]   Her dream-life images of wealth are like the apartment because they too make her unhappy. In her daydreams about life in a mansion, the rooms are large, filled with expensive furniture and bric-a-brac, and draped in silk. She imagines private rooms for intimate talks, and big dinners with delicacies like trout and quail. With dreams of such a rich home, she feels even more despair about her modest apartment on the Street of Martyrs in Paris.

[4]   The attic flat reflects the coarsening of Mathilde's character. Maupassant emphasizes the burdens she endures to save money, such as mopping floors, cleaning greasy and encrusted pots and pans, taking out the garbage, and hand-washing clothes and dishes. This work makes her rough and coarse, an effect that is heightened by her giving up care of her hair and hands, wearing the cheapest dresses possible, and becoming loud and penny-pinching in haggling with the local shopkeepers. If at the beginning she is delicate and attractive, at the end she is unpleasant and coarse.

---

*Central Idea
†Thesis sentence.

[5]   In summary, Maupassant focuses everything in the story, including the setting, on the character of Mathilde. Anything extra is not needed, and he does not include it. Thus he says little about the big party scene except the necessary detail that Mathilde was a great "success" (paragraph 52). It is this detail that brings out some of her early attractiveness and charm (despite her more usual unhappiness). Thus, in "The Necklace," Maupassant uses setting as a means to his end—the story of Mathilde and her needless sacrifice.

■ DEVELOP AND STRENGTHEN YOUR ESSAY THROUGH REVISION

After finishing a first draft like this one, you may wonder what more you can do. You have read the work several times, discovered ideas to write about through brainstorming techniques, made an outline of your ideas, and written a full draft. How can you do better?

The best way to begin is to observe that *a major mistake writers make when writing about literature is to do no more than retell a story or reword an idea.* Retelling a story shows only that you have read it, not that you have thought about it. Writing a good essay requires you to arrange your thoughts into a pattern that can be followed by a perceptive reader.

Use Your Own Order of References

There are many ways to escape the trap of summarizing stories and to set up your own pattern of development. One way is to stress *your own* order when referring to parts of a work. Do not treat details as they happen, but rearrange them to suit your own thematic plans. Rarely, if ever, should you begin by talking about a work's opening; it is better to talk first about the conclusion or middle. As you examine your first draft, if you find that you have followed the chronological order of the work instead of stressing your own order, you may use one of the prewriting techniques to figure out new ways to connect your materials. The principle is that you should introduce references to the work to support the points you wish to make, and only these points.

Use Literary Material as Evidence in Your Argument

Whenever you write, your position is like that of a detective using clues as evidence for building a case, or of a lawyer using evidence as support for an *argument.* Your goal should be to convince your readers of your own knowledge and the reasonableness of your conclusions.

It is vital to use evidence convincingly so that your readers can follow your ideas. Let us look briefly at two drafts of a new example to see how writing may be improved by the pointed use of details. These are from drafts of a longer essay on the character of Mathilde.

A comparison of these paragraphs shows that the first has more words than the second (158 to 120), but that it is more appropriate for a rough

1	2
The major extenuating detail about Mathilde is that she seems to be isolated, locked away from other people. She and her husband do not speak to each other much, except about external things. He speaks about his liking for boiled beef, and she states that she cannot accept the big invitation because she has no nice dresses. Once she gets the dress, she complains because she has no jewelry. Even when borrowing the necklace from Jeanne Forrestier, she does not say much. When she and her husband discover that the necklace is lost, they simply go over the details, and Loisel dictates a letter of explanation, which she writes in her own hand. Even when she meets Jeanne on the Champs-Elysées, she does not say a great deal about her life but only goes through enough details about the loss and replacement of the necklace to make Jeanne exclaim about the needlessness of the ten-year sacrifice.	The major flaw of Mathilde's character is that she is withdrawn and uncommunicative, apparently unwilling or unable to form an intimate relationship. For example, she and her husband do not speak to each other much, except about external things such as his taste for boiled beef and her lack of a party dress and jewelry. With such an uncommunicative marriage, one might suppose that she would be more open with her close friend, Jeanne Forrestier, but Mathilde does not say much even to her. This flaw hurts her greatly, because if she were more open she might have explained the loss and avoided the horrible sacrifice. This lack of openness, along with her self-indulgent dreaminess, is her biggest defect.

than a final draft because the writer does little more than retell the story. The paragraph is cluttered with details that do not support any conclusions. If you examine it for what you might learn about Maupassant's actual use of Mathilde's solitary traits in "The Necklace," you will find that it gives you but little help. The writer needs to consider why these details should be shared, and to revise the paragraph according to the central idea.

On the other hand, the details in the right-hand paragraph all support the declared topic. Phrases such as "for example," "with such," and "this lack" show that the writer of paragraph 2 has assumed that the audience knows the story and now wants help in interpretation. Paragraph 2 therefore guides readers by *connecting the details to the topic.* It uses these details *as evidence,* not as a retelling of actions. By contrast, paragraph 1 recounts a number of relevant actions but does not connect them to the topic. More details, of course, could have been added to the second paragraph, but they are unnecessary because the paragraph demonstrates the point with the details used. There are many qualities that make good writing good, but one of the most important is shown in a comparison of the two paragraphs: *In good writing, no details are included unless they are used as supporting evidence in a pattern of thought.*

Keep to Your Point

Whenever you write an essay about literature—or, for that matter, any essay about any subject—you must pay great attention to organization and to the correct use of references to the work assigned. As you write, you should constantly try to keep your material unified, for should you go off on a tangent you are no longer controlling but are being controlled. It is too easy to start with your point but then wander off and just retell the story. Once again, resist the tendency to be a narrator. Instead, be an interpreter, an explainer.

CHECK THE DEVELOPMENT AND ORGANIZATION OF YOUR IDEAS

It bears repeating over and over again that the first requirement of a good essay is to introduce a point or main idea and then stick to it. Another major step toward excellence is to make your central idea expand and grow. The word *growth* is a metaphor describing the creation of new insights, the disclosure of ideas that were not at first noticeable, and the expression of original, new, and fresh interpretations.

Try to Be Original

In everything you ever write, it is important that you try to be original. You might initially claim that you cannot be original when you are writing about someone else's work. "The author has said everything," might go your argument, "and therefore I can do little more than follow the story." This claim presupposes that you have no choice in selecting material and no opportunity to make individual thoughts and original contributions.

But you do have choices and opportunities to be original. One obvious area of originality is *the development and formulation of your central idea*. For example, a natural first response to "The Necklace" is "The story is about a woman who loses a borrowed necklace and endures hardship to help pay for it." Because this response refers only to events in the story and not to any idea, an area of thought might be introduced if the hardship is called "needless." Just the use of this word alone demands that you explain the differences between *needed* and *unneeded* hardships, and your application of these differences to the heroine's plight would produce an original essay. Even better and more original insights could result if the topic of the budding essay were to connect the dreamy, withdrawn traits of the main character to her misfortunes and also to general misfortunes. A resulting central idea might be "People themselves create their own difficulties." Such an idea would require you to define not only the personal but also the representative nature of Mathilde's experiences, an avenue of exploration that could produce much in the way of a fresh, original essay about "The Necklace."

You can also develop your ability to treat your subject freshly and originally if you plan the body of the essay *to build up to what you think is your most important and incisive idea.* As examples of such planning, the following brief outline suggests how a central idea may be widened and expanded:

Subject: Mathilde as a Growing Character

1. Mathilde has normal daydreams about a better life.
2. She takes a risk and then loses, in trying to make her daydreams seem real.
3. She develops by facing her mistake and working hard to correct it.

The list shows how a subject may be enlarged if you treat your exemplifying topic in an increasing order of importance. In this case, the order moves from Mathilde's habit of daydreaming to the development of her character strength. The pattern shows how you can meet two primary standards of excellence in writing—organization and growth.

Clearly, you should always try to develop your central idea. Constantly adhere to your topic, and constantly develop it. Nurture it and make it grow. Admittedly, in a short essay you will be able to move only a short distance with an idea, but you *should never be satisfied to leave the idea exactly where you found it.* To the degree that you can learn to develop your ideas, you will receive recognition for increasingly original writing.

Write with Your Readers in Mind

Whenever you write, you must decide how much detail to discuss. Usually you base this decision on your judgment of your readers. For example, if you assume that they have not read the work you are writing about, you will need to include a short summary as background. Otherwise, they may not understand your argument.

Consider, too, whether your readers have any special interests or concerns. If they are particularly interested in politics, sociology, religion, or psychology, for example, you may need to select and develop your materials accordingly.

Your instructor will let you know who your audience is. Usually, it will be your instructor or your fellow students. They will be familiar with the work and will not expect you to retell a story or summarize an argument. Rather, they will look to you as an *explainer* or *interpreter*. Thus, you may omit details from the work that do not exemplify and support your central idea, even if the details are important parts of the work. What you write should always be based on your developing idea together with your assessment of your readers.

USE EXACT, COMPREHENSIVE, AND FORCEFUL LANGUAGE

In addition to being original, organized, and well developed, the best writing is expressed in *exact, comprehensive*, and *forceful* language. At any stage of the composition process, you should try to correct your earliest sentences and paragraphs, which usually need to be rethought, reworded, and rearranged.

TRY TO MAKE YOUR SENTENCES MEANINGFUL. First of all, ask yourself whether your sentences really *mean* what you intend or whether you can make them more exact and therefore stronger. For example, consider these two sentences from essays about "The Necklace":

> It seems as though the main character's dreams of luxury cause her to respond as she does in the story.

> This incident, although it may seem trivial or unimportant, has substantial significance in the creation of the story; by this I mean the incident that occurred is essentially what the story is all about.

These sentences are inexact and vague, and therefore unhelpful; neither of them goes anywhere. The first sentence is satisfactory up to the verb "cause," but then it falls apart because the writer has lost sight of the meaning. It is best to describe *what* that response is, rather than to be satisfied with nothing more than that there *is* a response. To make the sentence more exact, we may make the following revision:

> Mathilde's dreams of luxury make it impossible for her to accept her own possessions, and therefore she goes beyond her means in order to attend the party.

With this revision, the writer could consider the meaning of the story's early passages and could contrast the ideas there with those in the latter part. Without the revision, it is not clear where the writer might go.

The second sentence is vague because again the writer has lost sight of the topic. If we adopt the principle of trying to be exact, however, we may bring the dead sentence to life:

> The accidental loss of the necklace, which is trivial though costly, supports the narrator's claim that major turns in life are produced not by earthshaking events, but rather by minor ones.

TRY TO MAKE YOUR SENTENCES COMPLETE AND COMPREHENSIVE. Second, in addition to being exact, it is vital to make sentences—all sentences, but particularly thesis and topic sentences—complete and comprehensive. As an example, consider the following sentence from an essay about "The Necklace":

> The idea in "The Necklace" is that Mathilde and her husband work hard to pay for the lost necklace.

Although this sentence promises to describe an idea, it does not do so. Instead, it merely describes the major action of the story. Therefore, it needs to benefit from additional rethinking and rephrasing to make it more comprehensive, as in these two revisions:

> In "The Necklace" Maupassant shows that hard work and responsibility are basic and necessary in life.
> Maupassant's surprise ending of "The Necklace" symbolizes the need for always being truthful.

Both new sentences are connected to the action described by the original phrasing, "Mathilde and her husband work hard to pay for the lost necklace," although they point toward differing treatments. The first sentence concerns the virtue shown by the Loisels in their sacrifice. Because the second sentence includes the word *symbolizes*, an essay stemming from it would stress the Loisels' mistake in not confessing the loss. In dealing with the symbolic meaning of their failure, an essay developed along the lines of the sentence would focus on the negative aspects of their characters, and an essay developed from the first sentence would stress their positive aspects. Either of the revised sentences, therefore, is more comprehensive than the original sentence and thus would help a writer get on the track toward an accurate and thoughtful essay.

Of course it is never easy to create fine sentences, but as a mode of improvement, you might create some self-testing mechanisms:

> ➤ **FOR TREATING STORY MATERIALS.** Always relate the materials to an idea or a point. Do not say simply that "Mathilde works constantly for ten years to help pay off the debt." Instead, blend the material into a point, like this: "Mathilde's ten-year effort shows the horror of indebtedness," or "Mathilde's ten-year effort demonstrates the emergence of her strength of character."

> ➤ **FOR RESPONSES AND IMPRESSIONS.** Do not say simply, "The story's ending left me with a definite impression," but state what the impression is: "The story's ending surprised me and also made me sympathetic to the major character."

> ➤ **FOR IDEAS.** Try to make the idea clear and direct. Do not say "Mathilde is living in a poor household," but rather get at an idea like this one: "The story of Mathilde shows that living in poverty reduces the quality of life."

> ➤ **FOR CRITICAL COMMENTARY.** Do not be satisfied with a statement such as "I found 'The Necklace' interesting," but try to describe what was interesting and why it was interesting: "I found 'The Necklace' interesting because it shows how chance and bad luck may either make or destroy people's lives."

Good writing begins with attempts, like these, to rephrase sentences to make them really say something. If you always name and pin down descriptions, responses, and judgments, no matter how difficult the task seems, your sentences can be strong because you will be making them exact.

SAMPLE ESSAY—IMPROVED DRAFT

If you refer again to the first draft of the essay about Maupassant's use of setting to illustrate Mathilde's character (page 258), you might notice that several parts of the draft need extensive reworking and revising. For example, paragraph 2 contains a series of short, unconnected comments, and the last sentence of that paragraph implies that Mathilde's dissatisfaction relates mainly to her husband rather than to her general circumstances. Paragraph 4 focuses too much on Mathilde's coarseness and not enough on her sacrifice and cooperation. The draft also ignores the fact that the story ends in another location, the Champs Elysées, where Maupassant continues to demonstrate the nature of Mathilde's character. Finally, there is not enough support in this draft for the contention (in paragraph 5) that *everything* in the story is related to the character of Mathilde.

To discover how these issues may be more fully considered, the following revision of the earlier draft creates more introductory detail, includes an additional paragraph, and reshapes each of the paragraphs to stress the relationship of central idea to topic. Within the limits of a short assignment, the essay illustrates all the principles of organization and unity that we have been discussing here.

Maupassant's Use of Setting in "The Necklace" to Show the Character of Mathilde

---

[1]   In "The Necklace" Guy de Maupassant uses setting to reflect the strengths and weaknesses of the main character, Mathilde Loisel.* As a result, his setting is not particularly vivid or detailed. He does not even provide a description of the ill-fated necklace—the central object in the story—but states no more than that it is "superb" (paragraph 47). In fact, he includes descriptions of setting only if they illuminate qualities of Mathilde's character. Her changing character may be related to the first apartment, her daydreams about mansion rooms, the attic flat of the Loisels, and the public street.†

[2]   Details about the modest apartment of the Loisels on the Street of Martyrs indicate Mathilde's peevish lack of adjustment to life. Though everything is serviceable, she is unhappy with the "drab" walls, "threadbare" furniture, and "ugly" curtains (paragraph 3). She has domestic help, but wants more servants than the simple country girl who does the household chores in the apartment. Her embarrassment and dissatisfaction are shown by details of her irregularly cleaned tablecloth and the plain and inelegant boiled beef that her husband adores. Even her best theater dress, which is appropriate for apartment life but which is inappropriate for more wealthy surroundings, makes her unhappy. All these details of the apartment establish that Mathilde's dominant character trait at the story's beginning is maladjustment. She therefore seems unpleasant and unsympathetic.

[3]   Like the real-life apartment, the impossibly expensive setting of her daydreams about living in a mansion strengthens her unhappiness and her avoidance of reality. All the rooms of her fantasies are large and expensive, draped in silk and filled with nothing but the best furniture and bric-a-brac. Maupassant gives us the following description of her dream world:

> She imagined a gourmet-prepared main course carried on the most exquisite trays and served on the most beautiful dishes, with whispered gallantries which she would hear with a sphinxlike smile as she dined on the pink meat of a trout or the delicate wing of a quail. (paragraph 4)

With impossible dreams like this one, her despair is complete. Ironically, this despair, together with her inability to live with reality, brings about her undoing. It makes her agree to borrow the necklace (which is just as unreal as

---

*Central Idea
†Thesis sentence

her daydreams of wealth), and losing the necklace drives her into the reality of giving up her apartment and moving into the attic flat.

[4]   Also ironically, the attic flat is related to the coarsening of her character while at the same time it brings out her best qualities of cooperativeness and honesty. Maupassant emphasizes the drudgery of the work Mathilde endures to maintain the flat, such as walking up many stairs, washing floors with large buckets of water, cleaning greasy and encrusted pots and pans, taking out the garbage, handwashing clothes, and haggling loudly with local tradespeople. All this reflects her coarsening and loss of sensibility, also shown by her giving up hair and hand care, and wearing the cheapest dresses. The work she performs, however, makes her heroic (paragraph 98). As she cooperates to help her husband pay back the loans, her dreams of a mansion fade and all she has left is the memory of her triumphant appearance at the Minister of Education's party. Thus the attic flat brings out her physical change for the worse at the same time that it also brings out her psychological and moral change for the better.

[5]   Her walk on the Champs-Elysées illustrates another combination of traits— self-indulgence and frankness. The Champs-Elysées is the most fashionable street in Paris, and her walk to it is similar to her earlier indulgences in her daydreams of upper-class wealth. But it is on this street where she meets Jeanne, and it is Mathilde's frankness in confessing the loss and replacement to Jeanne that makes Mathilde, finally, completely honest. While the walk thus serves as the occasion for the story's concluding surprise and irony, Mathilde's being on the Champs-Elysées is totally in character, in keeping with her earlier reveries about luxury.

[6]   Other details in the story also have a similar bearing on Mathilde's character. For example, the story presents little detail about the party scene beyond the statement that Mathilde is a great "success" (paragraph 52)—a judgment that shows her ability to shine if given the chance. After she and Loisel accept the fact that the necklace cannot be found, Maupassant includes details about the Parisian streets, about the visits to loan sharks, and about the jewelry shops in order to bring out Mathilde's sense of honesty and pride as she "heroically" prepares to live her new life of poverty. Thus, in "The Necklace," Maupassant uses setting to highlight Mathilde's maladjustment, her needless misfortune, her loss of youth and beauty, and finally her growth as a responsible human being.

Several improvements to the first draft may be seen here. The language of paragraph 2 has been revised to show more clearly the inappropriateness of Mathilde's dissatisfaction. In paragraph 3, the irony of the story is brought out, and the writer has connected the details to the central idea in a richer pattern of ideas, showing the effects of Mathilde's despair. Paragraph 5— new in this revision—includes additional details about how Mathilde's walk on the Champs-Elysées is related to her character. In paragraph 6, the fact that Mathilde is able "to shine" at the dinner party is interpreted according to the central idea. Finally, the conclusion is now much more specific, summarizing the change in Mathilde's character rather than saying simply that the setting reveals her "needless misfortune." In short, the second draft reflects the complexity of "The Necklace" better than the first draft. Because the writer has revised the first-draft ideas about the story, the final essay is tightly structured, insightful, and forceful.

SUMMARY

To sum up, follow these guidelines whenever you write about a story or any kind of literature:

➤ Never just retell the story. Use story materials only to support your central idea or argument.

➤ Throughout your essay, keep reminding your reader of your central idea.

➤ Within each paragraph, make sure that you stress your topic idea.

➤ Develop your topic. Make it bigger than it was when you began.

➤ Always make your statements exact, comprehensive, and forceful.

➤ Never just retell the story.

➤ **Never just retell the story.**

➤ *Never just retell the story.*

■ WRITING ABOUT RESPONSES: LIKES AND DISLIKES

Now that we have looked briefly at the processes of writing, with two drafts of the same essay for illustration, we are ready to apply the principles of development to another topic for writing—this one about likes and dislikes (already mentioned, pages 237–45). In writing about your responses, rely on your initial informed reactions. It is not easy to reconstruct your first responses after a lapse of time, so you will need your journal observations to guide you in prewriting. Develop your essay by stressing those characters, incidents, and ideas that interest (or do not interest) you.

As with many essays, you will be challenged to connect details from the work to your central idea. That is, once you have begun by stating that you like (or dislike) the story, you might forget to highlight this response as you enumerate details. Therefore you need to stress your involvement in the work as you bring out evidence from it. You can show your attitudes by indicating approval (or disapproval), by commenting favorably (or unfavorably) on the details, by indicating things that seem new (or shopworn) and particularly instructive (or wrong), and by giving assent to (or dissent from) ideas or expressions of feeling.

Organize Your Essay About Likes and Dislikes

INTRODUCTION. Briefly describe the conditions that influence your response. Your central idea should be why you like or dislike the work. Your thesis sentence should include the major causes of your response, which are to be developed in the body.

BODY. The most common approach is to consider specific details that you like or dislike. The list on page 241 may help you articulate your responses. For example, you admired a particular character, or you got so interested in a story that you could not put it down, or you liked a particular passage in a poem or play, or you felt thrilled as you finished reading the work. Also, you may wish to develop a major idea, a fresh insight, or a particular outcome, as in the sample paragraph on page 238, which shows a surprise ending as the cause of a favorable response.

A second approach is to explain any changes in your responses about the work (i.e., negative to positive and vice versa). This approach requires that you isolate the causes of the change, but it does not require you to retell the story from beginning to end.

1. One way to deal with such a change—the "bridge" method of transferring preference from one type of work to another—is shown in the sample essay below.

2. Another way is to explain a change in terms of a new awareness or understanding that you did not have on a first reading. Thus, for example, your first response to "The Necklace" might be unfavorable or neutral because the story may at first seem to move rather slowly. But further consideration might lead you to discover new insights that change your mind, such as the needs to overcome personal pride and to stop minor resentments from growing and festering. Your essay would then explain how these new insights have caused you to like the story.

CONCLUSION. Here you might summarize the reasons for your major response. You might also face any issues brought up by a change or modification of your first reactions. For example, if you have always held certain assumptions about your taste but like the work despite these assumptions, you may wish to talk about your own change or development. This topic is personal, but in an essay about your personal responses, discovery about yourself is legitimate and worthy.

Sample Essay

Some Reasons for Liking Maupassant's "The Necklace"

[1]   To me, the most likable kind of reading is adventure. There are many reasons for my preference, but an important one is that characters in adventure stories work hard to overcome obstacles. Because Guy de Maupassant's "The Necklace" is not adventure, I did not like it at first. But in one respect the story is <u>like</u> adventure: The major character, Mathilde, works hard with her husband, Loisel, for ten years to overcome a difficult obstacle. <u>Thus, because Mathilde does what adventure characters also do, the story is likable.</u>* <u>Mathilde's appeal results from her hard work, strong character, and sad fate, and also from the way our view of her changes.</u>†

[2]   <u>Mathilde's hard work makes her seem good.</u> Once she and her husband are faced with the huge debt of 18,000 francs, she works like a slave to help pay it back. She gives up her servant and moves to a cheaper place. She does the household drudgery, wears cheap clothes, and bargains with shopkeepers. Just like the characters in adventure stories who do hard and unpleasant things, she does what she has to, and this makes her admirable.

[3]   <u>Her strong character shows her endurance, a likable trait.</u> At first she is nagging and fussy, and she always dreams about wealth and tells lies, but she changes and gets better. She recognizes her blame in losing the necklace, and she has the toughness to help her husband redeem the debt. She sacrifices "heroically" (paragraph 98) by giving up her comfortable way of life, even though in the process she also loses her youth and beauty. Her jobs are not the exotic and glamorous ones of adventure stories, but her force of character makes her as likable as an adventure heroine.

[4]   <u>Her sad fate also makes her likable.</u> In adventure stories the characters often suffer as they do their jobs. Mathilde also suffers, but in a different way, because her suffering is permanent while the hardships of adventure characters are temporary. This fact makes her especially pitiable because all her sacrifices are not necessary. This unfairness invites the reader to take her side.

[5]   <u>The most important quality promoting admiration is the way in which Maupassant shifts our view of Mathilde.</u> As she goes deeper into her hard life, Maupassant stresses her work and not the innermost thoughts he reveals at the beginning. In other words, the view into her character at the start, when she dreams about wealth, invites dislike; but the focus at the end is on her achievements, with never a complaint—even though she still has golden memories, as the narrator tells us:

> But sometimes, when her husband was at work, she sat down near the window, and she dreamed of that evening so long ago, of that party, where she had been so beautiful and so admired. (paragraph 104)

A major quality of Maupassant's changed emphasis is that Mathilde's fond memories do not lead to anything unfortunate. His shift in focus, from Mathilde's dissatisfaction to her sharing of responsibility and sacrifice, encourages the reader to like her.

---

* Central Idea
† thesis sentence

[6]   "The Necklace" is not an adventure story, but Mathilde has some of the good qualities of adventure characters. Also, the surprise revelation that the lost necklace was false is an unforgettable twist, and this makes her more deserving than she seems at first. Maupassant has arranged the story so that the reader finally admires Mathilde. "The Necklace" is a skillful and likable story.

Commentary on the Essay

This essay demonstrates how a reader may develop appreciation by transferring a preference for one type of work to a work that does not belong to the type. In the essay, the "bridge" is an already established taste for adventure stories, and the grounds for liking "The Necklace" are that Mathilde, the main character, shares the admirable qualities of adventure heroes and heroines.

In paragraph 1, the introduction, the grounds for transferring preferences are established. Paragraph 2 deals with Mathilde's capacity to work hard, and paragraph 3 considers the equally admirable quality of endurance. The fourth paragraph describes how Mathilde's condition evokes sympathy and pity. These paragraphs hence explain the story's appeal by asserting that the main character is similar to admirable characters from works of adventure.

The fifth paragraph shows that Maupassant, as the story unfolds, alters the reader's perceptions of Mathilde from bad to good. For this reason, paragraph 5 marks a new direction from paragraphs 2, 3, and 4: It moves away from the topic material itself—Mathilde's character—to Maupassant's *technique* in handling the topic material.

Paragraph 6, the conclusion, restates the comparison and also introduces the surprise ending as an additional reason for liking "The Necklace." With the body and conclusion together, therefore, the essay establishes five separate reasons for approval. Three of these, derived directly from the main character, constitute the major grounds for liking the story, and two are related to Maupassant's techniques as an author.

Throughout the essay, the central idea is brought out in words and expressions such as "likable," "Mathilde's appeal," "strong character," "she does what she has to," "pitiable," and "take her side." Many of these expressions were first made in the writer's journal; and, mixed as they are with details from the story, they make for continuity. It is this thematic development, together with details from the story as supporting evidence, that shows how an essay on the responses of liking and disliking may be both informed and informative.

WEB RESOURCES

Web Resources can be found at **www.prenhall.com/troyka** under Instructor's Resources.

PART SIX

Workplace and Public Writing

by Linda Julian, *Furman University*

■ TEACHING "REAL WORLD" WRITING SKILLS

Most students expect that writing will comprise a large portion of their college course work. From essay exams to research papers, students receive a great deal of instruction and practice in the writing of the academy. What students may not realize, however, is the extent to which writing will be a part of their lives after their degree. Writing infuses most job situations, from corporate offices, not-for-profit agencies, schools, and health care facilities to farms and factories. And beyond the writing that will be expected in the workplace, many students will find themselves writing outside of work for activities or organizations they are involved in or issues or hobbies of interest.

In many ways, teaching a unit on business or public writing is similar to teaching a unit on essay writing. All workplace or public writing benefits from moving its way through the writing process, with particular emphasis on revision, editing, and proofreading. Consideration of audience, purpose, and tone are perhaps even more vital in workplace and public writing than they are in academic writing, and often those concepts are easier for students to understand when taught in a "real world" context. Additionally, like academic writing, students can expect to complete writing tasks both in print and online.

On the other hand, major differences exist between workplace or public writing and academic writing. One major difference between business writing and other kinds of writing is the emphasis on efficiency and timeliness in workplace writing. Students probably have never stopped to consider the most important principle governing most business writing: *Time is money.* A discussion of this point may make a striking beginning for a unit on business writing. Students generally do not equate the writing they do with saving or wasting money, but teachers can show them that when messages are unclear and have to be questioned in follow-up letters and calls, busy workers are wasting time and effort that could be better spent in making money. Have students investigate the cost a company incurs to write and mail a letter. This substantial expense may have to be doubled or tripled when follow-up communications are required by inadequate messages.

Students also must understand that with workplace or public writing, they may "never get a second chance to make a first impression." They need to know that every letter is a public relations statement about the writer and the company or organization, a first impression that can easily go wrong if the writer is careless and unconcerned about the impression created in business documents. In fact, business—or a job interviw—is lost sometimes on the basis of a poor first impression made by a sloppy or poorly written document. Students can readily see that a letter is like an introduction to a stranger: appearance and substance and tact either make the person want to get to know the newcomer—or not. A writer's tone and ethos also contribute to his or her credibility and effectiveness.

Business and public communication is often guided by strict policies and expectations. Students need to know that most workplaces will have strict policies regarding use of the organization's e-mail system and stationery. Using your work computer for personal e-mail or research may not be tolerated, and such activities can put the company's network at risk for viruses. Because employers have complete access to your business e-mail and print communication—in fact, they *own* all correspondence written, sent, or received in the workplace, they can use such documents as evidence of your job performance. Also, your business e-mail as well as communications you have written on company letterhead may be used as evidence in legal disputes. Recipients of workplace or public communications often expect certain standards of address, format, and language use; Chapter 43 in *The Simon & Schuster Handbook for Writers* provides valuable guidelines for e-mail and print workplace communications.

Students often have misconceptions about business writing which teachers should anticipate and deal with at the outset. Students sometimes think that workplace writing comes with a specialized vocabulary that smacks of governmentese and business lingo. Thus, they will labor to make simple and clear ideas sound "businesslike," usually by adding clichés and mixing phrases from the nineteenth century ("pursuant to," "beg to acknowledge," "per your request," for example) with inflated diction ("first and foremost," "in view of the fact that," "make an evaluation of the processes currently being used," for example). This inflated diction often results from overuse of the passive voice, linking verbs, circumlocution, and tautology. We need to make clear from the beginning that business writing—like all good writing—relies on using language appropriate to the audience and purpose. Students may be surprised to learn that workplace writing is not the most formal kind of writing and therefore usually contains contractions and simple, direct words put together effectively. It also relies on dynamic verbs.

Students may also be surprised to learn that the brevity of many letters and other business documents and the speed with which some are produced do not mean that these documents are easy to write or that they should be taken lightly by the writer. On the contrary, students should realize that often the brief letters are the most challenging. In addition, some students seem to have the mistaken impression that secretaries will "fix" their writing once they have a job. Not only may editing others' work fall outside many secretaries' job descriptions, the companies or organizations that hire the students will expect college graduates to have the excellent writing and editing skills necessary to do their own work. As teachers, we can emphasize the importance of careful editing and proofreading as well as teach students how to use handbooks and other resources to improve their writing.

General Characteristics of Workplace Writing

As in other kinds of writing, the most important decisions a business writer must make are the purpose of the document and the audience for it. Many business documents fail to achieve their goal because the writer tosses off a letter or report too quickly to plan the strategy appropriate to the audience and purpose. (See *The Simon & Schuster Handbook for Writers*, Chapter 1.)

Audience and purpose dictate major decisions about business documents: the choice of format, the organizational plan, the amount of background information necessary, the assumptions the writer can make about the reader, the level of language, the tone, and even the kinds of sentences appropriate for the task. Often students begin writing without knowing what they want to achieve with the piece of writing. For this reason, teachers may need to spend time having students analyze the purpose and audience for various types of business documents. In addition, many teachers require students to write a note, either on a cover sheet or in the upper-right hand corner of each assignment, identifying the intended audience and purpose. To emphasize the importance of audience and purpose, teachers may also want to have students write planning documents for each assignment, at least for the first few. Such a planning document might include answers to the following questions:

> - Who is my audience?
> - What do I know about my audience?
> - What level of language will be appropriate for this reader?
> - How much background information will I have to give this audience?

> On first glance, will the reader be receptive, neutral, or negative toward my message?
> What action do I want the reader to take?
> What strategies can I use to get the reader to take this action?
> What impression do I want this document to make on my reader?

In the business world, where time is money, students can also see that economical use of language is important. The most effective business documents avoid unnecessary passive voice, overuse of linking verbs, expletive constructions, tautological phrasing, and circumlocution. Students should also focus on the need for sentences that average fifteen to seventeen words so that documents may be read quickly, without the reader's having to reread in order to comprehend long, convoluted sentences. Also to engineer easy reading in business documents, teachers should point out the need for cumulative sentences as the dominant pattern rather than periodic sentences, which require readers to work harder at decoding the message.

Paragraphs, too, may be somewhat shorter in many business documents than they are in some kinds of essays. Students can see that shortening paragraphs and using a topic sentence at the top of each paragraph aids in quick, efficient reading. For longer documents, students may need to make use of headings to help readers quickly ascertain main ideas. Also, students need to know that many business documents are not read in their entirety, so headings and clear paragraph structure enable readers to skim documents, reading only the parts they have immediate interest in.

On the other hand, we must help students see that using the fewest number of words possible is not necessarily the best goal for a document. Economy does not mean brutally stripped-down language. Rather we need to emphasize that economy means using the fewest number of words to convey the tone and strategy of the message we are trying to send. Bluntness rarely wins friends and influences people—at least not in a positive way. And, at times, reducing the number of words can eliminate important details, making the document unclear.

Asked to identify the major differences between business writing and essay writing, students rarely think of these stylistic matters beyond making documents "sound" like business documents by using "business" language, but students quickly point out the differences in format. However, they underestimate how important adherence to conventional format is in workplace writing. As teachers, we can help them understand that readers of workplace communication usually expect documents to look a certain way and may be distracted if they do not. Writers want to avoid doing anything that may distract a reader from processing the message. Writers who do not follow conventional formats may communicate that they do not think such things important or that they have not bothered to learn what the conventions of business writing are, a message not likely to please a prospective employer or customer.

■ MAJOR KINDS OF WORKPLACE WRITING

All students know that workplace writing includes letters and memos, but many do not know that letters communicate between two companies or a company and individuals and use addresses that are outside the company and that memos communicate within a company. They usually do not know about the many kinds of reports, proposals, and public relations documents that require research, planning, revision, editing, and proofing just as more familiar kinds of documents do.

Furthermore, students have become so accustomed to using e-mail for friendly messages to friends and family that they generally lack real understanding of the ways e-mail functions in the world of work and the problems it can cause if not used carefully. (See *The Simon & Schuster Handbook for Writers,* Chapter 43d.)

A good way to begin a unit on workplace writing is to teach students how to write routine letters asking for information and then to have them write to companies or visit local companies requesting samples of some of the following kinds of documents:

Kinds of Workplace Documents

- ➤ Letter expressing favorable, neutral, or negative information
- ➤ Letter ordering a product or service
- ➤ Letter acknowledging an order
- ➤ Job application package—cover letter and résumé
- ➤ A letter of recommendation
- ➤ A letter of congratulations
- ➤ A letter report
- ➤ A letter proposal
- ➤ A memo expressing favorable, neutral, or negative information
- ➤ A memo explaining how to do something
- ➤ A memo analyzing how something works
- ➤ A feasibility report
- ➤ An informational report
- ➤ A proposal for changing a procedure or service

> ➤ A persuasive report
> ➤ A company brochure
> ➤ A news release
> ➤ An annual report
> ➤ A meeting agenda
> ➤ Meeting minutes
> ➤ An informal e-mail to colleagues
> ➤ A formal e-mail (internal or external; memo, letter, or report)

Students making such requests should ask the company to delete the names of the writer and addressee on letters and memos to protect the privacy of the employees who wrote them.

Discussion about the kinds of skills involved in writing these varied documents should prove fruitful. Students need to see that knowing such organizational plans as comparison and contrast, narration, cause and effect, process analysis, and argument is critical. They will also recognize that in the samples, the problems with grammar and format are distracting and potentially destructive to the success of the message.

■ STRATEGIES FOR LETTERS AND MEMOS

Writing effective letters and memos requires that the writer have a strategy for the document before beginning to write. In addition to thinking about the audience and emphasizing the reader by using second-person pronouns more than first-person pronouns, the writer also needs to decide where in the message to put the most important information. In deciding on placement, the writer must consider whether the message is likely to be received favorably, neutrally, or unfavorably.

Favorable letters and memos open with the important information and then follow up with the details. For example, a memo saying that an employee's trip has been approved would begin with that information. People enjoy receiving positive information and will usually continue reading the letter or memo to find out the details once they have been given the good news.

Neutral messages, often routine documents like orders, responses to inquiries, or acknowledgments of orders or shipments, should be handled in much the same way. Writers should, however, make an effort to be as positive and empathetic to the reader as possible, especially in the opening and closing sentences.

Unfavorable news, sometimes called a "bad news message," requires a different approach—a much less direct beginning. Readers who read bad news in the first line of a letter or memo may not read the reasons for the bad news or notice the helpful alternatives, which an unskilled writer may have put after the bad news in the document. An effective bad news letter usually reverses this process, beginning with a positive tone and giving the reasons for the unfavorable news—and only then giving the bad news. The advantage of this arrangement is that the reader's disappointment or anger is more likely to be softened if he or she can see the reasoning explained in stages from the beginning. This kind of letter or memo can be even more effective when the writer can help the reader by suggesting other ways the reader might achieve the goal or solve the problem.

■ EMPLOYMENT DOCUMENTS

Résumés

Most students have at least heard of a résumé, though most do not know how to write an acceptable one. Few seem to understand that a job application package has two parts: the résumé and the job application letter, also known as a cover letter. They also need to know about additional kinds of letters that are involved in getting a job, such as thank you letters following interviews, inquiries about the status of an application, and letters accepting or rejecting a job.

One of the most difficult lessons to teach about employment documents is that they must be perfect and conventional. One of the best ways to make this point is to invite a human resources director or other executive to the class to discuss the number of résumés that are rejected simply because of sloppy appearance or a misspelling. Students need to hear that their résumés may not be read at all if the layout conveys a lack of attention to convention. (See 43k in *The Simon & Schuster Handbook for Writers* for guideliness for résumé writing.)

Before they even begin drafting a résumé or looking at sample résumés, students should be encouraged to spend time doing a thorough self-analysis. In particular they should list their previous or current jobs, activities, academic qualifications, and skills (especially experience with computers, foreign languages, money management, and travel). School and community activities can reveal leadership, experience with financial management, and organizational skills.

Some students are discouraged about beginning a résumé because they think they do not have anything to put on one. That empty-résumé feeling, however, is rarely the case. Students need help in seeing that their four years' work with a sorority or a service group has taught them much about planning, public relations, budgeting, and accountability. On the other hand, students must learn that employers are on the lookout for padded résumés, those which contain inflated—or even dishonest—descriptions of routine jobs or activities. Once students have done some brainstorming about their own achievements, they are ready to think about how résumés ought to look. At this point, teachers may find it useful to have the class critique both effective and ineffective résumés. Career Placement personnel at the school may be able to come to class to discuss the most recent trends in résumé writing.

The most common kind of arrangement for résumés of graduating or continuing students is the reverse-chronological résumé. Under its three or four main headings—Education, Employment Experience, Activities and Honors, and Personal—activities are cited from most recent to oldest. Because the educational block is generally the most important for students, it comes first. Often it will include a subheading for school-related activities. This section normally does not refer to high school activities or graduation unless they were extraordinary (attending high school abroad, for example), though students who are not graduating from college may wish to list their high school and graduation date.

As with employment history, this educational history needs to be accurate in terms of exact dates. If gaps of a year or more appear, these need to be explained in the cover letter.

Many job placement experts suggest that in the educational block, students should give their GPA (but only if it is above 3.0 on a 4.0 scale), note that percentage of their college expenses they have earned themselves, and list special courses outside the major that show additional expertise that might attract an employer's eye—for example, particular computer programs, foreign language proficiency, journalism courses, etc.).

As part of this block, often under a heading like *Activities and Awards*, students should list their memberships and achievements. The most difficult part of this section is that many students have difficulty in making parallel the elements of such a list. They need to be reminded to clarify (in parenthesis) unclear, abbreviated, or Greek titles of organizations and to explain briefly what certain responsibilities might mean if an office has an unusual title. Similarly, in the *Employment Experience* section, students should succinctly describe the duties of a position they held, particularly if the job title is not descriptive. When describing job duties, students should write telegraphicallly, beginning with verb phrases rather than with the word "I."

Job-seekers who have been out of school for a while or who are in specialized or creative fields may prefer to do an Emphatic Résumé, one which highlights special talents and achievements first, following these with *Education* and *Activitie*s sections.

Job placement experts disagree about two elements on résumés, and they seem evenly split in their vote. Some favor the use of a *Job Objective* at the beginning of the résumé, but others argue that such an objective is a waste of space that could be better used for more specific details about the applicant. Those who do not favor their use argue that it is the cover letter that tailors the job application package to the job, not the résumé.

Similarly, these experts are divided about whether or not applicants should list references on the résumé or simply state that they are available. Those who favor listing references on the résumé argue that doing so saves the company a step and may, in a time of urgency in hiring, expedite consideration of those résumés that have them listed. Those who argue against listing them say that references may change and that the list takes space better used to show the qualifications of the applicant. Whether or not references appear on the résumé, students need to be reminded that listing someone as a reference is rude unless permission to do so has been arranged beforehand. If students opt not to list references on their resume, they need to bring an updated reference list with them to their job interviews. Also students need to be told that family friends and ministers are not useful references. They should instead list professors, employers, or supervisors.

The résumé, like the cover letter, should appear on business weight stationery, not photocopy paper. The paper should be white or off-white, and the printer cartridge should be fresh and dark.

Cover Letters

Job application letters have one major purpose: to win a job interview for the writer. These letters, which usually accompany resumes, should be no longer than a page and should avoid overusing first-person pronouns such as *I* and *me*, even though the letter is about the writer. Such pronouns should be positioned within sentences and paragraphs rather than at the beginning, where they receive more emphasis.

In general, cover letters have three parts. The first paragraph should explain how the writer learned about the job. The applicant should say that the letter is in response to an ad in a particular newspaper or magazine, giving the date of the ad and the title of the position as it was listed in the ad. Or, if the applicant found out about the job through a contact, he or she should mention the person who made the job information available.

If the letter is a blanket letter, a job solicitation letter, that the applicant is sending to many firms in a particular geographic area or a specialization, the opening should make clear that the writer knows what kinds of positions are typically open so that he or she avoids a vague and negative opening like "I would like to apply for any entry-level job with your company" or "Please consider me for any new positions in management." Such statements usually result in the application's immediate rejection.

The second paragraph should highlight qualifications, though it should not simply list what is on the attached résumé. This paragraph also provides an opportunity for the writer to explain potentially negative impressions such as gaps in dates on the résumé, low grades, a major in a field different from the area in which the applicant is pursuing a job, the lack of extracurricular activities, or reasons why employment was brief or terminated at a particular company.

The third paragraph, which, like the first, should be only four or five lines long, should request an interview. Career experts are divided on whether the applicant should offer to call the employer to set up the interview or whether the applicant should simply express willingness to have an interview at the employer's convenience, leaving it to the employer to make the initial contact. (Chapter 431 in the handbook provides sample cover letters and advice for writing cover letters.)

Other Employment Letters

Students should be aware that looking for jobs may require letters beyond job application letters. Among the kinds of letters they may need to write are letters requesting recommendations, letters requesting applications, letters thanking a prospective employer for an interview, letters inquiring about the status of an application, letters accepting or declining a job, and letters responding to a rejection letter from a company.

Job-seekers should telephone or write former teachers, current teachers, or former employers and request permission to list them as references on applications or resumes. Such a letter of request should be brief. If requesting that a letter be sent to a potential employer, the writer should give complete information to the person writing the recommendation: to whom it should be sent (complete name, title, and address) and the deadline for receipt of the recommendation. If some time has passed since the writer worked for or was the student of the person being asked for the recommendation, he or she should remind the person writing the recommendation about the past job or courses when they knew one another. As a courtesy, the writer should say that he or she will let the reader know about the outcome of the application.

Letters requesting applications should specify the exact position for which the application is being requested and ask about the deadline for returning it. Similarly, letters soliciting information about possible openings should make clear the exact kind of job the writer seeks.

Once job-seekers have had an interview, they should write promptly to thank the appropriate personnel for the interview. This brief letter reinforces the job candidate's interest in the job at the same time that it acknowledges the time and energy expended on the interview. It should mention some comments that were made in the interview or allude to something the candidate learned about as a result of the interview. Such a letter should be sent to the primary interviewer, though it should be sent also to anyone who spent a considerable amount of time with the job-seeker.

In some cases a person who has had an interview with a company may not hear immediately about the status of the application. If the applicant has several offers but has not heard about the status of the application at his or her top choice, the applicant should write a letter of inquiry. Such a follow-up letter gives the applicant a chance to share any additional information that might strengthen the application, and it gives the applicant an opportunity to express continued interest in the company.

A letter accepting a job should begin with the positive information of the acceptance, ask whatever practical questions may have arisen since the interview, and express enthusiasm about the opportunity. The writer should begin by thanking the firm for the confidence in him or her expressed in the offer. Like other "bad news" letters, a letter turning down a job should briefly give the reasons for declining the offer before it makes the statement of rejection.

When the applicant is turned down by a company—usually in a rejection letter—the applicant should respond. Occasionally, such responses, especially those that show appreciation for the interview process and continued interest in the company, may keep the applicant's file alive for future consideration.

Most students do not understand that companies expend much money and time in the process of hiring. Hiring is expensive. Applicants should always express their appreciation for interviews and for job offers, even those they decline.

■ PROPOSALS AND REPORTS

Two of the most common kinds of workplace documents are proposals and reports. These documents occur in many kinds of formats and serve many kinds of purposes in the workplace, everything from documenting travel expenses to studying the feasibility of installing a new air-conditioning system in a factory. Both kinds of documents may be extremely brief or extremely long, and they may be either formal or informal, depending on the purpose and audience.

Most students will have had only the most cursory acquaintance with many of these kinds of documents, though teachers can remind students that many of the documents students handle routinely are versions of these workplace documents. For example, students are familiar with agendas and minutes for meetings, and often they have sent school administrators requests for funding or arguments for changes in policies or facilities.

Students usually need to be told that some overlapping occurs with the terms *proposal* and *report*. Proposals are always persuasive: They always argue for some kind of change. Many documents that are called reports are, in fact, proposals. For example, feasibility reports always analyze the need for and potential success of change, but when they go so far as to argue for particular change based on the findings, they become proposals.

Reports may be informative or persuasive. Many routine business documents are informative reports: summaries of articles or speeches, travel reports, inspection reports, instructions, budget reports, procedural reports, and research reports, to name only a few.

Reports and proposals are often classified as *formal* or *informal*. These terms have nothing to do with length, and the terms *formal* and *informal* do not refer to the relative difficulty of the material, the tone, or the level of language. Both informal and formal proposals and reports may take the form of letters or memoranda. The major distinction is that a formal report usually is bound and usually contains subordinate documents of various kinds.

Formal Reports

Formal reports may be as brief as five to ten pages or as long as several hundred pages. The defining characteristics of formal reports are the numerous supplementary parts, many of which students will never have seen.

Parts of Formal Reports in the Order of Appearance in the Report

TITLE PAGE—A page that gives the title of the report, the name of the company requesting the report, the date, the name of the writer of the report, and the company represented by the writer of the report.

LETTER OR MEMO OF TRANSMITTAL—A communication that accompanies the final report and is addressed to the person designated to receive the report. A letter is used when the report goes to someone outside the writer's firm; a memo is used when the report goes to someone within the firm. **Table of Contents—A listing of the page on which each part of the report appears.**

LIST OF FIGURES—A list by title of graphs, charts, and other visual aids and the pages on which they are found.

ABSTRACT OR EXECUTIVE SUMMARY—A one-page summary of the main findings of the report. Abstracts are more technical and are meant for specialized readers; executive summaries are intended for more general managers.

BODY—The text of the report, which may be single- or double-spaced.

CONCLUSIONS—The findings of the report, often summarized in a numbered list. In informative reports, this is the last part of the report before the appendices and bibliography.

RECOMMENDATIONS—In persuasive reports, this is a list, usually numbered, of actions that should be taken based on the conclusions drawn in the study.

APPENDIX—Usually titled and lettered consecutively (Appendix A, Appendix B, etc.), appendices are used for information that may be of interest to the reader but which would interrupt the focus if it were in the body of the report.

BIBLIOGRAPHY—A listing of sources used in the report. These may be classified under such headings as *Primary Sources* and *Secondary Sources*, or they may be combined in a list alphabetized by last name of the author. Bibliographies in workplace writing may use any of the major style sheets, but most often they use either the MLA style or the APA style for documentation.

Unlike informal reports, these kinds of reports are often bound like books or have other kinds of special binding. Many companies generate formal reports internally for their own use, but many others hire consultants to analyze conditions or to study the feasibility of projects.

Informal Reports and Proposals

Like formal reports, informal reports may be brief or lengthy. Although they do not include the many parts of a formal report, they may include such parts as conclusions, recommendations, appendices, and a bibliography.

If the informal report or proposal is being sent within the company, it usually has a memorandum heading. If it is being sent outside the company, it may take the form of a letter, or it may have a letter as a cover document.

An informal proposal, like a formal one, has four special parts in the body. The introduction gives the background information necessary for the reader to understand the proposal. The second section is the proposal itself. The third section is the budget, and the fourth section is conclusions, which ties the parts of the document together and discusses negative and positive results of proceeding with the plan as it is discussed in the document.

Headings in Reports

Both formal and informal reports and proposals use headings for separate sections. The major reason for using headings is to make it possible for the reader to easily find the parts he or she wants or needs to read. Rarely is a report or proposal read in its entirety. A busy executive, for example, may read only the executive summary, the budget part of the body, and the conclusions and recommendations.

Students need to understand, however, that headings do not replace transition. Headings are required in addition to all of the kinds of transitional devices good writers use in any kind of writing—repetition of key words, use of transitional words and phrases, use of pronouns, and use of parallelism. In a formal report, the headings may correspond to entries in the table of contents.

The placement and size of headings suggest the relative importance of the information introduced by them. Writers have five levels of headings from which to choose. These levels are similar to the levels in a traditional outline that uses Roman numerals, capital letters, Arabic numerals, small letters, and so on. Here are the kinds of headings, and information about their relative placement:

FIRST DEGREE HEADING

This level can be used for the title of the report and for major sections in a long report. It is all capitals and centered.

Second-Degree Heading. This level is used for major sections in a short report and major subdivisions in a long one. Only the first letters in words are capitalized, and the heading is underlined.

Third-Degree Heading. This kind of heading looks like a second-degree heading, but it begins at the left margin.

Fourth-degree heading. This heading is on the same line as the sentence it precedes. Only the first word is capitalized, and the heading begins at the left margin.

Fifth-degree headings are part of the sentence that they introduce. They begin at the left margin, and only the first word is capitalized.

Most students will have had little if any experience in using headings, and as a result, they will have some predictable problems. As with outlining, they need to be taught that if a section of a report cannot be divided into at least two sections, it cannot be divided: that is, any heading must always have at least one other at its level. Similarly, as writers work to achieve structural parallelism in topic outlines, they must also make subordinate headings in a given section parallel with one another. In addition, students need to be reminded that headings are not mixtures of sentences and phrases. Most headings in workplace writing are phrases. (See section 45d in handbook for more information about headings.)

Just as students generally dislike outlining, they also resist working to write precise, effective headings. This part of report writing is best left until students have done enough research and writing to have become interested in the project.

In addition to learning about headings, students may also be learning about visual aids, often referred to as graphics, in reports and proposals. Although visuals are used in most lengthy reports and proposals, they also figure prominently in other kinds of workplace writing, especially oral presentations. (See section 45f in handbook for more information about incorporating visuals into a report.)

■ Public Writing

Part of our responsibility as teachers is helping students understand how to express themselves on issues important to their own lives. They may want to write their mayor or senator. They may need to rally neighbors to protest reduced services by the city. They may want to argue their positions in a letter to the editor, or they may need to write a news article or press release to publicize a fundraising event for a sorority or fraternity or for a children's group. In addition, students are increasingly posting Web logs and other materials on the Internet.

In all of these cases, students must learn how to write for an audience that they do not know and they must learn to establish credibility as a public spokesperson.

We must teach students to analyze what they have in common with prospective readers, what experiences they bring to the debate that lend credibility to their argument, what reputable sources they can cite to shore up their views, and what facts they have found that will strengthen their position. (See Chapters 1, 5, and 44 in *The Simon & Schuster Handbook for Writers*.)

As in any good argument, students writing to share views in a debate should concede that the opponents may be right on certain points, because doing so shows that the writer has thought carefully about the issue from many points of view. The writer should maintain a positive tone, refraining from name-calling and insults to those who think differently.

Dear Editor:

The recent debate over the cost of enforcing "No Littering" laws has led to confusion among some citizens of this community, and as a resident of Mobile for the last twenty years, I would like to share some thoughts about this important issue.

Surely the projected cost of $73,000 for two full-time officers to oversee the prosecution of those who trash our streets, parks, and other green areas is a small price to pay for the many benefits our community will reap if we can penalize those who litter.

Not only will the fines imposed on those caught off-set a third of this cost, according to the recent report of consultants hired by the city, but the added revenue from taxes paid by new businesses will more than pay for the rest.

The 2001 reports by two area Chambers of Commerce as well as a recently released ten-year study by the state's Economic Development Commission document that last year alone, our part of the state lost eighteen businesses that explored opening here because of the "trashy appearance of the major roads leading into the city," according to the state analysis of economic development.

Littering is a selfish, wasteful act that must not be ignored by our community. We can easily afford to pay for the proposed employees. Indeed, we can't afford not to.

Miguel Sanchez
115 Edgemont Road

Writing a news release is an important skill for our students to learn, whether they eventually need to do so as part of a job or as a result of non-profit activities in the community. A news release should look professional. Its heading should list the name, address, and telephone number as well as an e-mail address of the contact person responsible for verifying information or giving further details. The heading also should include the release date for the information.

The body of the news release should answer the journalistic questions of *who, what, where, when, why*, and *how* in a brief, clear statement that begins with the most important information to be publicized.

Students should know that many organizations and businesses attempt to use news releases to promote an individual or publicize a product or service rather than pay for advertising. Releases that are padded with promotional details that obscure the news value are likely to be discarded without a careful reading.

Here is a news release announcing a festival that will raise money for local nonprofit arts groups.

FOR IMMEDIATE RELEASE

CONTACT: Edwin Conners
12 Stonegate Terrace
Charleston, S.C.
843-928-4768

SPRING FLING TO AID ARTS GROUPS

A Spring Fling April 9–10 in downtown Charleston will raise money to benefit six local nonprofit groups.

Festival-goers will be able to sample specialties of 18 local restaurants, hear six jazz and chamber music groups, enjoy four folk dance groups, and take in a wide array of arts and crafts from a three-state area. Games and rides will be available for children ages 3–10.

On both days Meeting Street will be closed to traffic from 10 a.m. to 11 p.m. in the two blocks around the Visitors' Center to accommodate stages, display areas, and temporary food court.

Admission to the festival is free, but musical events will cost five dollars, food tickets will cost two dollars for each sample, and games and rides will cost one dollar.

Visitors may browse through the arts and crafts areas at no charge. Ten percent of the sales of arts and crafts items will be donated to the proceeds of the festival.

Benefiting from the festival's proceeds will be the Carolina Youth Chorale, the Young Artists of the Low Country, the Charleston Children's Theater, the Symphony's Candy Concerts, the Lowenthal Ballet Troupe, and the Goosecreek Youth Orchestra.

* * *

■ ACTIVITIES FOR TEACHING WORKPLACE AND PUBLIC WRITING

In addition to suggestions in other sections of this supplement, teachers may wish to try some of these activities to interest students in the complexities of workplace writing and to further their understanding of public writing.

Letter and Memo-Writing Activities

1. Students enjoy role-playing, and teachers can increase students' enthusiasm for writing by assigning roles in small groups and having them solve problems by writing letters, memos, and e-mails. For example, one student in a group might be a disgruntled parent writing to a teacher to complain about a class policy; another student might be the teacher, who must write both to the parent and to inform his or her principal; the student who takes the role of the principal may need to write to the school board about the continued harassment of teachers by parents, etc. Many such scenarios give effective opportunities for students to practice letter- and memo writing. These scenarios also provide students with good practice in ascertaining audience and purpose.

2. Students can assume roles having to do with employment scenarios. They can practice writing all of the kinds of employment documents they may encounter in trying to find out about jobs, apply for a job, thank someone for an interview, check on the status of their application, etc.

3. Students particularly enjoy writing real letters of complaint to companies and organizations from whom they had poor service or products and sharing the responses with the class. The responses provide great texts for class discussion of strategy and tone.

4. Students often ask teachers for letters of recommendation, but rarely have had the chance to write one themselves. Students can develop a letter of recommendation for themselves or can recommend a friend, classmate, family member, or colleague for a job, award, scholarship, or other recognition.

5. Students can practice the conventions of e-mail, letter, and memo-writing by composing class-related communication in these types of formats, i.e., writer's memos describing their revision of a particular essay, formal e-mails to instructor regarding questions or requests, and cover letters describing the strengths, weaknesses, and learning reflected in an essay or portfolio.

Report and Proposal-Writing Activities

1. To teach students about precision in language, have groups of them draft questionnaires all on the same subject, but a subject they could actually poll the student body at large about. Comparing the ways each group went about the questioning and the differences in tone and precision will teach students a lot about efficiency in language.

2. Students could role-play a student government or city council meeting regarding a specific problem or issue. In groups, students can develop solution or action proposals to address the issue at hand and present them

to the "council" at an in-class meeting. The council will then evaluate the proposals they receive and make a decision on which action to take.

3. Ask students to request sample formal and informal reports from local companies. Then have them analyze the parts of each report and offer suggestions for improving it.

4. For an original experience with a formal report, ask students to come up with an issue at the school to investigate. For this they might use a questionnaire for students, interviews with several key people, primary documents at the school, and secondary reading. With a topic as simple as "The Campus Security Force: Overcharging for Parking Violations?" students have the opportunity to write everything from a letter of transmittal to conclusions and recommendations. You may wish to require a number of visual aids and an appendix or two.

5. Another way students can gain experience writing formal reports is to offer to draft a report for a campus or community organization. Students can gather and report on data for the organization; for example, the campus writing center may be curious about how satisfied students are with their drop-in services. Alternatively, students can synthesize data an organization has already collected into a formal report or proposal; for example, the local library may have facts and statistics about why they would like to extend their services to include Sunday evenings, and students could use that information to produce a formal document for the library.

Public Writing Activities

1. Ask students to write a letter to the editor (or respond to a letter to the editor) in the campus or community newspaper, or have students write a letter to the dean or president of the college arguing that a certain policy or requirement should be changed.

2. Students can write a review of a book they have recently read, a performance they recently attended, or a local eatery to post online.

3. Students can use information from a club or organization they are involved in to create a portfolio of items such as a news release for an event, a newletter article about a recent fundraiser, or blog updates about activities or members.

4. Ask students to use Internet resources to find the name and contact information for their U.S. senators and/or representative and to write a letter of support or opposition to a current issue.

5. In groups, have students publish a Web page for the class or for a campus or community organization. For example, students can take the information they gathered in their formal report writing activities above and publish the report online.

WEB RESOURCES

Web Resources can be found at **www.prenhall.com/troyka**.

SUGGESTED READING

Adler-Kassner, Linda, Robert Crooks, and Ann Watters. *Writing the Community: Concepts And Models for Service-Learning in Composition.* Washington, DC: American Association for Higher Education, 1998.

Bailey, Edward P., Jr. *The Plain English Approach to Business Writing.* New York: Oxford UP, 1990.

Blackburn, Elizabeth, and Kelly Belanger. "You-Attitude and Positive Emphasis: Testing Received Wisdom in Business Communication." *The Bulletin of the Association for Business Communication* 56.2 (June 1993): 1–9.

Blase, Dean Woodring. "A New Sort of Writing: E-Mail in the English Classroom." *English Journal* 90.2 (Nov. 2000): 47–51.

Boone, Louis E., David L. Kurtz, and Judy R. Block. *Contemporary Business Communication.* Englewood Cliffs, NJ: Prentice Hall, 1994.

Brusaw, Charles T., Gerald J. Alfred, and Walter E. Oliu. *The Business Writer's Handbook.* 6th ed. New York: St. Martin's, 2000.

Collins, Paul S. *Community Writing: Researching Social Issues Through Composition.* Mahwah, NJ: Lawrence Eribaum Associates, 2001.

Conlin, Joseph. "The Write Stuff." *Sales and Marketing Management* (Jan. 1998): 71–75.

Coogan, David. "E-Mail Tutoring: A New Way to Do New Work." *Computers and Composition* 12.2 (1995): 171–81.

Elliot, Norbert, Margaret Kilduff, and Robert Lynch. "The Assessment of Technical Writing: A Case Study." *Journal of Technical Writing and Communication* 24.2 (Winter 1994): 19–37.

Faidman, Anne. "Mail." *The American Scholar* 69.1 (Winter 2000): 7–11.

Fredericksen, Elaine. "Letter Writing in the College Classroom." *Teaching English in the Two-Year College* 27.3 (Mar 2000): 278–84.

Greenly, Robert. "How to Write a Resume." *Technical Communication* 40 (Feb. 1993): 42–48.

Guffey, Mary Ellen. *Business Communication: Process and Product.* 3rd ed. Belmont, CA: Wadsworth, 1999.

Henry, Julie. "E-mail Style is :-(for Writing." *The Times Educational Supplement* 4392 (Sept. 1, 2000): 5.

Hoffman, Marvin. "On Teaching Technical Writing: Creative Language in the Real World." *English Journal* 81.2 (Feb. 1992.): 58–64.

Hyde, Paul. "E-mail: Is It a Blessing or Curse?" *The Masthead* 52.2 (Summer 2000): 20.

Jablonski, Jeffrey. "Teaching the Complexity of Business Proposals." *Business Communications Quarterly* 62.3 (Sept. 1999): 108–12.

Jackson, Tom. *The Perfect Resume.* New York: Doubleday, 1990.

Kowalski, Kathiann M. "Dear Editor . . . (How to Write Letters to the Editors of Newspapers)." *Cobblestone* 22.2 (Feb. 2001): 20.

Krajewski, Lorraine, and Gwendolyn Smith. "From Letter Writing to Report Writing: Bridging the Gap." *Business Communication Quarterly* 60.4 (Dec. 1997): 88–91.

Krause, Tim. "Preparing an Online Resume." *Business Communication Quarterly* 60.1 (March 1997): 59–61.

Lauer, Janice M. "Persuasive Writing on Public Issues." *Composition in Context: Essays in Honor of Donald C. Stewart.* Ed. W. Ross Winterowd and Vincent Gillespie. Carbondale, IL: Southern Illinois UP, 1994: 62–72.

McCune, Jenny C. "Get the Message." *Management Review* 86 (Jan. 1997): 10–11.

Moran, Charles. "Notes Toward a Rhetoric of E-mail." *Computers and Composition* 12.1 (1995): 15–21.

Munro, John, and David Howes. "The Effect of Cognitive Style on Learning to Write a Letter of Complaint." *The British Journal of Educational Psychology* 68.2 (June 1998): 243–54.

Patterson, Valerie. "Resume Talk from Recruiters." *Journal of Career Planning & Employment* 56.2 (Jan. 1996): 33–39.

Pirto, John. "University Student Attitudes Toward E-mail as Opposed to Written Documents." *Computers in the Schools* 14.3–4 (1998): 25–32.

Rabb, Margaret Y, and Richard Scoville. "Tips for Great Reports." *PC World* 10.4 (April 1992): 224–31.

Shafer, Gregory. "Using Letters for Process and Change in the Basic Writing Class." *Teaching English in the Two-Year College* 27.3 (Mar 2000): 285–92.

Subramanian, Ram, Robert G. Insley, and Rodney D. Blackwell. "Performance and Readability: A Comparison of the Annual Reports of Profitable and Unprofitable Corporations." *Journal of Business Communication* 30.2 (1993): 49–61.

Troyka, Lynn Quitman. *Majoring in the Rest of Your Life: College and Career Secrets for Students*. Englewood Cliffs, NJ: Prentice Hall, 1999.

Vassallo, Philip. "U-mail, I-mail—More Effective Business E-Mail." *Etc.* 55.2 (Summer 1998): 195–203.

PART SEVEN:

Integrating Computers into the Writing Classroom

by Linda Julian, *Furman University*

■ TECHNOLOGY IN THE NEW MILLENNIUM: TOOLS FOR READING AND RESEARCH

Today most college students, as well as those from kindergarten through high school, either own a computer or have access to one in their classrooms, computer labs, or school libraries. In fact, many young children know more about computer resources and using computers than their teachers do. Public school teachers and college instructors must embrace the new possibilities of the computer age if they are to educate their students as productive citizens of the twenty-first century.

All teachers of writing must understand how to use technology best to help students improve their skills in writing and research so that they will not be left behind their peers in entering the workforce or going into graduate programs. If we do not help all students use computer technology as a tool for their learning and work, we teachers are, to a great degree, abdicating our responsibilities to them.

Those teachers who use computers in teaching composition have done so to greater and lesser degrees. Some have put their entire course online, everything from the syllabus and assignments to chat rooms and other resources for their students. Others are wading in slowly, using word processing programs to help their students come up with ideas, outline essays, write drafts, and revise them. Some, in fact, limit their use of computers in the classroom to showing students how to do research online.

Troyka & Hesse's *Simon & Schuster Handbook for Writers*, 9th ed., offers much help in using technology for teachers and students alike (see especially Chapters 1, 33–35, 42, 45, and 46). In addition, Troyka & Hesse's emphasis on the process of writing (see Chapter 2) easily enables teachers to adapt some of the stages of writing to computer instruction, even if they choose to limit the use of computers. A glossary of basic computer terminology is included at the end of this chapter of the supplement. Finally, Prentice Hall, the publisher of Troyka & Hesse's handbook, and its partners offer many online resources for both the teacher and student. (See the online resources on the Web at www.prenhall.com /troyka.)

■ ADVANTAGES AND DISADVANTAGES OF TEACHING WITH COMPUTERS

Using computers in the classroom offers both disadvantages and advantages for students and teachers, though most instructors find the benefits far outweigh the challenges.

Disadvantages

Among the disadvantages to computer-assisted instruction mentioned by some teachers are these:

- ➤ Valuable time may be spent teaching word processing and research skills that could be better spent working on students' writing.
- ➤ Class time may be wasted if the technology is not functioning properly.
- ➤ Students who lack access to or experience with technology are disadvantaged in classrooms that emphasize computer use, especially if they do not have strong keyboarding skills.
- ➤ Some students will be tempted to surf the Net or play computer games rather then concentrate on instruction.
- ➤ Teachers may need special training.
- ➤ Students may not learn how to do library research and may rely on unreliable, but easily accessible Web sources for research.
- ➤ In online courses instructors may need to do far more individualized instruction, which is time consuming.
- ➤ Plagiarism can be harder to detect, and it is easier for students to access "paper mill" essays.

Many of these reasons for not using computers are only minor concerns at best today, when most students know more technology than many of their teachers. Those who teach in colleges where a number of their students still lack basic word processing skills or access to computers at home will find that, although the computer-assisted classroom may require writing instructors to spend more time developing computer skills, this time is time well spent; the ability to use technology will be essential to students' success in their academic and professional lives.

Advantages

The advantages seem more significant than the disadvantages of using computers to teach writing:

> Many students find composing on computer easier than first composing by hand.

> Students will develop skills necessary for them to become more independent learners.

> The students can more easily identify and move through the stages of writing, especially revision and editing, and this ease will underscore Troyka & Hesse's philosophy that students must see writing as a process, not a product.

> Students can utilize various software programs designed to help them brainstorm, organize, or revise their work.

> Many word processing programs provide templates for various types of documents students will be asked to produce.

> Students will learn skills that will help them in the job market. In fact, not being able to word process and use the Internet usually disadvantages students seeking jobs.

> Students will learn writing and research skills that will empower them in their other courses.

> Students may develop a greater sense of the importance of document design and creating professional looking final products.

> Students will likely learn to work in a more individualized way— a real plus since teachers want students to see that they have their own styles and methods, unlike those of other students.

> Students can use online spelling and grammar checks (though we must explain that these are not infallible).

> Doing peer review and other interactive assignments on the computer may lead to valuable interaction among students.

> The computer-assisted classroom provides a fruitful place for students to work on collaborative writing projects.

> Teachers can collect disks or have students e-mail their papers as attachments. This method can also be used for peer-response.

> E-mail can mean contact with the teacher or classmates twenty-four hours a day, seven days a week, so students will likely feel more connected to the teacher and classmates.

> Technology enables students to give more professional and effective presentations by using presentational software.

➤ Technology allows teachers to develop more creative and motivating assignments, including designing Web pages, blogs, and developing electronic portfolios.

➤ Teachers can supplement classroom discussion with threaded discussions and chat rooms; they can supplement print materials with Web links.

➤ Learning to use technology can make teachers more marketable and more effective.

■ USING COMPUTERS TO TEACH WRITING SKILLS

Today, almost all college writing projects require computer use. Most instructors will ask for word processed final drafts of papers. However, the computer can be used for more than typing up a final draft; the computer can be useful at all stages of the writing process.

PREWRITING WITH COMPUTERS

Many of our students complain that they do not know anything to write about, but some brainstorming and other prewriting exercises using the computer can help them see that they, in fact, know much more than they realize and that they have things to say that will interest readers. (See Troyka & Hesse, Chapter 2 for prewriting activities that can be adapted for use on the computer.)

Teachers may also find that invention exercises using only a word processing program work well. Having students use the outlining feature to break down topics to give them a narrowed enough focus for a thesis can work. Also effective is having the students turn off their monitors while they do free-writing as brainstorming. Although some may be uncomfortable at first not seeing what they are writing, most will come to feel comfortable and see the value in letting ideas flow freely without constant self-censoring. Once students have topics narrowed, pairing students to ask questions about the topic and its development through e-mail can stimulate the invention of further ideas.

Word processing programs and e-mail may be used to great advantage to help in early drafting stages. One technique is to divide the class into groups of three and ask them to huddle around one computer, with one of them as typist. You might have them take an overly general thesis, which you could submit to all machines at once, and try narrowing it collaboratively and drafting an introduction together.

You could use this kind of collaborative assignment to reinforce skills related to any part of the essay. For example, if you are stressing transitional paragraphs, you might send them an essay lacking these and have them collaboratively write them. Or, you might ask each group to do communal brainstorming, coming up with several workable theses they have pulled out of a too-general statement. On the paragraph level, one can have small groups write certain types of paragraphs (definition or compare and contrast, for example).

Prewriting skills can also be enhanced through the use of interactive, Web-based tools, such as WebCT or Blackboard, which make collaboration and online discussion even easier. Online discussion of readings or chats about new paper assignments can be fruitful ways for students to come up with topic ideas. Many textbooks also provide CD-Rom or Web-based resources that supplement the textbook's lessons.

Going online can help students in a variety of ways. Narrowing topics may involve research, and the use of the computer to do research is a great benefit. (See Using Computers for Research, below.) Additionally, students can access one of the many online resources to support their writing at all stages of the writing process. One example is http://owl.english.purdue.edu/, one of the foremost writing help-centers online.

DRAFTING AND REVISING USING THE COMPUTER

Composing with a word processor can make it easy for students to highlight their thesis and topic sentences and stay on track rather than going off on tangents. Students can make use of the "highlight" or font color function available on most word processing programs to call attention to questions or parts of an essay, which helps their teachers check for understanding. Highlighting the thesis, topic sentences, transitions, and perhaps even examples or other supporting details can reveal when the reality of what they underline does not match what they think they have written. Once they have considered the highlighted material, they can easily see what kinds of organizational and substantive change they need to make. Highlighting questions they want to ask peers or their teacher also makes it easy for them to get help in the late stages or the process.

Writing with the computer can also make it easier for students to move from one part of the paper to another, writing parts out of order or testing different organizational strategies. Of course having typed drafts also makes it easier for peers to share each other's essays than trying to read often-illegible handwriting. When students are ready to receive feedback on a draft, the computer, whether through e-mail or an interactive, online classroom management tools, such as WebCT or Blackboard, can make the commenting process easier for peers and instructors alike. Students can still make use of teacher-generated questions or directions for commenting, even if the peer response session takes place outside of class time. (Troyka & Hesse's handbook offers much help with all stages of revision and editing in Chapter 2.) Some online tools lend themselves to more global comments, preferred by many instructors on early drafts. However, for those who want students to help edit one another's texts, most word processing programs also have tools in which students can track changes made to their text, allowing peers to make comments or changes while still enabling the writer to accept or reject suggestions or changes. Many colleges also have online versions of their writing centers, which students can use to ask questions, access resources, or receive feedback.

When editing, students will, of course, rely on the spellcheckers and grammar checkers, but teachers must point out the problems with totally relying on these tools. Spellcheckers have much smaller dictionaries that those in the average desk dictionary, so they often will not have words the students need to spell. Similarly, grammar checkers, while they may help with some errors, often do not identify other errors; and sometimes they give wrong or incomplete advice. Looking at these tools will not lead the students too far astray, but students need to be made well aware of their shortcomings and limitations. Students can be taught to use the "Find" command to seek out their individual writing problems, such as confusing "there" and "their" or using wordy phrases.

As students move from one draft to another, they should be encouraged to keep hard copies of each draft as well as copies on their disks or jump drives, perhaps using a different computer folder for each revision. They should also keep a revision log, keeping up with the kinds of changes they made in each draft. Such records may help them understand better their own composing process. Keeping a computer list of errors the teacher points out on each final draft can show them particular types of errors they need to concentrate on in the proofing and editing process. Finally, students must be reminded to back up all of their course work frequently on a separate disk or drive.

Finishing the Final Draft and Designing the Document

Once all of the revision has ended, the student must think about how he or she wants the document to look. Making the document look consistent from page to page, easy to read, harmonious, and unified throughout, the student can show the instructor and peers that he or she took the assignment seriously. Good document design helps students make a good first impression on both peers and the teacher (see Troyka & Hesse's *Simon & Schuster's Handbook for Writers*, Chapter 45).

The first step in designing a document is identifying the genre of the document (essay, report, etc.), the audience for whom it is intended, and the purpose of the document—the same questions a writer asks at the beginning of the writing process. The answers to these questions help determine design, to some extent, but the writer also has some personal choices.

Among these choices are decisions about using visuals, page layout, white space, headings, highlighting, borders and margins, bulleted or numbered lists, colors, and boxed information, clip art, charts, and graphs as well as justifying text, adding headers or footers and choosing an appropriate font. Troyka & Hesse also includes information about designing Web pages (see Chapter 46).

Many word processing programs, such as Microsoft Word and Corel WordPerfect, have easy-to-use features that insert charts, graphs, and tables as well as headers and footers. Such page layout software as Adobe Page-Maker and Microsoft Publisher help students to place text and visuals precisely. Graphic design software such as Macromedia Freehand or Adobe PhotoShop can help students create and edit graphics, pictures, and other kinds of visuals. The student must then save these visuals in a format compatible to his or her own word processing system so that they can insert them in appropriate places in the document.

Students will generally find documenting a paper easier than ever. Most word processing programs offer guidelines or templates for the major styles of documentation, especially MLA, APA, and CM. WordPerfect has a template for APA format.

Students love to play with design features on the computer, especially the more unusual typefaces, so teachers need to help them understand which ones are appropriate for the document in question and which ones are the most readable. Fonts are either serif (they have little "feet" at the top or bottom of each letter) or sans-serif (these are without extensions at the top or bottom of the letter). Serif fonts are usually chosen for text because they are more comfortable to read, especially in a long text. One of the most common of these is Times New Roman.

Sans-serif fonts may be more easily read from a distance, so they may be the better choice for charts and signs. They are often used also for headings in documents.

Font sizes are measured in points ranging from six points to seventy-two, but many teachers stipulate a particular size (usually 12-point) to ensure readability as well as to help students write the appropriate amount of text if they have stipulated that an assignment be a certain number of pages.

■ Using Computers to Do Research

Most students will need to access the Internet even to find library-based materials in the campus library. And beyond college library holdings and databases, the Internet is a rich source of information for students when they know how to use it effectively. Our instruction should involve explanations of what the Internet and the Web are, how to use search engines to locate the information they need, how to evaluate the information they find, and how to use information without violating privacy or copyright laws.

Understanding the Internet

The Internet is a network of sites found at universities, businesses, research centers, and government agencies worldwide.

The best way for students to access the Internet is through the **World Wide Web**, a collection of what are called **Web pages** or **websites**. These interlinked Web pages each have their own **home page**, a catalogue of what the site offers and directions for finding information.

Not a replacement for all library research, the Internet offers more up-to-date information than libraries are able to, so accessing the Internet is especially important for research on current topics.

Students access the Web through a **browser**, a **search engine** that helps them locate the kind of information they are seeking. They need to understand that a **URL** is an address on the Internet that should be typed into the search box of the browser. **URL** is an acronym for "Universal Resource Locator." (Chapter 34 of the handbook discusses how to locate information on the Internet.)

Well known browsers include Apple Safari, Mozilla Firefox, and Microsoft Internet Explorer, though there are many other browsers available. Most recent computers will have an icon on the start-up page listing at least one of these among other programs available on that computer.

Places to Begin

Jumping into an Internet search is not the best beginning for most research projects. First, students need to have a general idea of the narrowed topic they want to find out about and some of the key terms that will help in the online search for information. Often a preliminary online search can help students narrow the topic even further, taking an angle that they had never thought of.

Before they can make the best use of online resources, students need to be instructed by the teacher or an information technology specialist in the school's library about the most efficient ways to use keywords to search, the ways to narrow searches, and the ways to use Boolean operators to help reduce frustration. Boolean operators are various combinations of words and symbols like *and, or, not,* and *near* and symbols help narrow the search and to stipulate what kinds of related words made of the keyword the student would like to check. Different search engines use variations on these Boolean operators and symbols. For those unfamiliar with Boolean operators, most search engines allow users to limit searched by selecting the "Advanced Search" option.

In addition, some keywords can be truncated so that related words containing that root will also be searched if the searcher types in a symbol like *. For example, in some searches * typed at the end of the keyword's root checks for all related words with that root: if the student is searching for information on *communism* and types in the root *comm*, the search will turn up such words as *common, communal, commune,* and *community,* along with *communist* and *communism.* Many of the terms have nothing to do with the subject of the search, so to avoid such frustrating paths, students must be carefully instructed about using truncation in a search.

Once students are on the Internet, however, they have many other browsers at their fingertips. Among the most popular are these:

➤ AltaVista, a fairly comprehensive engine that searches both the Web and news sources: www.altavista.com

➤ Excite, a large database that searches by both subject and keywords: http://www.excite.com

➤ Infoseek, which searches by keyword and subject: www.go.com

➤ Northern Light, which sorts information into requested folders: www.nlsearch.com

➤ Webcrawler, which finds information with either a keyword or subject: www.Webcrawler.com

➤ Yahoo!, which searches by keyword and subject directory: www.yahoo.com

In addition to these basic search engines, the Web offers several that are called metasearch engines, because they search several of the browsers simultaneously. Among the best known are these:

➤ Ask Jeeves at www.ask.com

➤ DogPile at www.dogpile.com /
➤ Google at www.google.com
➤ Savvysearch at www.search.com (This one translates the search term into the appropriate form for each search engine it checks.)

Also available online are many other sites to check out, including those of university libraries, the Library of Congress, and government as well as standard references such as the Oxford English Dictionary and encyclopedias. Language students may find help and practice accessing foreign language sites.

Some sites are general; some are narrowed to subject areas. A sampling includes these:

➤ Encyclopedia Britannica at www.britannica.com
➤ Bartlett's Familiar Quotations at www.bartleby.com /bartlett
➤ Center for Responsive Politics at www.crp.org
➤ How Stuff Works at www.howstuffworks.com
➤ American Statistical Index at www.fedstats.gov
➤ FindLaw at www.findlaw.com
➤ Library of Congress Research Tools at www.loc.gov/rr/tools.htm l
➤ National Institutes of Health at www.nih.gov/
➤ American Chemical Society's ACS Web at www.acs.org
➤ Math Archives at http://archivesm ath.utk.edu
➤ National Academy of Sciences at www.nasonline.org

School libraries also have databases that include newspapers, periodicals, current business information, book reviews, and many others. These may be available on the library's own network or CD-Rom.

EVALUATING RESOURCES ON THE INTERNET

Researchers with online information must always approach that information cautiously. Knowing what is reliable, what is questionable, and what is downright unreliable comes with experience. New computer users do not realize that almost anyone can put a website on the Internet without regard for its authenticity, fairness, or accuracy. Researchers should always ask these questions of a site:

➤ What is the purpose of this site—to inform, persuade, sell something?

➤ Who is the author of this website and what are his or her qualifications? Does the site offer contact information?

➤ Does the site explain where its information has come from?

➤ How current does the information seem to be?

➤ Is there a bibliography or other list of sources?

➤ How well developed is the site's content, especially when compared to that offered by other sites?

➤ Can you detect any bias in the information that suggests the site has an agenda?

➤ Is the information recent? How often does the site seem to be updated?

The site is more likely to be reliable if it is from an educational or nonprofit organization, government organization, those with Internet addresses ending in **edu**, **org**, **gov**, or a country abbreviation, such as **us** or **uk**. Students should be alerted, however, that when country abbreviations, such as **uk**, appear in the URL, the site's information is often not relevant to U.S.-specific topics. Another criterion is whether the author is someone respected and well known in his or her field. We can teach students to learn who is respected by checking out this person in the library's catalogue, reference books, or bibliographies given by other writers in the field. Online versions of well-known print sources, such as newspapers, magazines, or journals are just as reliable as the print versions. Students should be taught to look for copyright or update dates and sponsor or publisher information. Credible sites generally make publication and sponsorship information clear, including copyright information. Reliable sources should be current or recently updated and should provide evidence in a balanced, unbiased manner, often with links to other reliable sources of information and in-text cites or bibliographies. Much of what is posted on the Internet may be plagiarized from other sources. Students should learn to be overly cautious and suspicious of all sources on the Internet. (Refer students to Chapters 34 and 35 of the handbook for more information on evaluating Internet sources and avoiding plagiarism.)

HANDLING COPYRIGHT ISSUES AND PLAGIARISM

Many kinds of dishonesty appear as a result of the openness of the Internet and ease with which students can view others' work and share papers online. However, some strategies and resources help teachers cope with these kinds of problems.

The best tool for reducing plagiarism is usually the instructor him- or herself. Becoming familiar with each student's writing style by frequently reviewing student work often enables teachers to detect shifts in syntax or surprisingly sophisticated vocabulary. Typing a sentence from a suspicious portion of a student's essay into a search engine will often reveal if the students has copied the text from an online source. Teachers should steer clear of assignments that make it easier for students to copy from others: using fresh paper topics each term, requiring references to specific class-related readings, and requiring multiple drafts of essays will all help reduce plagiarism. Teachers can also help prevent plagiarism by ensuring students both understand the severe consequences plagiarism carries and know how to use and document sources correctly in their work.

These days buying a term paper is easier than ever. If a student types in "term papers," he or she has access to thousands of papers.

When teachers find papers that they believe to have been plagiarized, they can access several helpful Internet sites:

- **http://www.academicintegrity.org** (This site is by the Center for Academic Integrity.)
- **http://chronicle.com/free/v46/i12/12a04701.htm** ("How to Proctor from a Distance")
- **http://chronicle.com/free/v46/i12/12a04901.htm** ("Web Services Help Professors Detect Plagiarism")

Many teachers, departments, or colleges also subscribe to sites offering plagiarism detection software, such as **www.turnitin.com**, **www.mydropbox.com**, or **http://plagiarism.com**.

The freedom of the Internet has also brought thousands of copyright problems and questions, many still unresolved. Teachers must help students understand what kinds of information they need to document and what they must request permission to use. In some cases, teachers need to request permission for their students to access a site.

Generally students may link to any site on the Web that is available to the public. However, Netiquette suggests that you ask permission of every site you plan to send your students to. Some sites, not equipped to handles numerous hits at one time, may crash if all your students sign on at once when many others are also using the site. Although government sites can be accessed without permission, Netiquette suggests that one should ask permission of city, county, and state sites.

Students and teachers must never copy material from a site and post it on their own websites—unless the owner gives permission. In Chapter 33 of their handbook, Troyka & Hesse also give general information about avoiding plagiarism.

To learn more about copyright and the Internet, teachers can access this site:

> ➤ "Copyright Office Study on Distance Education" from the U.S. Copyright Office: http://www.loc.gov/copyright/disted/ "The Code of Best Practices in Fair use for Media Literacy Education," from National Council of Teachers of English and Center for Social Media: www.cenerforsocialmedia.org/resources/ publications/code_for_media_literacy_education

■ GLOSSARY OF BASIC COMPUTER TERMS

Bit— The smallest amount of information read by a computer.

Blog— A Web log is a website on which a writer posts a series of messages, whether personal diaries or interest-based commentary, that anyone can read through on the Internet.

Bookmark— A method of telling the browser to save a particular Internet address so that one can more easily access it again.

Boolean operators— Words like *and, or, but, near* and certain symbols that help users narrow or define keywords for a search.

Byte— Eight bits treated as a unit of information that takes up the space of about one character on a typed page.

Cable modem— A fast modem that uses cable TV lines to connect Internet sites.

CD-Rom— "Read Only Memory," that is, a computer disk that cannot be changed, containing references works. These are available for purchase or for use in libraries.

Cookie— A tiny bit of information left on your computer by a site, especially a commercial site, to help the sender recall your last hit at the site and to enable other websites to see what sites you have accessed.

Cyberspace— The medium where electronic communication over networks occurs.

Digital portfolio (or electronic portfolio)— A collection of several texts in electronic format that allows a writer to represent his or her range of skills and abilities.

Download— Copying information from the Internet to your hard drive or a disk.

FTP— "File Transfer Protocol," a way of moving files between Internet sites.

HTML— "Hypertext Markup Language," the code used to create Web pages and to enable users to move from one Web page to another. It includes regular words as well as codes.

Hypertext— A document that provides links that allow access to other sites when the user clicks on the links.

Kilobits— The speed of transmitting 1,000 bits per second.

Megabits— A speed of one million bits per second.

Message board— A site where users can post questions or make comments on a particular topic.

Modem (sometimes known as a Dial-up Modem)— a device that uses telephone lines to access the Internet.

Newsgroup— A discussion group among users who post messages for all users in the group.

Operating System— The controlling system for a computer, such as Windows and Mac OS.

Podcast— Brief sound files that are shared over the Internet, somewhat like online radio broadcasts.

RAM— "Random Access Memory." The part of a computer's memory that enables the computer to run programs.

Secure website— A site that requires certain protocols, like a password and a user name, for viewing it.

Spamming— Sending unsolicited messages to mass mailing lists, often to advertise products or services.

Subject directory— A list of categories of information with links to related websites.

Truncation— Listing only the first few letters of a keyword in a search so that the search will also look for closely related terms. The truncation is usually noted by a symbol such as *.

URL– A Universal Resource Locator, a specific address on the Internet.

Virus– A destructive program, often from an unknown source, that can destroy or scramble data or programs. Once imported, computer viruses can spread quickly through your system and can infect any users you send messages to.

Webmaster– A person who maintains the content and operation of a website.

Wiki– A website that allows multiple readers to change its content.

WEB RESOURCES

Web Resources can be found at www.prenhall.com /troyka

SUGGESTED READING

Anson, Chris M. "Distance Voices: Teaching and Writing in a Culture of Technology." *College English* 61.3 (Jan. 1999): 261–80.

Barksdale, Karl, and John Steffee. *Writing with Computers.* Cincinnati, OH: Computer Literacy Press, 1998.

Beals, Timothy J. "Between Teachers and Computers: Does Text-Checking Software Really Improve Student Learning." *English Journal* 87.1 (Jan. 1998): 67–73.

Benson, Angela, and Elizabeth Wright. "Pedagogy and Policy in the Age of the Wired Professor." *T.H.E. Journal* 27.4 (Nov. 1999): 60–62.

Berzsenyi, Christyne A. "How to Conduct a Course-Based Computer Chat Room: Enabling a Space for Active Learning." *Teaching English in the Two-Year College* 28.2 (Dec. 2000): 165–74.

Blair, Kristine L. "Literacy, Dialogue, and Difference in the 'Electronic Contact Zone.'" *Computers and Composition* 15.3 (1998): 317–29.

Chapman, David W. "A Luddite in Cyberland, or How to Avoid Being Snared by the Web." *Computers and Composition* 16.2 (1999): 247–52.

Coogan, David. *Electronic Writing Centers: Computing the Field of Composition.* Stamford, CT: Ablex, 1999.

Crafton, Robert E. "Promises, Promises: Computer-Assisted Revision and Basic Writers." *Computers and Composition* 13.3 (1996): 317–26.

Drechsel, Joanne. "Writing into Silence: Losing Voice with Writing Assessment Technology." *Teaching English in the Two-Year College* 26.4 (May 1999): 380–87.

Faigley, Lester. *The Longman Guide to the Web.* New York: Longman, 2000.

Forbes, Cheryl A. "Cowriting, Overwriting, and Overriding in Portfolio Land Online." *Computers and Composition* 13.2 (1996): 195–205.

Hansman, Catherine A., and Arthur L. Wilson. "Teaching Writing in Community Colleges: A Situated View of How Adults Learn to Write in Computer-Based Writing Classrooms." *Community College Review* 26.1 (Summer 1998): 21–42.

Hawisher, Gail E., Sibylle Gruber, and Margaret F. Sweany. *Computers and the Teaching of Writing in American Higher Education, 1979–1994: A History.* Norwood, NJ: Ablex, 1996.

Hewett, Beth L. "Characteristics of Interactive Oral Computer-Mediated Peer Group Talk and Its Influence on Revision." *Computers and Composition* 17.3 (2000): 265–88.

Holdstein, Deborah H. *Computers and Composition.* 2nd ed. Upper Saddle River, NJ: Prentice Hall, 1997.

Huot, Brian A. "Computers and Assessment: Understand Two Technologies." *Computers and Composition* 13.2 (1996): 231–43.

Inman, James, Jeffrey M. Buchanan, Shawn Christian, and Cathryn A. McFaul. "Making Every Voice Count: Constructing on Online Community of Writing Instructors." *Writing Instructor* 16.3 (Spring 1997): 127–35.

Kastman, Breuch, Ann M. Lee, and Sam J. Racine. "Developing Sound Tutor Training for Online Writing Centers: Creating Productive Peer Reviewers." *Computers and Composition* 17.3 (2000): 245–63.

LeCourt, Donna. "Critical Pedagogy in the Computer Classroom: Politicizing the Writing Space." *Computers and Composition* 15.3 (1998): 275–95.

—— and Luann Barnes. "Writing Multiplicity: Hypertext and Feminist Textual Politics." *Computers and Composition* 16.1 (1999): 55–71.

Marshall, James. "Electronic Writing and the Wrapping of Language." *Journal of Philosophy and Education* 34.1 (Feb. 2000): 135–49.

Mauriello, Nicholas, Gian Pagnucci, and Tammy Winner. "Reading Between the Code: The Teaching of HTML and the Displacement of Writing Instruction." *Computers and Composition* 16.3 (1999): 409–19.

Meel, David E. "Email Dialogue Journals in a College Calculus Classroom: A Look At the Implementation and Benefits." *The Journal of Computers in Mathematics and Science Teaching* 18.4 (1999): 387–413.

Moran, Charles. "From a High-Tech to a Low-Tech Writing Classroom: 'You Can't Go Home Again.'" *Computers and Composition* 15.1 (1998): 1–10.

Norton, David W., Matthew Segaard, and Ann Hill Duin. "The HTML Decision-Making Report: Preparing Students for the Information Age Workforce." *Computers and Composition* 14.3 (1997): 377–94.

Pagnucci, Gian S., and Nicholas Mauriello. "The Masquerade: Gender, Identity, and Writing for the Web." *Computers and Composition* 16.1 (1999): 141–51.

Palmquist, Mike. *Transitions: Teaching Writing in Computer-Supported and Traditional Classrooms.* Greenwich, CT: Ablex, 1998.

Peckham, Irvin. "If It Ain't Broke, Why Fix It?: Disruptive and Constructive Computer-Mediated Response Group Practices." *Computers and Composition* 13.3 (1996): 327–39.

Pirto, John. "University Student Attitudes Toward E-Mail as Opposed to Written Documents." *Computers in the Schools* 14.3–4 (1998): 25–32.

Price, Jonathan. "Electronic Outlining as a Tool for Making Writing Visible." *Computers and Composition* 14.3 (1997): 409–27.

Rea, Alan, and Doug White. "The Changing Nature of Writing: Prose or Code in the Classroom." *Computers and Composition* 16.3 (1999): 421–36.

Regan, Alison E., and John D. Zuern. "Community-Service Learning and Computer-Mediated Advanced Composition: The Going to Class, Getting Online, and Giving Back." *Computers and Composition* 17.2 (2000): 177–95.

Selfe, Cynthia L., and Susan Hilligoss. *Literacy and Computers: The Complication of Teaching and Learning with Technology.* New York: Modern Language Association, 1994.

Sharples, Mike. *Computer Supported Collaborative Writing.* London/New York: Springer-Verlag, 1993.

Shirk, Henrietta Nickels, and Howard Taylor Smith. "Emerging Fair Use Guidelines for Multimedia: Implications for the Writing Classroom." *Computers and Composition* 15.2 (1998): 229–41.

Slattery, Patrick J., and Rosemary Kowalski. "On Screen: The Composing Processes of First-Year and Upper-Level College Students." *Computers and Composition* 15.1 (1998): 61–81.

Sorapure, Madeleine, Pamela Inglesby, and George Yatchisin. "Web Literacy: Challenges and Opportunities for Research in a New Medium." *Computers and Composition* 15.3 (1998): 409–24.

Strickland, James. *From Disk to Hard Copy: Teaching Writing with Computers.* Portsmouth, NH: Boynton/Cook, 1997.

Sullivan, Laura L. "Wired Women Writing: Towards a Feminist Theorization of Hypertext." *Computers and Composition* 16.1 (1999): 25–54.

Sullivan, Patricia, and James E. Porter. *Opening Spaces: Writing Technologies and Critical Research Practices.* Greenwich, CT: Ablex, 1997.

Taylor, Todd W., and Irene Ward. *Literary Theory in the Age of the Internet.* New York: Columbia UP, 1998.

Tobin, Lad. *Using Computers for Collaborative Writing: An Interdisciplinary Project.* Washington, DC: U.S. Department of Education, 1991.

Tornow, Joan. *Link/Age: Composing_in_the_Online_Classroom.* Logan, Utah: Utah State UP, 1997.

Van Hoosier Carey, Gregory. "Rhetoric by Design: Using Web Development Projects in the Technical Communication Classroom." *Computers and Composition* 14.3 (1997): 395–407.

Varone, Sandy. "Voices from the Computer Classroom: Novice Writers and Peer Response to Writing." *Teaching English in the Two-Year College* 23 (Oct. 1996): 213–18.

Wienbroer, Diana Roberts. *Rules of Thumb <For Online Research>.* Boston: McGraw Hill, 2001.

Whitaker, Elaine E., and Elaine N. Hill. "Virtual Voices in 'Letters Across Cultures': Listening for Race, Class, and Gender." *Computers and Composition* 15.3 (1998): 331–46.

Wolfe, Joanna L. "Why Do Women Feel Ignored? Gender Differences in Computer-Mediated Classroom Interactions." *Computers and Composition* 16.1 (1999): 153–66.

Yagelski, Robert P., and Jeffrey T. Grabill. "Computer-Mediated Communication in the Undergraduate Writing Classroom: A Study of the Relationship of Online Discourse and Classroom Discourse in Two Writing Classes." *Computers and Composition* 15.1 (1998): 11–40.

PART EIGHT:

The Role of Visual Rhetoric in Writing

by Susan Loudermilk Garza, *Texas A&M University—Corpus Christi*

When we think about teaching visual rhetoric, the tendency often is to focus on advertisements and how the creators of such ads attempt to create some action in readers. (See *Simon and Schuster Handbook, 9/e, and Quick Access: Reference for Writers, 6/e.*) And while advertisements are one mechanism through which to study visual rhetoric, focusing on visual rhetoric from this view may keep us from seeing the larger picture of what visual rhetoric is, what it does, and how we can use it to make meanings. When we ask ourselves what do we mean when we talk about writing today, when we examine what we need to do to teach our students to write, can we afford to look away from the important and expanding role that visual rhetoric plays in making meaning in today's world? Kathleen Blake Yancey in her chair's address at CCCC 2004, "Made Not Only in Words: Composition in a New Key," states that our students "compose words and images and create audio files on Web logs (blogs), in word processors, with video editors and Web editors and in e-mail and on presentation software and in instant messaging and on listservs and on bulletin boards—and no doubt in whatever genre will emerge in the next ten minutes" (298). Carolyn Handa, in the Introduction to *Visual Rhetoric in a Digital World*, points out that "outside of our writing classrooms, students surround themselves with multimedia and cybertexts. . . . manipulate and edit images. . . use Web browsers to create pages that almost always include visual elements. . . . create their own visuals, even their own typography" (3). And Charles A. Hill adds that "since so many of the texts that our students encounter are visual ones, and since visual literacy is becoming increasingly important for everyday social functioning and even for success in the workplace, it would seem obvious that

> Our present understanding of rhetoric and its tradition can no longer account for ways that the visual functions rhetorically. . . . To understand visual rhetoric better, we need to reanimate its tradition, and in doing so, reconsider our conception of rhetoric itself as primarily a verbal art. (Blakesley)

> Though classroom teaching often assumes essay organization as the norm, outside the classroom visually informative prose is pervasive, and not just in scientific or technical fields. (Bernhardt 95)

our educational institutions should be spending at least as much time and energy on developing students' visual literacies as these institutions spend on developing students' textual literacy" (109).

How do we go about bringing the study of visual rhetoric into our writing classes? One tendency might be to introduce PowerPoint activities into the syllabus. While this is certainly one way to help our students begin to think about visual rhetoric, we are limiting their understanding of what visual rhetoric can do if we limit our study of it to only certain types of documents. And PowerPoint has been so overused and incorrectly used that students can miss the point of the importance of the visual elements in presentation documents. In fact, Edward Tuft, in "PowerPoint is Evil," likens PowerPoint to "a widely used and expensive prescription drug that promised to make us beautiful but didn't," and "induced stupidity, turned everyone into bores, wasted time, and degraded the quality and credibility of communication." PowerPoint, Tufte continues, "elevates format over content, betraying an attitude of commercialism that turns everything into a sales pitch."

Students tend to automatically default to a PowerPoint presentation as the only way to do a presentation. When I assign a presentation, students will ask, "You want us to do a PowerPoint?" We have to make sure that our students understand that when they need to present any type of information, they need to focus on audience and purpose, and one of the first questions they need to ask is, "What tool(s) should I use?" to develop the presentation. PowerPoint is one type of presentation tool and it can be used in myriad ways, but we seldom discuss its use and effects on audience. As Tufte explains, PowerPoint can be an effective tool, "but rather than supplementing a presentation, it has become a substitute for it. Such misuse ignores the most important rule of speaking: Respect your audience." So let's not let our students simply take content, copy and paste it into slides, put in a few pictures, and most dreaded of all, use those sound or motion elements indiscriminately just because they seem to provide some whizbang. And, we shouldn't let ourselves as teachers do this either!

While many of us may see ourselves as being progressive if we allow our students to create those ever present PowerPoint presentations to accompany the essays they write for our classes, or to create a PowerPoint presentation in place of one essay, how much do we really know about this overused tool, and how much do we know about how to use it well?

The study of visual rhetoric is not just about studying ads or creating PowerPoint presentations or Web pages that have pictures and color added to text, although these are documents in which visual rhetoric does play an important role. Even traditional ways of writing, essay writing for example, are shaped by visual rhetoric. Visual rhetoric functions in every document we create, often without our knowledge of its presence or its effects. Even a blank document has elements of visual rhetoric built into it, so we begin to write with these elements, often unaware of their presence. Open a blank document, then click on "Format" and choose "Style." This will display the visual elements of a blank/default document. Under the "List:" section, "Styles in use" will probably be displayed as the default selection. Click on the drop-down menu and choose "All styles." This opens up a longer list of options of visual elements that the user can add to a word document.

> If teachers would begin to look at naturally occurring discourse forms which have evolved outside the classroom, they would begin to develop a descriptive base for visual design. A preoccupation with conventional essay format allows little attention to visual features. Instead of helping students learn to analyze a situation and determine an appropriate form, given a certain audience and purpose, many writing assignments merely exercise the same sort of writing week after week, introducing only topical variation. (Bernhardt 103)

I am still amazed at how many of my students are not aware of the "Styles" function, even though in general they have more computer knowledge and experience than their predecessors. So first steps for incorporating visual rhetoric into our teaching may require that we discover the tools that are available and increase student awareness of those tools.

■ WHAT IS VISUAL RHETORIC?

> Before we, as composition instructors,
> can begin to construct
> a coherent pedagogy of the visual,
> we might ask ourselves what we need
> to understand about our discipline
> and what our assumptions about teaching are,
> exactly.
> Why do some writing curricula
> continue to focus only on words
> when today's documents are increasingly
> hybrids of words, images and design?
> In what ways might
> we begin to address
> the visual on par with the verbal
> in our classrooms?
> (Handa 9)

Why format this quote as right-aligned text rather than simply formatting it as block text indented five spaces,

> Simply applying methods and concepts designed specifically for verbal language to persuasive images is not the most productive or accurate way to develop a methodology for the study of visual rhetoric; doing so often results in misleading (or sometimes simply

useless) assertions about the ways in which persuasive images work. (Hill 27)

or simply centered text?

The range of visual elements
that could be considered rhetorical is vast ...
(Hill 25)

Placing text in the right-aligned position illustrates how much visual rhetoric affects our engagement with texts (online as well as more traditional hard copy types of documents) and how changing one element of visual presentation creates a change in the reading experience. Most readers probably would pay more attention to text that is right-aligned because it goes against the norm. However, when we think of visual rhetoric, we don't usually focus on using right-aligned text. When I ask students to think about and use visual rhetoric, their first tendencies often are to center and bold text, use many different fonts, use lots of color, and put in lots of pictures, all reflective of misconceptions of just what it means to apply visual rhetoric to a document. Just think about the types of flyers that are part of every campus culture. Many are student-made and reflect these misconceptions. Once I get students to realize the effect that these actions have on the readers of the documents, it becomes easier to get them to focus on other elements of visual rhetoric that are readily available in most word processing programs, such as the following:

Headings	Guide readers from section to section.
Bulleted lists	Help readers see the relationships among items by chunking information.
Lines	Break up the visual plane and/or provide motion across the visual space.
Boxes	Can be used to separate one part of a text from another. (Note the use of boxes within this discussion to draw attention to some of the quotes.)
Links	Create paths and connections. Usually thought of as part of Web pages, but can be useful in other types of documents as well. (For example, they are highly underused in those overused PowerPoint documents.)
Pictures/Images	Supplement explanation for written text, but perhaps the most misused/overused element.
Typography	Shows relationships. Fun to play with, but using one-two fonts is usually more visually effective.
Location on Page/Layout	Helps reader navigate.

Color	Affects mood. Easy to overuse, but using one-two colors is usually more effective.

(For a more extended discussion of these elements, see *Teaching Visual Rhetoric*, Prentice Hall Resources for Writers, by Susan Loudermilk Garza, 2006.)

While it is interesting, and perhaps even fun, to incorporate these elements into the way we teach writing, we should not lose sight of the importance of understanding the rhetorical reasons for using them. Our purpose should be to get students to think about how writers work, how writers make decisions that affect audience and purpose, including decisions about elements of visual rhetoric, "how textual elements capture an audience's attention and convey a point of view" (Handa 4). We should make decisions about visual rhetoric part of the process of teaching writing and help students understand that different decisions are required for each audience situation. We can help our students understand that even an essay has multi-genre elements so that they can begin to see an essay as being more than just a flat, linear surface, as more than the flatland that Tufte attempts to move us away from: "Escaping this flatland is the essential task of envisioning information—for all the interesting worlds (physical, biological, imaginary, human) that we seek to understand are inevitably and happily multivariate in nature. Not flatlands" (12).

So when we teach students in our writing courses now, if we don't talk about concepts such as white space, chunking, and gridding, are we providing them with a complete understanding of the rhetorical nature of writing?

> Writing teachers today are living through a revolution in literacy brought about by the capability of computers to combine blocks of text—or verbal lexias—with graphic images, sounds, video, and other multimedia. . . . We are forced—at times by our failures—to grapple with the potential relationships between the ubiquitous and chaotic new visual and the comfortingly familiar, more linear verbal. Awash in both good and bad examples—on the Web, but also on TV and, lest we forget, still in traditional print—we are discovering that it is no longer enough to fragment our concepts of literacy, bracket off our traditional blocks of text, and just stick to what we know. (Hobbs 55)

The visual creates meaning in our written texts; "visual and verbal literacies have become increasingly interdependent" (Handa 4). So we must teach students the rhetorical concepts of picturing ideas. And before we can do this, we need to understand the role of visual rhetoric in various texts. Bernhardt provides a good starting point:

We might think of texts arranged along a continuum, from texts at one end which convey relatively little information visually, to texts at the opposite end which reveal substantial information through such visible cues as white space, illustrations, variation in typeface, and use of nonalphabetic symbols, such as numbers, asterisks, and punctuation. In terms of this continuum, an essay would fall well toward the nonvisually informative end. Certainly, paragraph indentation, margins, capitalization, and sentence punctuation provide some information to the reader, but such information is extremely limited, with most of the cues as to organization and logical relations buried within the text. At the other extreme of the continuum would be texts which display their structure, providing the reader/viewer with a schematic representation of the divisions and hierarchies which organize the text. (94)

And although essays "fall well toward the nonvisually informative end," we can begin to incorporate more elements of visual rhetoric into these documents, especially since our sharing and reading of such texts are occurring more and more in online environments, allowing us to implement more physical movement into the process.

■ HOW SHOULD WE TEACH VISUAL RHETORIC?

It is one thing to argue that university students should be exposed to more explicit instruction about the uses of visual communication, and it is quite another to develop a workable pedagogy for dealing with visual rhetoric. Such a pedagogy has not yet been developed, partly because no one recognizable discipline has staked a claim around the immense and vaguely defined area that is variously referred to as "visual communication," "visual rhetoric," or "visual literacy." (Hill 111)

With a visible text, it may not be fruitful to talk about paragraphs in terms of topic sentences and support, or opening and closing sentences, or sentences of transition. In fact, it may not be useful to speak of paragraphs at all, but of sections or chunks. In the visible text, the headings take over the task of generalizing or identifying the topic. Levels of subordination are indicated by variation in typeface, type size, or placement of headings, rather than through subordinators or cohesive ties which indicate semantically dependent relations. (Bernhardt 101)

We design every time we write. We either choose the visual elements in a word document—elements of white space, font, color, headings, etc.—or they are chosen for us if we go with the blank/default document. What we see when we look at a text defines how we will understand it, so visual elements are very important when we think about how they will affect the reader.

In *Picturing Texts*, Faigley et al. offer that good design

- Directs the reader
- Provides clear emphasis
- Conveys the writer's message
- Makes the text memorable
- Sets an appropriate tone
- Builds the writer's credibility
- Helps persuade the reader to take the text seriously. (454)

Robin Williams in his book *The Non-Designer's Design Book*, a favorite among design teachers, focuses on the elements of proximity, contrast, alignment, and repetition. Williams's list is another example of how we can engage students in a discussion of visual design. And Tufte reminds us that we make decisions about visual rhetoric to serve many purposes: "We envision information in order to reason about, communicate, document, and preserve that knowledge—activities nearly always carried out on two-dimensional paper and computer screen. Escaping this flatland and enriching the density of data displays are the essential tasks of information design" (33). And we have the tools available to us today to enrich our information presentations and create environments that function as multi-dimensional documents.

When I teach writing I try to impress upon students what I call "The Elements of Good Design":

- Simple is best
- Determine one focal point
- Don't decorate just for the sake of decoration
- Focus on purpose/audience
- Try to achieve balance on the page
- Use easily readable fonts
- Use different sizes and styles of one font, rather than several different fonts
- Use color sparingly for effect, not decoration
- Think about how the reader will move through the document
- Strive for consistency

While simple and clean are usually best practices for designing documents, students love to play with new tools, especially if they have never played with them, or never been allowed to use them before. I usually begin with an easy activity that will allow students to play, and at the same time allow those who may not be comfortable with technology to learn how to use these tools.

In this section I include some of the activities I use to incorporate the study of visual rhetoric into my writing classes. I begin with one easy activity that I use to introduce students to the study of visual rhetoric.

Analyze and Redesign a Flyer

Flyers are everywhere, so they are a good resource for teaching visual rhetoric. Have students leave the classroom and look at the various bulletin/message boards that they encounter. Students can do this individually or as a group. Have them decide which flyer grabs their attention first. Also have them bring back a flyer (preferably one that is no longer current) that they want to redesign. Using "The Elements of Good Design" list, have students analyze the flyer and then redesign a flyer based on those guidelines. Students can use a basic word program to develop the flyers. PowerPoint is also useful for this type of activity as the program has many elements of visual rhetoric already built in, such as grids, centered text, ready-made backgrounds, color contrast, etc.

Perform the "Squint Test"

When we look at a text we usually take in the entire page/screen simultaneously, then we look at individual elements. One activity that illustrates this is the "squint test." I ask students to perform this test when they are analyzing documents created by others, and then to analyze documents they have created. To do the squint test, first squint your eyes, then look at a document and whatever stands out on the page is the element that will first draw the reader into the document (Hilligoss and Howard 97). In designing documents, it is a good practice to determine what element of the document the reader's eye will be drawn to first. In a basic essay document, that element would most often be the title, which is why having a catchy title is important to editors.

Analyze Video Game Documents

Most of our students today have some experience with video games. All video games have licensing, instructions, and other types of documentation. Ask students to find an example from a video game and analyze how the information is presented using elements of visual rhetoric. Students can also examine how the visual presentation differs from one game to another and determine which presentation is better and why. Games that are played online present different challenges related to visual rhetoric, which opens up a wider discussion of how information is presented in different formats. Students could also rewrite the documents they find.

Analyze Your College's Catalog

This is an activity I did with one of my classes, and it worked very well. Ask students to examine the catalog for your school. Most colleges/universities have both hard and online copies of their catalogs, so in addition to analyzing one or the other, students can compare the two and determine what types of visual elements work best in each of the environments. Students can also examine catalogs from other schools and determine which documents do the best job at reaching the intended audience. Students can also compare their school's catalog to the catalogs of other schools. When I did this activity with my students I also asked them to make suggestions for changes to the catalog.

Write a *Parade* Essay

We are so used to formatting/designing essays in the same way, including starting with the generic heading, or a standard cover page format. Ask students to find examples of documents that go beyond the traditional essay format. Students are exposed to many of these different formats, but they may not be aware of how the presentation formats affect the ways readers interact with the documents. One example is the "In Step With" essay that appears in the weekly *Parade* magazine published in many Sunday papers throughout the country. This type of document is an excellent example for discussing chunking information, or how we group information in a document.

Ask students to focus on the layout of the page and how the information in each of the sections relates to the information in the other sections. What kind of information should go in the box on the right-hand side of the page and how does that information relate to the main text? Have students create a grid in a word document similar to the grid in the *Parade* document, like the example in Fig. 1.

Students could create a different grid layout based on the type of document they are producing. The *Parade* essays are biographies, but students could adapt the visual layout to many other types of essays. For example, if students are working on an argument essay, how could the boxes be used

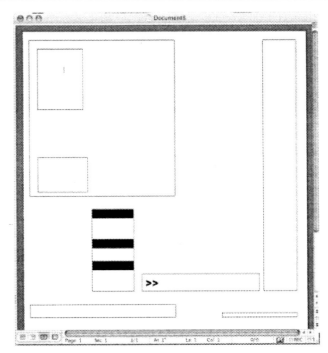

Fig. 1 *Parade* Essay Grid

to illustrate relationships among information in an argument? The *Parade* essay has a picture of the person who is being highlighted that week, which provides an excellent opportunity for discussing whether pictures or other images would be useful for other types of essays/documents. To use the argument example again, what pictures/images could be included in such a document that would increase the effect of the argument on the reader? And where should the pictures/images be placed? By bringing documents such as the *Parade* essay to the attention of our students, we encourage them to expand their thinking in regard to writing essays and to incorporate some of the same visual practices into their own documents.

Use the Tools of Word Programs for Invention

While most of the examples included to this point focus on the format of finished documents, visual rhetoric is a useful tool for students to use during the invention stage of the writing process as well. Headings and links are useful visual rhetoric tools to use during invention. As students begin thinking about putting together their documents, encourage them to post their initial thoughts as headings and/or links. For example, in the early stages of putting together this document, my invention page looked like the document in Fig. 2.

In this document I listed the main elements that I initially thought about including. As I thought of what I wanted to say or found information from other sources that I wanted to include, I would place that information under one of the headings. As students begin to write they can dump information below the headings where they think the information belongs at that point in the writing process. As headings fill up with lots of information, students can then make the headings into links and move the information to another page. As students write, the visual elements of headings and links on the page help them to see the relationships among the important points of the document. So rather than indenting five spaces and starting a new paragraph (or skipping one line and starting a new paragraph), a practice that shows very little about the informational relationships, by using headings as they add and work with the information, students will visually see these relationships and more actively manipulate the chunks of information in the document. By using headings and links students can easily move information around, combine information, and even see what information no longer fits and should be cut.

Fig. 2   Invention Example

Write an Essay Modeled on *The Way to Rainy Mountain*

In *The Way to Rainy Mountain*, N. Scott Momaday uses elements of visual rhetoric to recount the story of his family heritage. Momaday includes three different versions of one story displayed across two pages, as illustrated in Fig. 3.

In the text box on the left-hand page, Momaday recounts the story as it was told within the tribe. In the top text box on the right-hand page, Momaday includes historical information related to the story. And in the box below that, he tells the story from his own point of view in first person. Students could follow a similar format by laying out three parts of an essay/document in this manner. One of the misconceptions we have about the use of visual rhetoric is that it is useful for creative types of documents, but the same elements can be useful in other types of documents as well. So while Momaday's story is a biographical story, we can borrow his use of layout and adapt it to other types of documents.

Analyze and Design Menus, Brochures, Websites

These are documents that students encounter quite often, and they offer opportunities for analyzing and practicing the use of visual rhetoric. Again using "The Elements of Good Design" list, students can find and analyze sample documents and then redesign those documents, or use what they

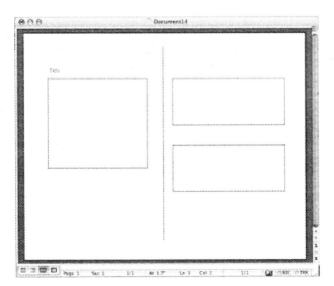

Fig. 3 *The Way to Rainy Mountain* Layout

learned to create new ones. It is important, as Hill points out, to teach students to understand how documents "are used to create action in readers," to understand "the psychological processes by which images persuade," to understand "the psychological processes that are brought to bear while interpreting and reacting to persuasive images," to understand "that images are not just ornamental supplements to written texts, but complex texts in their own right," and to consider "their own responses to such images" (119-122).

Re-view Reality Using the *Turnabout Map*

I was first introduced to the *Turnabout Map*, created by Jesse Levine, as a graduate student. I still remember the impact it had on how I view and interpret visual representations. The map shows the usual view of the Americas; however, the map is flipped with south at the top and north at the bottom. Introducing students to the *Turnabout Map* will emphasize the importance and impact of visual rhetoric on beliefs and ideas, how visual rhetoric shapes knowledge. After discussing the *Turnabout Map*, students can find other examples of visual representations that create/subvert meaning in this way. Then students can redesign the representations to affect the meaning of the visual, in the same way that Levine did with the *Turnabout Map*. Ask students to write about how the elements of visual rhetoric create meaning in the original representation, and how they used the elements of visual rhetoric to change the meaning.

Examine Images from Other Cultures

With the emphasis today on international events and the global nature of our world, students are more aware of the rhetorical elements of other cultures. And it is important to increase their awareness of the importance of the rhetoric of other cultures and to create documents based on this awareness. "Students need to learn to appreciate the power of images for defining and for reinforcing our cultural values and to understand the ways in which images help us define our individual roles within society" (Hill 116). Ask students to identify elements of visual rhetoric in documents from other cultures and analyze those elements, including how the use of these elements compares to the use of the same elements in their own cultures. Then ask students to create documents with an international audience in mind. Students can then describe the different decisions they made in designing the documents based on the international audience.

I have attempted to utilize in this document many of the elements of visual rhetoric that I have discussed, thus creating a multi-layered feeling to the text, and perhaps creating a different type of reading experience. As we move more and more into the online environment, our reading experiences will continue to change and visual rhetoric will receive more emphasis as a tool for creating texts. But even if you continue to focus on the traditional essay as a tool for teaching writing, you can still introduce and encourage the use of visual rhetoric, as I have attempted to illustrate. So have fun as you endeavor to learn more about visual rhetoric and add it to your pedagogy, but don't forget the importance of visual rhetoric as a tool for making meanings.

RESOURCES FOR TEACHING VISUAL RHETORIC

Online Resources

Blakesley, David. "What Is Visual Rhetoric, and What Is Its Tradition?" Position statement for the Alliance for Rhetoric Society Conference (Sept. 11-14, 2003). <http://www.comm.umn.edu/ARS/Tradition/blakesley,%20tradition.htm?

Cortés, Claudia. *Color in Motion.* 2003. Excellent Flash demonstration of the implications of color, including social and cultural symbolism. <http://tc.eserver.org/24857.html>

Howard, Rebecca Moore. *Visual Rhetoric: Some Sources.* Syracuse University. Extensive bibliography of scholarship, including sources on film and art. <http://wrt-howard.syr.edu/Bibs/Visual.bib.html>

Iowa State University. *First-Year Composition Web Center.* Online resource provided for teachers and students with practical lessons on visual design and visual literacy. <http://learn.ae.iastate.edu/omega/Anthony/FYC/FYC.html>

Pinkel, S. *The On-Line Visual Literacy Project.* Pomona College, Claremont, CA. A comprehensive introduction of many of the basic elements of visual rhetoric. <http://www.pomona.edu/Academics/courserelated/classprojects/Visual-lit/intro/intro.html>

Propen, Amy. *Visual Rhetoric Portal.* University of Minnesota. One of the most extensive resources available. Includes lists of online resources, journals and conferences. <http://www.tc.umn.edu/~prope002/visualRhet.htm>
Also available at <http://mattlevy.home.mindspring.com/rhetcomp/visual.html>.

Richardson, James F. "The Visual Dimension of Writing." Very interesting and different approach to thinking about writing using elements of visual rhetoric. <http://www.intellectbooks.com/iconic/writing/ writing.htm>

Visual Communication–Visual Rhetorics. University of Iowa Department of Communication. List of resources in the field of communication, with an emphasis on film and media studies. <http://www.uiowa.edu/ ~commstud/resources/visual.html>

"Visual Rhetoric." *E-server Library.* This cooperative library for technical communicators provides links to over 100 scholarly articles related to the topic. <http://tc.eserver.org/dir/Visual-Rhetoric>

"Visual Rhetoric for Students." OWL. Purdue University. Handout provided to introduce students to the concept. Covers color, images, and overall design. <http://owl.english.purdue.edu/handouts/vizrhet/>

Zulik, Margaret. *Sources in Visual Rhetoric.* Wake Forest University. List of articles in communication journals and recommended art theory and history of rhetoric and art articles and books. <http://www.wfu.edu/ ~zulick/454/visrhetbib.html/>

Syllabi/Course Websites

Blakesley, David. "Visual Rhetoric and Composition." Purdue University, Spring 2002. <http://web.ics.purdue.edu/%7Eblakesle/680/ 680course.html> "Visual Rhetoric," Fall 1999. <http://www.sla.purdue.edu/people/engl/dblakesley/visual/>

Bowers, Bege K. "Document Design and Production." Youngstown State University, Summer 2000. <http://cc.ysu.edu/~bkbowers/ bowe944.html>

Dubinsky, Jim. "Visual Rhetoric and Document Design." Virginia Tech. <http://www.english.vt.edu/~dubinsky/5334_vr/syllabus.htm>

Kimme Hea, Amy C. "Spatial & Visual Rhetorics." University of Arizona, Spring 2003. <http://www.u.arizona.edu/~kimmehea/svrhet/ svrhet.htm>

Murray, Joddy. Washington State University. Several examples of courses related to visual rhetoric. <http://www.tricity.wsu.edu/%7Ejmurray/>

Salvo, Michael. "Visual Rhetoric: Argument, Persuasion, Narrative." Purdue University, Spring 2004. <http://web.ics.purdue.edu/~salvo/680V/ info.htm>

Vitanza, Victor J. "Rhetoric, Poetics, and Cultural and Digital Studies." University of Texas at Arlington, Spring 2001. <http://www.uta.edu/ english/V/digital/>

Weisberg, Meredith. "Persuasion in a Digital Age." Purdue University, Fall 2000. <http://web.ics.purdue.edu/~weisberg/103c/>

Zemliansky, Pavel. "Visual Rhetoric." James Madison University, Spring 2005. <http://courses.pz-writing.net/sp05/node/122>

Articles

Bernhardt, Stephen A. "Seeing the Text." *College Composition and Communication* 37:1 (Feb 1986):66-78. Rpt. In *Visual Rhetoric in a Digital World: A Critical Sourcebook.* Ed. Carolyn Handa. Boston: Bedford, 2004. 94-106.

Blakesley, David and Collin Brooke. "Visual Rhetoric." Special Edition of *Enculturation: A Journal for Rhetoric, Writing, and Culture* 3:2 (2001). <http://enculturation.gmu.edu/3_2/>

Freenzweig, Tim. "Aesthetic Experience and the Importance of Visual Composition in Information Design." *The Orange Journal* 2001. <http://tc.eserver.org/10285.html>

George, Diana. "From Analysis to Design: Visual Communication in the Teaching of Writing." *College Composition and Communication* 54:1 (Sept. 2002), 11-39.

Tufte, Edward R. "PowerPoint is Evil." *Wired Magazine* 11:9 (Sept. 2003). <http://www.wired.com/wired/archive/11.09/ppt2.html>

White, Jan V. "Color the Newest Tool for Technical Communicators." *Technical Communication Online* 50:4 (Nov 2003).

Yancey, Kathleen Blake. "Made Not Only in Words: Composition in a New Key." *College Composition and Communication* 56:2 (Dec 2004): 297-328.

Books/Chapters

Faigley, Lester, Diana George, Anna Palchik, and Cynthia Selfe. *Picturing Texts.* New York: W. W. Norton & Company, 2004.

Garza, Susan Loudermilk. *Teaching Visual Rhetoric.* Prentice Hall Resources for Writing. Upper Saddle River, NJ: Pearson Education, Inc., 2006.

Handa, Carolyn, ed. *Visual Rhetoric in a Digital World: A Critical Sourcebook.* Boston: Bedford, 2004.

Hill, Charles A. and Marguerite Helmers, Eds. *Defining Visual Rhetorics.* Mahwah, NJ: Lawrence Erlbaum Associates, 2004.

Hill, Charles A. "Reading the Visual In College Writing Classes." *Intertexts: Reading Pedagogy in College Writing Classrooms.* Ed. Marguerite Helmers. Mahwah, NJ: Lawrence Erlbaum Associates, 2003. 124-150.

Hill, Charles A. "The Psychology of Rhetorical Images." Eds. Charles A. Hill and Marguerite Helmers. *Defining Visual Rhetoric.* Mahwah, NJ: Lawrence Erlbaum Associates, 2004. 25-40.

Hilligoss, Susan and Tharon Howard. *Visual Communication: A Writer's Guide.* New York: Pearson, 2002.

Hobbs, Catherine L. "Learning from the Past: Verbal and Visual Literacy in Early Modern Rhetoric and Writing Pedagogy." *Language and Image in the Reading-Writing Classroom.* Eds. Kristie Fleckenstein, Linda T. Calendrillo and Demetrice A. Worley. Mahwah, NJ: Lawrence Erlbaum Associates, 2002. 27-44. Rpt. In Handa.

Mitchell, W. J. T. *Picture Theory.* Chicago: The University of Chicago Press, 1994.

St. Clair, Robert N. "Visual Metaphor, Cultural Knowledge, and the New Rhetoric." *Learn in Beauty: Indigenous Education for a New Century.* Eds. Jon Reyhner, Joseph Martin, Louise Lockard, and W. Sakiestewa Gilbert. Flagstaff: Northern Arizona University, 2000. <http://jan.ucc.nau.edu/~jar/LIB/LIB8.html>

Stephens, Mitchell. "By Means of the Visible." *Rise of the Image: Fall of the Word.* Oxford University Press, 1998.

Tufte, Edward R. *Envisioning Information.* Cheshire, CT: Graphics Press, 1990.

Tufte, Edward R. *Visual Explanations.* Cheshire, CT: Graphics Press, 1997.

Williams, Robin. *The Non-Designer's Design Book.* Berkeley, CA: Peachpit Press, 1994.

Works Cited

Bernhardt, Stephen A. "Seeing the Text." *College Composition and Communication* 37:1 (Feb 1986):66-78. Rpt. *In Visual Rhetoric in a Digital World: A Critical Sourcebook.* Ed. Carolyn Handa. Boston: Bedford, 2004. 94-106.

Blakesley, David. "What Is Visual Rhetoric, and What Is Its Tradition?" Position statement for the Alliance for Rhetoric Society Conference (Sept. 11-14, 2003). <http://www.comm.umn.edu/ARS/Tradition/blakesley,%20tradition.htm>

Faigley, Lester, Diana George, Anna Palchik, and Cynthia Selfe. *Picturing Texts*. New York: W. W. Norton & Company, 2004.

Garza, Susan Loudermilk. *Teaching Visual Rhetoric*. Prentice Hall Resources for Writing. Upper Saddle River, NJ: Pearson Education, Inc., 2006.

Handa, Carolyn, Ed. *Visual Rhetoric in a Digital World: A Critical Sourcebook*. Boston: Bedford, 2004.

Hill, Charles A. "Reading the Visual in College Writing Classes." *Intertexts: Reading Pedagogy in College Writing Classrooms*. Ed. Marguerite Helmers. Mahwah, NJ: Lawrence Erlbaum Associates, 2003. 124-150. Rpt. In Handa.

Hill, Charles A. "The Psychology of Rhetorical Images." Eds. Charles A. Hill and Marguerite Helmers. *Defining Visual Rhetoric*. Mahwah, NJ: Lawrence Erlbaum Associates, 2004. 25-40.

Hilligoss, Susan and Tharon Howard. *Visual Communication: A Writer's Guide*. New York: Pearson, 2002.

Hobbs, Catherine L. "Learning from the Past: Verbal and Visual Literacy in Early Modern Rhetoric and Writing Pedagogy." *Language and Image in the Reading-Writing Classroom*. Eds. Kristie Fleckenstein, Linda T. Calendrillo and Demetrice A. Worley. Mahwah, NJ: Lawrence Erlbaum Associates, 2002. 27-44. Rpt. In Handa.

Momaday, N. Scott. *The Way to Rainy Mountain*. Albuquerque, NM: University of New Mexico Press, 1976.

Tufte, Edward R. *Envisioning Information*. Cheshire, CT: Graphics Press, 1990.

Tufte, Edward R. "PowerPoint is Evil." *Wired Magazine* 11:09 (Sept. 2003). http://www.wired.com/wired/archive/11.09/ppt2.html

Williams, Robin. *The Non-Designer's Design Book*. Berkeley, CA: Peachpit Press, 1994.

Yancey, Kathleen Blake. "Made Not Only in Words: Composition in a New Key." *College Composition and Communication* 56:2 (Dec 2004): 297-328.